Praise for *The ...*

'An astonis...'
Sebastian Faulks, *New Y...*

'This is a story every Australian should read . . . a complex mixture of love of family and a hard-edged determination to survive in a brutal, unforgiving world.'
Bruce Elder, *Sydney Morning Herald*

'The adventures make *Les Misérables* look like plain sailing. Unforgettable.'
The Guardian (UK)

'The most extraordinary book. It has opened my eyes in a life-changing way.'
Missy Higgins

'A must-read . . . It's an illuminating tale in the context of the asylum-seeker debate . . . A thriller and an inspirational story.'
Jane Sullivan, *Saturday Age*

'As gripping as it is chilling.'
Paul Morgan, *Australian Book Review*

'A story that had to be told.'
Weekend Australian

'Tight, powerful and extraordinarily well written. A book which glories in the strength, courage and compassion of the human spirit.'
Bruce Haigh, *Canberra Times*

'While giving us the details of Al Jenabi's plight, the dramatic narrative holds strong . . . Compelling.'
Dianne Dempsey, *The Age*

PENGUIN BOOKS

THE
PEOPLE
SMUGGLER

THE PEOPLE SMUGGLER

THE TRUE STORY OF
ALI AL JENABI,
THE 'OSKAR SCHINDLER OF ASIA'

ROBIN DE CRESPIGNY

PENGUIN BOOKS

PENGUIN BOOKS

UK | USA | Canada | Ireland | Australia
India | New Zealand | South Africa | China

Penguin Books is part of the Penguin Random House group of companies
whose addresses can be found at global.penguinrandomhouse.com.

Penguin
Random House
Australia

First published by Penguin Group (Australia), 2012
This edition published by Penguin Random House Australia Pty Ltd, 2017

Design by Adam Laszczuk © Penguin Random House Australia Pty Ltd
Cover photographs © Getty Images; vladphotos/Alamy
Typeset in Adobe Caslon by Penguin Random House Australia Pty Ltd
Colour separation by Splitting Image Colour Studio, Clayton, Victoria
Printed and bound in Australia by Griffin Press, an accredited ISO AS/NZS 14001
Environmental Management Systems printer.

National Library of Australia
Cataloguing-in-Publication data:

de Crespigny, Robin
The people smuggler / Robin de Crespigny
9780143569183 (paperback)

Al Jenabi, Ali.
Human smuggling – Australia.
Human smuggling – Asia.
Detention of persons – Australia.
Refugees – Australia.
Boat people – Australia.
Iraqis – Australia.
Refugees – Government policy – Australia.

penguin.com.au

For Ahmad.

And for my sister Paddy,
who died during the writing of this book.

CONTENTS

AUTHOR'S NOTE

I began the long journey of writing this book when refugee advocate Ngareta Rossell came to me in 2008 with the idea of writing a film script based on the life of Ali Al Jenabi. The epic breadth of his story is so great, with its cast of thousands, military conflicts, desperate mountain treks, boats on high seas, and a journey across two continents and at least six countries, each with its own unique culture and language, that I somewhat gratefully took the suggestion of screenwriter John Collee to tell the story in book form first.

Thus began an expedition of more than three years working intensely with Ali. He is an Arabic Muslim man and I am a Western agnostic woman. Gaining each other's trust, especially after what he had been through, meant that initially we focused on the events and not the internal story. What fascinated me most was not only Ali's moral fibre and strength of spirit, but the depth of his self-awareness. This was accompanied by an infectious sense of humour that seemed to transcend even the most severely traumatic incidents. In truth, despite Ali's remarkable memory, it was tremendously hard for him to dredge up the details of his life for months on end.

We met every few weeks, often over lunch at Ngareta's home. I recorded all our conversations, then spent long hours meticulously transcribing them. By the time I had mapped out the complex sequence of events in his story we had grown to know each other better, so returning to the start I asked more personal questions, and bit by bit we traversed the emotional depths of his odyssey. For me the meat of the story is the life-changing moral choices he faced while carrying so much responsibility for others, and the internal process by which he made his decisions.

As we went deeper I found the emotions involved were ones we can all identify and empathise with. In this way I believe it is a universal story about one individual in the storm of life, and that by travelling with him we can understand the bigger picture of why people make the choices they do to get on leaky boats, and how none of it is black and white. This is a story not so much about people smuggling, as about a man who happened to become one.

Half a lifetime of extraordinary events with hundreds of encounters has demanded some truncation of incidents and merging of minor characters. Also some names have been changed or omitted. This is particularly notable in the chapter dealing with the hearing in the Darwin Magistrate's Court. The Commonwealth DPP refused to agree to co-operate with the lifting of a suppression order on witnesses, despite the relevant details being freely available on the internet.

Like all refugee stories where trauma is a daily fact of life, it has not always been possible to tie down exact dates, and very occasionally I have had to reconstruct incidents with the fragments of memory available, offsetting them where possible against more certain recollections, or lining them up with known historical incidents. However, the tone and emotional experience is always accurate.

I made the decision to write this book in the first person to enable the reader to experience Ali's life at first hand by being placed in his shoes. Until Ali reached Australia he spoke Arabic, Kurdish, Farsi and Indonesian, but very little English. So the voice is essentially a construct of him and me, in the English language as he might have used it. As all the events are through his eyes, the view of those events reflect Ali's recollections.

I feel privileged that Ali has allowed me to preserve his story and pass it on to the world.

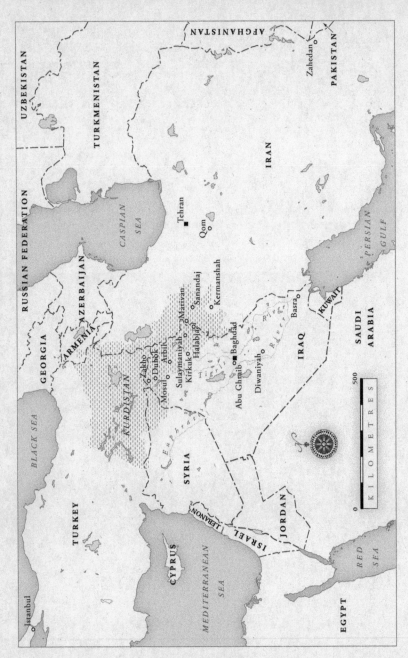

The Middle East

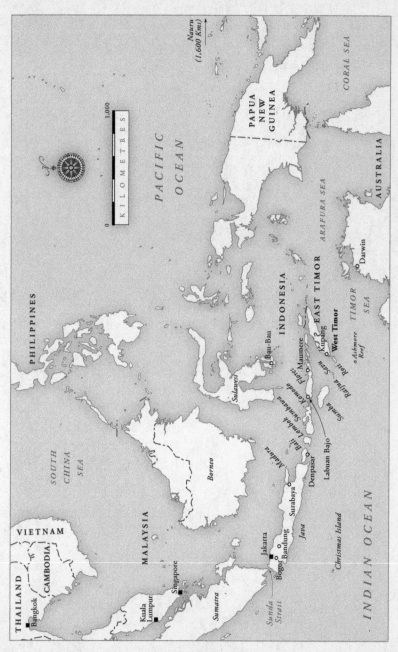

South-East Asia

PART ONE

IRAQ

1970 — 1999

HASSAN PILOT

I am the oldest son, which meant my parents gave me everything. I was lavished with attention, but that was not what inspired my affection for my father. He was a man with an indomitable spirit. Once a proud and dignified man. Once the centre of my universe. He was full of fire yet tender, outraged but calm. For the first ten years of my life I loved everything about him.

It seemed to my young eyes that he was made of steel, yet every morning when I was little he would walk me to school. I would patter alongside gazing up at his towering figure. Once there, he would let go my hand and put a dinar in it. 'Just in case,' he would say.

I would wrap my tiny fingers around it with a sense of growing independence, which he would then destroy by asking for a kiss. As he watched me go, I loved the feel of his eyes on my back. I knew he was proud of me, but he would never say it, he wanted me to be tough.

My father had a reputation as an individual, he was the son of the Pilot. Not that the Pilot flew planes, on the contrary, but one night when my grandfather was particularly drunk he stood on the roof and said, 'They think I can't fly. I fly!' And he jumped off and broke half the bones in his body.

It became a story amongst the people of our city who named my grandfather Pilot, so my father, Hassan, became known as Hassan Pilot.

My grandfather walked with difficulty on two crutches for the rest of his life, but like my father in those early years he remained jovial and good-humoured. When he was on his deathbed Hassan Pilot took me to see the dying Pilot, but I was only six and was confused by his sickly smell, and the sucking in and out of breath, and I ran from the room. I did not yet know about death.

When I was a little older my four brothers and I would wait in the afternoon for my father's return from his shop, where he made windows and doors to keep our family in the middle-class comfort my mother was accustomed to. We would sit in the house guessing if those were his footsteps, or if that was his voice singing, as he so often did. And then the door would fly open and we would all leap on him.

He would have a shower and then he was ours. He would do whatever we wanted. Our favourite was eating kebab. 'Okay, let's go,' he would say when he emerged smelling of fresh soap and dressed in clean slacks and a short-sleeved shirt. My mother never left the house without her hijab, yet my father always wore Western-style clothes. But of course this was the 1970s, when most of the cities of Iraq were becoming prosperous and cosmopolitan. These were the early years of Saddam Hussein's influence.

My father would swing Basim, the youngest then, onto his shoulders and off we would go to the kebab shop. As the sun set over our little city of Diwaniyah in southern Iraq, we would gorge ourselves on char-grilled lamb while Hassan Pilot told us stories about the last King Faisal of Iraq, who came to the throne at the age of four after his father died in a car accident, or the legendary Hanging Gardens of Babylon, built by the great Nebuchadnezzar the Second. My father loved his country.

Other times he would take us to the movies. Everyone knew my father, because in all of Diwaniyah there was never a girl in the cinema, but when my sister Afrah was old enough he would always take her.

We would all sit excitedly in one of the little opera boxes on the mezzanine level, oblivious of the outrage we were causing. Some people thought it was wrong, some would want to bring their daughters too but couldn't. I didn't know why not, but before there was fear of Saddam, there was always fear of defying our own customs.

Without thinking about it, my father was unafraid of being different. In fact he was afraid of nothing, not even Saddam Hussein when he became president in 1979 and began his reign of terror. I saw Iraqi men who were strong and tough but under Saddam they were terrified. Yet in this land that became ruled by fear, my father remained utterly fearless.

Back then when things were still normal and he was training for the army, he would get a week off out of every four. His homecomings were always a celebration. My brothers and I would squeeze pomegranate, grape and watermelon juice for him – no alcohol of course because we were Muslim. My mother would make samak mazguf, kebabs, and our favourite, hot pita bread and jelly. There was hugging and singing and laughing. He and my mother were happy then. We were all happy.

After eating we would wait with great anticipation. My father had a breadth of knowledge because he was an avid reader, but he never read to us. He preferred to tell us stories.

We would gather around him on the floor, or next to him on the couch, as he began. 'Once there was a boy whose mother sent him to buy chickpeas. He bought the peas and put them in his pocket, but there was a hole, and by the time he got home all the peas but one had gone.' We would settle in happily. We loved this story.

'The boy couldn't show his mother only one pea, so he asked a friend to hide it, but next day his friend said, "Sorry, the rooster ate it."'

We giggled, and the younger ones climbed on my father's lap and played with his moustache as he talked. He would swat them off without missing a beat. He truly relished the telling of this tale, which was part of our enjoyment.

So the boy demanded the chickpea or the rooster. He got the

rooster, which he gave to another friend to mind, but it was killed under a pile of timber, and so it went. The timber was burnt in an oven, which was broken by a cow, which was eaten by a family having a wedding party for their daughter. As the story progressed my father would take on the voices of the characters.

'When he went back to get the cow the boy said, "Give me the cow or the girl."' My father would imitate the boy's trembling expectation. We shrieked with laughter, with the little ones tumbling all over him. 'So he took the girl and went back home singing, "From the chickpea to the rooster, from the rooster to the timber,"' and we would all join in, even my mother. 'From the cow to a girl,' singing and laughing and laughing.

It was about this time that I betrayed my father, but his unconquerable spirit was never quashed, not even by the torture he endured as a consequence of my error. They broke him as a man and they fractured his mind, but somewhere inside that spirit remained intact.

So now he is taking another beating and this time I am with him. It is 1991 and I am twenty. We are in Abu Ghraib, Saddam's most notorious prison. The size of a small town, where cells are little more than human cages, and torture and mass executions are carried out daily.

I am humming. To myself. Fists clenched around iron bars as I steady my nerves for what is to come. Behind me prisoners, silenced by their fear, are packed together as far away from the bars as they can get. I put everything I have into my humming but the shouting of men, the crashing of batons, and the thud of fists on human flesh cuts through.

I fix my gaze on a naked bulb emitting a sickly yellow half-light down an eerie passageway, which reverberates with the violence they are doing to my father.

They picked us up together after the Shiites rose up in the south.

My father, my next and closest brother Ahmad, and myself. On arrival they separated us, but now four prison guards haul Hassan Pilot towards me, blood-splattered and beaten. He doesn't see me, the blood runs into his eyes from a gash on his forehead.

They bash him to his knees then lash out with heavy boots to make him crawl towards the wall of bars near me. I suspect this humiliation is part of the process of intensifying my distress. I am sure I am the one they want most. I am not only Shiite of fighting age, but for two years I have dodged compulsory induction into their army.

I can't extend my head to see, but I can hear them heaving my father against the bars and shackling him. They march away but soon return, their jackboots echoing threateningly as they reappear dragging my eighteen-year-old brother. I hear my father stop struggling against his chains and fall silent.

I call to Ahmad but his face is rigid with fear and he doesn't seem to see either of us. He is as yet unhurt. Maybe they will release him when they realise he is in the army and no threat. I call again, but he is disappearing down that hideous passageway and my voice is swallowed up by the noise of slamming gates and guards herding prisoners. Then I hear my father, frothing with impotence and rage, howl above the din, 'Saddam is a bastard!'

I had heard him say this so many times in our home as a child I had finally, unintentionally spouted it in a game at school, and in no time was hauled up in front of the headmaster for an explanation. While I knew not to say I had heard that Saddam was a bastard from my father, at ten I didn't entirely understand the severity of my crime, so nor did I deny it. I wasn't punished, just reprimanded, so I headed home with a light heart, glad my parents had not been called in.

But that night my father disappeared and our lives changed forever.

Next morning, after many miserable hours of worry, my mother, knowing nothing of what had happened the previous day at school, insisted I go as usual. I was wary and on guard when I arrived. Later I stared out the window, longing for my father, willing him to be home when I got there, and missing most of a lesson that would have aided my political awareness had I listened. It wasn't until years later that I paid any attention to how our great leader had found his feet.

I had no experience of anything other than the Baathists. They had taken over government in a bloodless coup in 1968, two years before I was born. They innocently made the relatively unknown Saddam Hussein, a Sunni, head of national security, and unbeknown to anyone but my father it seems, Saddam began to slowly build a new political force.

With the proceeds of oil he became a man of the people, redistributing stolen tribal lands and providing free health facilities and education. The universities were open to the West, men and women, Sunni and Shia, and were soon amongst the best in the Middle East, turning out doctors, engineers and scientists, creating a thriving new middle class. Then in 1971 he was involved in nationalising the Iraq Petroleum Company, which, to much public applause, brought billions more oil dollars into our country.

This enabled him to build more hospitals, schools, universities, and a vast amount of new infrastructure, and to dramatically expand and modernise the armed forces. However, during this golden age there was a darker side to things. When Saddam became vice president to Ahmed Hassan al-Bakr in 1975, he used his power to restructure the Mukhabarat, with its secret police and intelligence bureaus, to control the Iraqi people and the military.

By 1979 Saddam was ready to make his move. A charming yet uneducated brute of a man, he ousted al-Bakr in another bloodless coup and made himself President, Prime Minister and General Secretary of the Baathist Party. In his first year, a third of the highest ranking Baathists were executed, and any dissidence, from any walk of life, would cause you to disappear. Thus, under the cloak of prosperity,

Saddam became one of the worst tyrants of his time, but tragically, not unlike Hitler's Germany, the general population were initially blinded by his achievements.

But as I ran all the way home from school that afternoon I had little interest in any of this. I threw the door open and stood panting; I needed no more than a glimpse of my mother's face to tell me my father was not there, and so began a desperate period of our lives.

For the first few months we searched for him almost every day. It was now 1981 and the fear with which Saddam had begun to rule the nation had already seeped under the skin of most Iraqis, and nobody wanted to know about someone who had vanished, in case by association they were contaminated.

We must have gone to every police station in Diwaniyah. My mother would stand at the counter virtually ignored, surrounded by her children, our eyes alive with hope, as she tried to get someone's attention. 'My husband is missing.' The police attendant would look at her with disinterest; it was an everyday affair.

After a while my mother would go in alone. Outside, the younger children doodled in the dust. I sat on the steps staring off, with Ahmad sitting silently next to me, waiting for the terrible disappointment on my mother's face, and the ensuing sense of paralysis that flooded through my body when I let my mind imagine how different our lives would be if I had lied to the headmaster.

Then, taking my mother's hands, we would walk dejectedly on to the next police station. Our father had held our family together, but now we were rudderless in a sea of uncertainty and loss.

Once home my mother would cook whatever she could find. We were often hungry. We depended on the charity of our extended family. We were too young to work, and even if my mother had been educated she would have found it hard to get a job, but she was not even literate.

Sometimes my uncle, who was a colonel in the army, brought us food, but when there was a knock at the door my mother would grab the children and hold us to her. Then a voice, 'It is me. Uncle,' and we would relax.

One day, after another of our fruitless searches for my father, the colonel arrived looking anxious. 'I have found out where Hassan is.'

My mother gasped, her face softening with relief.

'He is in Section 5 Prison. But you must try to get to see Saddam as soon as possible, as they …' He glanced at the children and tapered off.

He poured himself some tea from the pot near my mother and bent close to her. I was allowed to listen because I was the oldest son and in the absence of my father the head of the family. 'They torture him very badly. You must hurry.'

I turned to my uncle in fright. While I had no interest in politics, I did understand enough to know they were hurting my father. For a moment I had the strangest sensation that I was going to pee, then bile surged up in my throat.

My mother, always a fighter, suddenly looked old and afraid. 'How can I go to Saddam Hussein? He will lock me up too, or kill me, and then who feeds the children?'

'No,' my uncle explained, 'he has sessions where he takes requests for clemency from ordinary people. You don't need to be afraid. To him you are no threat, so he will either help you or ignore you. Anyhow, what choice do you have?'

I looked forlornly at my mother as she leaned heavily on the kitchen bench, head hanging low between her shoulders, dredging up the strength to gird her loins again. I knew she could do it. I had seen her in action. After my father's first brush with the law in 1978, if it hadn't been for her he would have gone to prison then.

Despite Saddam's general popularity at that time, and his self-promotion as a man of the people, my father already saw through him. While not affiliated with any group or party, Hassan Pilot loved a good discussion about politics. Riding home in a taxi one night, he let it slip to the driver that Saddam would destroy Iraq. Unfortunately the driver worked with the secret police. He taped his passengers and delivered up any suspicious conversations. The next day Hassan Pilot was arrested.

When the matter went to court my mother sat in the public seating surrounded by her five small children. As the judge was about to pronounce a hefty jail sentence my mother stood up, ready for a fight.

She interjected and addressed the judge across the courtroom. 'If you are going to take my husband, take all the children too.' She pushed us towards him. I looked at her in horror as I stumbled forward. I endured her moods, her unpredictability and her stubbornness, but I was not prepared to be offered up for a jail sentence.

'I can't feed them without him. So take them all.'

There was an intake of breath around the courtroom as everyone froze. The judge, shocked, looked at our faces and then at my mother. He must have foreseen trouble he didn't want to have, because he backed down. He gave my father a fine instead of a prison sentence. I never found out what she would have done if the judge had agreed to take us. I was too afraid to ask.

Although we thought my mother was a tyrant back then, we still had plenty of fun at her expense. Ahmad and I grew up doing everything together. We played together, we went to school together, we shared our lunch together. We were of one mind. The thing we always remembered with affection about my mother was the way we defied her to get our first bicycle.

It was before my father disappeared, and we were normal, happy, innocent kids. My mother, like my father, is full of contradictions. She has the wile and courage of a wolf, yet is always afraid of tomorrow. If she can't find something to be frightened about she will make something up. She said no to a bicycle. She was scared a car would run over us.

My mother had a daughter who died before I was born. She believed there was a curse, so when I came into the world she would let no one see me in case they cursed me too, which possibly explains her over-protectiveness. Her distress was so severe she kept me hidden away for two years. But we were little children. We knew nothing of this, and even if we had we would not have understood. We just wanted a bicycle.

So Ahmad and I saved the coins our father gave us to buy sweets until we had a reasonable stash. Then we went to the bicycle shop. At first the owner thought we had stolen the money, but when we told him Hassan Pilot was our father he believed us and gave us a bicycle for what little we had. We were so happy we sang and laughed all the way home. When we arrived my mother glared and took it straight back.

Some weeks later I won a big pile of marbles in a game with our neighbour, who said he had a bicycle he would exchange for them. Ahmad and I were over the moon, but then we saw the bicycle. It was old, small, and had no tyres. We stared at it for a moment then looked at each other, nodded, and said, 'Okay, no problem, we're happy with that.' It was a bicycle, and it had the distinct advantage that no one would steal it if we left it outside, which we would have to do to hide it from our mother.

So off we went, Ahmad pushing and me riding. We fell many times but we hid our scratches and bruises. After about three days my mother came out of the house and saw us on the bicycle. I said, 'Ahmad, push, push,' and Ahmad pushed and she called, 'Come here, come here,' and we yelled, 'No, you can't take it,' and pedalled and pushed like crazy as she ran behind, waving and yelling, all around the neighbourhood.

Because the bicycle had no tyres, the steel rims made a terrible noise, so we woke everyone who was having an afternoon sleep. Windows flew open and angry people swore and threw things at us. We swore back, laughing, but then we saw a flying egg hit our mother as she came around the corner and we knew we were in trouble. But we didn't care. We were happy. We had a bicycle. We kept running and she kept chasing, eggs flying, people yelling.

As time passed I came to see my mother not as a tyrant, but as a woman so bold she would do anything to protect her family. Whereas very few people would have taken on one of Saddam's judges to free their husband, fronting Saddam himself took far greater courage. When my uncle came that night with news of my father's imprisonment and torture it was more than she could take. So, alone, she marched right into the lion's den.

On the day, Ahmad and I helped the younger children get ready in silence. Everyone was nervous. When my mother appeared, dressed as always in her black hijab, the now six of us huddled together with her and caught the train to Baghdad. When we arrived at the palace we stood outside staring up at it in awe. I had never seen such a massive building, or one so beautiful, but even though I was only ten I recognised it for the symbol of power and indulgence that it was.

My mother held baby Afrah in her arms and a letter in her hand. I could see she was afraid but I knew she wouldn't admit it. 'Don't go,' I said.

'I must. It is organised now. It will be all right.' She took a deep breath, passed the baby to me, and stepped up to the gates. We all stood frozen as we watched three guards with automatic weapons collect our mother and march her away.

My little brothers, Khalid and Asad, panicked and tried to follow, but were pushed back by the guards. Ahmad pulled some marbles from his pocket and we began, with the baby nestled on my lap, to play in the dust. It soon distracted the younger children, and once they got involved Ahmad and I sat back and watched them. But it was hard for us to concentrate. We kept looking anxiously at the palace.

'She should have let us have a bicycle,' I said, glancing from the marbles to Ahmad. It took him a while but finally he grinned. Her mad run through the streets could always be relied on to bring a smile to our faces. But then I thought of her fear of losing me as a baby.

She must not have been more than seventeen when she lost her first daughter.

'It was her fault she got hit by an egg,' Ahmad said with a grin, and we managed to laugh for a moment, but we soon fell silent again. We looked back up at the palace. Saddam could have her killed on the spot. He needed no reason or justification. My mother was as brave as my father was fearless.

She later told me that inside the palace she had to sit in a long row of women with letters trembling in their hands. Armed guards stood at the doors. An attendant, revolver on his hip, moved along the row collecting letters and speaking in a threatening tone.

'You do not speak. If he has a question he will ask you but otherwise you say nothing.'

Then he looked at a list and called the first name. When my mother's turn came she got up cautiously, straightened her shoulders and marched through a metal-detector and into the inner sanctum of Saddam Hussein.

Unlike the rest of the palace the room was very plain. Saddam stood in the middle in military fatigues with a large pistol in a holster on his belt. He read the brief letter I had written for my mother with his back to her. She was trembling but she mustered her strength.

'I have something to say.'

Saddam paused. 'Your letter says it.'

'No, not everything is in my letter.' She knew it would take more than a few written words to distinguish her case from the others.

Saddam lowered the letter and turned to her. My mother could be very appealing with her fiery determination. He looked bemused rather than angry. He half smiled, charmingly. 'Okay. Say what you want.'

Disarmed by his charisma, she burst forth with months of pent-up passion. 'My husband is a good man. He does nothing wrong. He is training in the army. He provides for his family very well. For nine months he has been in prison and we don't know why. We have many children and now they go hungry. I do not have the education to get a job. We are a good Iraqi family but without my husband things are very bad. And he is one less good man that you have to fight for Iraq.'

Saddam contemplated her for a moment without expression. 'Okay.'

She stared at him with no idea of what this meant. He nodded for her to leave. The attendant led her out and pointed her back to her seat.

Meanwhile, after hours of waiting anxiously, we finally saw my mother being escorted towards us. She was alive, but as she got closer I could see she was not happy. I looked away, unable to bear the disappointment.

She came out the gate and one of the guards gave her a letter. She passed it to me and took the baby. I opened it slowly. It was enough to see my mother's face, I could not stomach seeing it in black and white as well. But I must, so I took a deep breath and read it out. 'Hassan Al Jenabi will be freed and waiting for you at the Central Mosque at two pm in three days.'

I blinked. I felt dizzy. I started leaping and bounding down the street, waving the letter in the air. The children ran behind. There was laughter and my mother, at last, was smiling.

For three days it was hard for us to sleep. My mother borrowed money and began to cook up a feast: spicy kibbe, stuffed roast lamb, kebab, red lentil soup, wheat pudding and candied citrus peel. We talked about how it was going to be with all of us together again.

At night I heard my mother weeping. She was exhausted from carrying the load, and now, after nine months of secretly believing my father was dead, she nervously anticipated seeing him again.

At last three days had passed. My mother dressed us all in our best, and with baby in arms and children in tow we set off for the mosque. When we arrived we hurried inside, each one of us ready to run to my father, to throw ourselves into his arms kissing and hugging like we used to do when he returned from the army.

We scanned the vast interior of the mosque but there was no sign of him. My mother gestured us forward to kneel and pray. We knelt in a row. She was smiling. I was happy. I squeezed my eyes closed and I prayed. I had never been sure if there was a God and I heard nothing. But then I felt a presence beside me and I knew my prayers had been answered. My father had arrived. I was bristling with excitement as I turned to him, hungry for that first embrace ... but I faltered.

I was unsure if it was him. He was skin and bone. His shoulders sagged, his face was sallow, his eyes sunken and bloodshot. A shell of a man ... But it was him. I knew this. This was my father. He could not look at us, but it was him.

I reached for his hand. He flinched away from my touch.

That day we intuitively knew it was the end of the happy childhood we had known. Saddam's henchmen were waiting outside the mosque to take Hassan Pilot to a mental asylum, presumably because the torture in Prison 5 had sent him insane. First they used electric shock to torture him, now they would use it to make him better. This was how things went.

As we headed home my mother's anguish was palpable and her face hardened with the pain. It was a relief she wanted to walk alone, with the children trailing behind in silence, each in our own way already steeped in grief.

Just to compound our sadness, it seemed our sentiments were paralleled by what was happening in our nation. A major loss of innocence had begun for the Iraqi people who had turned a blind eye to the dangers of Saddam for the sake of the boom times he was delivering.

Riding on the affluence that oil had brought to Iraq in the '70s, and secure in the power of the army he had developed, in September 1980 Saddam declared an unprovoked war against Iran. It bogged the country down for eight years, almost bankrupting it, and leaving nearly a million soldiers dead or wounded, with over fifty thousand taken prisoner, many thousands of civilians killed, and millions made refugees. Even those who hadn't encountered the savagery of Saddam were soon disillusioned.

The rules at the mental hospital were different from those of the prison. My mother was allowed to visit my father. After her first trip she came home full of rage. 'They can't bear that they can't break him, and now that they have they want to fix him.' I could tell by her tone she knew it was too late, and she confirmed this by her next remark. 'You'll have to start to work the markets after school, Ali.'

The rest of the children looked up from squabbling over the last of the lentil soup. They were never hungry before Hassan was taken. This and the idea of their ten-year-old brother going to work brought home the reality of our situation.

'What about my homework? If I fail they'll put me in the army,' I protested, though I knew this would not be a threat for a few more years.

My mother passed her piece of bread to Ahmad to share. 'So what happens to Afrah and your brothers?'

I felt anger rise up in me that I was being called on to play the parent's role when I was still a child. 'I'm no good at the markets. I can't do it,' I threw back at her.

Needless to say the next afternoon, when I got home from school, my mother was waiting with a box of batteries, and I compliantly headed off for the markets. I felt shy and awkward as I pushed my way through busy stalls of fresh fruit, colourful fabrics, woven baskets, pots and pans and clothes, to find a place to stand to sell my batteries. I was afraid I would see someone I knew. I felt unsafe, and ashamed for my family to be seen as not providing.

On the perimeter I found a shoe shop with a big glass window. If I saw someone I knew I could turn around and pretend to be looking in the shop. It also had the advantage that I could see in the reflection when they had gone.

I placed my box at my feet and laid out the batteries, small, medium and large. I stood patiently for several hours, but nobody wanted to buy. I watched the other sellers spruiking but I couldn't bring myself to attract even more attention. Finally, in a weak voice, I forced myself to call, 'Batteries. Anyone want batteries?' I glanced around to see if anyone heard but no one took the slightest notice.

The sun was getting low in the sky. I watched the people selling cigarettes. Without doing a thing, they had a constant stream of customers. By dusk I was getting cold and desperate. A man looked down as he passed and paused. I felt a glimmer of hope. 'You want batteries?' I asked, but he turned to go. 'You pay anything. I want to go home.'

My mother, strung out by worry about tomorrow, flew into a fury when I told her. She whacked my legs with a belt, yelling, 'Are you crazy? That's quarter what I paid for them.'

It stung my flesh but not as much as my pride. I glared at her. 'You go sell the damn batteries yourself.' She hit my legs again. If only she could have imagined how she was compounding the humiliation of my day. I flew back at her, 'I told you I can't do it.'

She started to cry, which I couldn't bear. No matter how angry she made me, she was my lynchpin to life. I was full of love and hate for her, but by anybody's standards we were exceptionally close. She gestured to the children. 'Is it better that they starve?' She had me in a corner. What was I to do? I curbed my rage, rubbed my stinging legs and said quietly, 'I'll get better at it.'

As time went on I became less self-conscious and my confidence grew. I changed from batteries to cigarettes. At first my mother bought them but she got the wrong ones – Arabic cigarettes, made in Jordan. You had to light them up several times and nobody wanted them. They wanted cigarettes from Europe. Eventually I discovered the black market and did the deals myself. I soon learnt to work out margins and what to buy and sell for. At last I began to make enough to provide for the family.

After a few months Ahmad turned eight and joined me. We started at one o'clock, straight after class, and finished after dark, then had to get up early next day for school. We could never do our homework, so the teachers would get angry and sometimes beat us. We were ashamed. We didn't want to admit our father had been in prison and was now in a mental hospital, and that we had to support our family. No other kids in our classes were in this situation. They declared their Baathist allegiance and did their homework. So every time we would bring a new excuse and try to bear our punishment.

Usually we made more money because there were two of us, but sometimes we lost it because there were thieves in the markets and we didn't yet know how to protect ourselves. We would have to go home with nothing and our mother would be angry, then we would go to school the next day and the teacher would be angry, and finally we got angry too and started to bash people.

We became violent kids that no one wanted to touch. They didn't steal from us any more, and we began to experience a different kind of respect, which was dangerously intoxicating.

These were tough times, but being children we imagined if we could hold on somehow, our father would eventually return and take over. Sometimes we were so exhausted after getting home late and leaving early for school that we would go for a week without a shower. It was miserable, and my mother became increasingly nervous about our situation. If we came home with too little profit she would hit us, only if we brought home plenty would she smile with relief.

But Ahmad and I still found ways to make fun when we could. In the summer, when it was really hot, most of the older people would go home for lunch and a siesta, leaving younger members of the family to run their stalls. So on the street there were just children, who were left for those few hours to play freely. It was kid heaven.

Ahmad and I were our own bosses, so when a friend came by and suggested, 'Apples?' we couldn't resist abandoning our post. There was a very small green apple which we all loved to eat. You bite a little bit from it, dab it in salt and then you eat it. It is delicious. So while the adults slept we went from house to house to find an apple tree. Fences in Iraq are made from stone, brick and mud and are very high, two to three metres. You can't see what is behind them, so we looked for a wall with protruding branches and then, because Ahmad was the smallest, lifted him up to check the coast was clear.

We soon found one and quickly got Ahmad on our shoulders.

'Do you see anyone?' I whispered.

'No,' he replied. But as we let him down I saw a glint in his eye. I could always read Ahmad and without a word I knew he had seen something and was playing. So when I went up next and saw the owner was not sleeping but watching, I kept Ahmad's game going.

'No one. Your turn,' I told my friend.

He climbed onto my shoulders and by now the guy was ready and waiting with a stick. So when my unfortunate friend popped his head over, the guy whacked him twice before he fell back with me on top of him, and little Ahmad almost hysterical with the giggles.

I grabbed Ahmad's hand and we ran laughing all the way back to the markets, with my friend in hot pursuit. Ten years later, whenever I saw that friend, he would still remember and laugh. 'You and your brother,' he would say, shaking his head.

Seven months after being taken to the mental hospital, my father was finally released. We came home from school to eat lunch one day and there he was, sitting in his chair. He had gained a little weight but still looked gaunt and distant.

There was no hugging and laughing, no jokes. The children stood staring at him, waiting for a response. Finally Hassan smiled and our eyes lit up. I felt a surge of relief. Maybe all was well after all.

My mother watched hopefully. 'Tea, Hassan?' She passed him a cup and he sipped it.

'Ah, very good coffee.'

I looked at him strangely, unsettled again. 'It's tea, Baba.'

He smiled. 'Yes, of course. Very good tea.'

The disappointment began to bite and I looked away from him. I tried to catch my mother's eye but she avoided mine. It was as if the substance had gone out of him and he was imitating what he remembered of himself for our benefit.

For some weeks my father sat quietly in his chair with a haunted look, while the pain and rage bubbled underneath. He never drank before he was tortured but now he discovered the anaesthetic powers of alcohol. Initially it got him by, but then Khalid, my second brother, died.

Ahmad, Khalid and I had been running home from school. There was a strong wind blowing dust down the street. We stopped at the local store to find some game cards you could get off ice-cream wrappers. The wind was getting worse. Ahmad and Khalid began going madly through the bins.

Suddenly there was a wild blast of dust. I pulled their heads out of the bins and yelled that we had to go. I had them each by the scruff and didn't release them until we had begun to run. The wind roared. There was almost no visibility but I thought I could hear them both behind me.

When we arrived home, Ahmad and I flew in the front door followed by a blast of sand, but Khalid was not with us.

After several days of the family desperately searching, we discovered that on that day the wind had blown the cover off a wastewater well on the footpath near the shop.

We received this news in deathly silence. Then my father turned on me. 'How could you have left him? He was your little brother, your responsibility. How could you?'

Khalid was epileptic. His life had not been easy, and now to imagine him drowning alone in a well was too unthinkable. I began by defending myself. 'The dust, we couldn't see … Don't blame me.' Then, in a rush of uncontrolled anger, I flew at him. 'I'm not the parent, you had the children, you should look after them. All this time you've been gone and now you've come back you're still no father...' I managed to stop myself. My father, bleary-eyed from anger and drinking, suddenly looked pitiful. He grabbed me and held me to him, a look of anguish on his face.

The well cover was removed, the colonel arrived with a pump, and I, as the oldest of the family who could fit, was lowered down through the small opening on a rope. The wet, stone walls were covered in slime. The water was black and putrid. It dripped and echoed around the eerie space. Above was the sound of the pump, below the receding surface of the water. Then beneath me a shape began to emerge.

The last thread that was holding my father's mind together snapped. After Khalid's death his rage became uncontainable. It was about that time that the army decided he was well enough to return to duty. They sent him to the front for seven years of brutal, purposeless war with the Iranians. The army only paid enough for him to survive, so there was no way out, Ahmad and I had to continue working.

When he came home on leave there were no celebrations. Where once we sat in excited anticipation, now it was with dread that we waited to discern the level of his drunkenness by his singing or his footsteps. Once home he would drink and take his rage out on his family. After smashing up the house he would attack my mother, who invariably made things worse by fighting back. When he started chasing us with threats and blows she would pull us all into one room and lock the door, but then he would try to bash it down.

His rage would increase until he was too drunk to do anything but plead. By then the night was over and, sleepless, we would have to go to school, where I lived under the increasing threat of having to go into the army if I failed.

Nine months of torture in jail would be enough to send most people mad, but for my father this was followed by seven months in the mental asylum and then seven years fighting a war he profoundly disagreed with. He never had a chance of restoring his mind, and now, only two years later it is 1991 and they have got him again. But this time with Ahmad and me.

There is no justice to why the three of us are here in Abu Ghraib. Despite Iraq being virtually crippled by eight years of war with Iran, and with barely three years of relative peace, Saddam invaded Kuwait. When the Americans drove him out, offering the Shiites support if we rose up against him, we believed them. But as soon as the uprising started, the US left us to our fate, and the full weight of Saddam's army was turned on us.

They moved swiftly through the mostly Shiite southern cities, imprisoning, torturing and killing all the young men and anyone suspicious.

When we heard Saddam's army was coming everyone ran out of the city. It made no sense because there was nowhere to hide, but our options were fight or flight, and we knew we could not fight AK-47s, so we flew.

There were eleven of us by 1991, nine children plus my parents, but my father refused to go. Perhaps by now he and Saddam were as mad as each other, but he yelled, 'I won't run from Saddam, he destroyed our country, he should be running from us,' and stood firm. There was no moving Hassan Pilot once he had made up his mind, or perhaps he knew there was a limit to how long he could last without a drink, but either way we had to give up and flee without him.

My mother's last baby, Hashim, was only one. I was carrying him in my arms as we ran through the streets. When we were about a kilometre from the city we saw a helicopter. Maybe some of the remaining Americans were coming to save us after all. But when it got close we could see it was one of Saddam's, and then it began shooting at us.

We scattered and ran towards a cluster of date palms. I clutched the baby to me and tried to cave my body around him as I ran, while the helicopter circled and dived on us, spraying bullets.

I leapt beneath some low fronds with the baby. Ahmad was already there, trying to shield our little sisters, Afrah, Ahlam and Inas. My mother clutched my other brothers. Ahmad and I caught each other's eyes. This had to be the end, the palms were virtually no cover. With guns blazing, the helicopter circled again and began its final approach. All the children were crying now, and baby Hashim, sensing his siblings' fear, screamed hysterically.

I held his tiny body tightly to me and looked again at Ahmad. He was shaking with terror, yet he tried to smile at me. 'It's okay, at least we go together,' he whispered. Overhead the roar of the helicopter and the guns got louder, but then, the firing ceased.

I looked up to see the belly of the helicopter, but to the left of it was a passing American plane. The shooters had pulled in their guns and the helicopter was backing off. Within minutes it had disappeared and the US plane continued on its way. Maybe it was just heading home to the USA but one way or another it inadvertently saved our lives. God bless America.

We went on, out into the desert, but there was no food, water or shelter and we had little children. We gathered with at least a hundred other families at a monument near a small village that had nothing to share with us. We stayed for three days in the cold and rain, then my father, who knew our destination, appeared with the news that the city was calm and we could go back. I suspected this was one of the army's tactics to lure the people home, but the misery of the children was agonising so we agreed to return.

The journey home was painfully slow as the children were sick from hunger, fear and sleepless nights on wet ground. I knew one of my uncles had begun to build a house on the outskirts of the city before he was killed in the war. It still stood in its incomplete state, and my father and I had planned to come and finish it as a memorial to him. We managed to find it and spent the night in its empty shell.

It rained all night and I lay listening to the water drip into pots around me like small gunshots in our ears. I was scared to go back to

Diwaniyah. It didn't matter if you had done anything or not, the secret police and the army were like animals, they had AK-47s and you were guilty. Things might be quiet for the moment but the city would be under martial law by now, and you could not argue with that.

A few days after we returned I wished I had paid more attention to my instincts. This morning they took Ahmad and me off the street. Ten men with guns in black Toyotas stolen from Kuwait. They said, 'Get in the car.' And we couldn't say no or they would shoot us. Once they had us they drove to our house and got my father. Then they brought the three of us here to Abu Ghraib.

The guards reappear to the jarring beat of their jackboots. They unshackle my father from the bars and drag him so close to my cell I can smell his sweat above the stench of the prison. I think he sees me as he cries out again, 'Saddam is a bastard!' Batons rain down on his head and back, *thud, thud*. My eyes wild, I grip the bars and hiss, 'Shut up, Baba. They'll kill you.'

A guard hears me but I don't care, it's better they hit me than him. He swings his baton at my hands, *smash*, but I keep holding the bars. He challenges me by raising it to strike again, but I swallow the pain, glare back and continue to hold my grip.

I don't know why I'm doing this. I can only end up with broken hands. There is nothing that I can win, but somehow it feels like a united stand with my poor crazy father, who has nothing left but the ability to stand back up. 'Saddam is a bastard! Saddam —'

Crunch. A baton is driven into his gut and he crumples forward. He hits the floor and the guards begin a frenzy of kicking. Blood spurts from his mouth, yet he keeps up his protest until it is just a spluttering whisper. I beg him, 'Baba, stop.'

My mind flashes to my father's friend Munam, my first encounter with the results of Saddam's wrath. Was this the prison where it happened? Is this how it went? I was only a child, maybe eight or nine.

Munam was a Communist. The Baathists hated the Communists, who had thrived on Iraq's high level of education in the '70s, making it a breeding ground for Marxism. Now, presenting some of the strongest opposition to Saddam's regime, they were subject to barbaric punishment.

Munam's body was shattered when the secret police released him from interrogation. His mouth was a strange gaping hole where his teeth had been and his body was swollen and purple. He was close to death, he had no family, he was alone in his house, and everyone was too afraid to help him. Except my father, of course. With no thought of the consequences, he took Munam food, prepared it and fed him through his broken mouth with a spoon. Munam could no longer speak but his eyes were gentle and full of gratitude.

One day, when I went with my father, his friend was gone. The secret police had come again and taken him for another, and no doubt last, round. It was the only time I saw Hassan Pilot close to tears.

When my father is finally kicked into unconsciousness the guard turns and smiles at me. 'That's nothing compared to what we are going to do to you.' I continue to clench the bars with my swelling hands. I haven't backed down. I'm still hanging on. I'm standing with you, my broken father.

They drag his unconscious body away and I try to face the reality that I might not see him again. I am comforted by the thought that they have never killed him before, and they have certainly had plenty of goes at it. The precious love of our first decade and the misery of what followed swirl madly in my head as I crane my neck to watch him disappear into the bowels of the prison. Then I hear his spluttering voice again in the distance, echoing back to me. 'Saddam is a bastard!'

In that most horrible of moments I begin to smile. No matter what they do, they can't silence him. Even in his mania he says what he believes. I am proud of him. Behind me the watching prisoners cower. What has Saddam done to our people?

I strain to hear him one more time. I am both laughing and crying now. I look down at my swollen hands, then back into the void. I had never told him that it was my fault he got arrested that day, because of my silly schoolyard game.

I am still clinging to the bars when our cell gate flies open. The guards march in, rottweilers on the hunt. But I am aching with the injustice of my father's plight. I loved the part of him that never accused others, nor lied or cheated. In my first ten years he was a gentle man who was never angry. Nor was he envious or jealous. He didn't care that others had more than him. He didn't care if some guy had a million dollars, he would look at us and say, 'Don't lie, don't swear, don't steal.'

'Bring him!' cuts across my thoughts and I realise it is now my turn.

I know what I am in for. I am twenty and every twenty-year-old has heard about the arsenal of instruments Saddam's henchmen use. If you haven't been through it, someone close to you has. It's said their methods are so refined they can make a camel speak English within an hour. But like my father, the tortured don't talk about it afterwards, you just piece it together from what comes out in their drunken rages and their nightmares.

The guards swoop on me and drag me out. Down that hideous passageway, reeking with the stench of stale sweat and blood. My father's blood.

When they push open a heavy wooden door I am desperately trying to steel myself to withstand more physical pain, but what I see is worse than hell. My little brother Ahmad is tied to a chair, his bloodied hands in front of him, nailed to a table. His face bashed and bleeding.

The guards see the rage on my face. 'Each time you won't answer a question we take another finger off.'

Another sears my brain. I can hardly stomach looking, but in a glance I see his little finger is already severed and lies in front of him on the table.

'We took that one for your father.'

The blood pounds in my temples. I imagine my poor father, after all he had been through, being held down and made to watch his son's mutilation.

I steady myself and try to stay calm. I look at Ahmad. I can see his relief. I have come, like I always did, to fight off the school bullies or the thugs on the street.

'Let him go. This is a mistake. He is in Saddam's army, he fought in Kuwait.'

The guard shoots back, 'He deserted.'

I struggle to control my voice. I was always a bad liar. 'He did not. He came home for urgent family matters. He was going back to the army tomorrow.'

Unlike me Ahmad had done what was asked of him, he had joined up. I try not to remember the night he came home after deserting, how he had suffered being amongst death. My little brother was too sensitive to be one of Saddam's killers.

'He is a deserter and you and your father are part of a political group. What is its name?'

'I know nothing about politics.' This time I don't have to lie. Despite my father's protests, which always just seemed like part of his personality, and despite what they had done to him, I never analysed what had befallen us as being the result of politics, just the pathological brutality of Saddam. My father was never part of a party, just a persistent critic of the regime, and would not be forced to say that what was happening to our country was good. I try to explain to the guards, but they have a job to do, the orders come down from above and they want to get on with it.

'You will answer the question or we take off another finger.'

I look at Ahmad. My sweet, gentle brother. I was his protector when my father was no longer able. Together we worked the markets to support the family. Together we laughed and made the best of things. He is my best friend, my brother, my first love.

I feel panic rising in my throat. I can't answer their questions. Even if I lie, what names will I give them? I don't know any political groups or resistance fighters. I have always been too busy making a living to get involved. If I make up names it will only hold them off for a few hours while they investigate. Then they will come back fuelled with revenge for my deception. 'I know nothing,' I say, trying to buy time.

In a flash they take another finger. The axe comes down with such speed I hardly see it, but blood spurts across the room. 'You think we are joking?' Ahmad doesn't cry out, but the terror on his face is so profound that it is a stake through my heart and I bellow like a bull being held down for slaughter.

I was a wrestler in my youth and in that moment I become a madman. I forget their weapons and I howl tears of fury as I kick, bash and tear at eye sockets, noses, groins, and as they swing their batons into my face, my head, I yell, 'Saddam is a bastard!' I know now what my father meant. I become my father. Hollering for my brother. For my family. For what is left of Iraq.

As they drag me from the room I try to look back at Ahmad, but they kick my head around so I can't. He of all of us is so ill-equipped to face the slow and painful death they are about to inflict on him, and I cannot save him. I can't even see him one last time.

They drag me into a stone-walled cell and hitch me by my wrists to the ceiling. They throw cold water over me and turn an old air-conditioner on to freezing. My arms begin to pull from their sockets but I feel nothing. They can do anything they want to me now. They can't hurt me any more.

How long will it take you to die, Ahmad? My brother. My sweet brother.

THE KINDNESS OF STRANGERS

I am seven years old and I am running with Ahmad down a street near my home. We each have a bicycle wheel with no tyre, which we propel with sticks as we race each other down the gentle incline of the dirt road. Ahmad is five and he is winning. I am letting him because he needs to know he can, and Khalid, too small to hoop a wheel, gleefully gallops beside him.

Then suddenly an army truck is coming towards us. The roar of the engine fills my ears. It is getting too close to Ahmad and Khalid. They are focused on their wheel. They are laughing. The truck comes straight towards them. I try to cry out but my voice is swallowed up by the noise of the engine. I try to run but my legs hang from my body without touching the ground and my arms are lashed above my head.

I am struggling and yelling, 'Ahmad! Khalid!' when a metal door flies open and two guards appear. I stare at them, not sure which reality I am in. One of the guards shouts, 'Wake up! Wake up. Time for you to rest. You hang for eight hours, you rest for two, then you tell us what we want to know or you hang for another eight.'

My breath has frozen on my lips and I am only semiconscious. The air-conditioner roars like the engine of the truck as it pumps air so cold that small stalactites have formed beneath the unit. My legs have buckled and any weight I may have been taking on my toes has gone. Now I am hanging with my full weight on my arms, which miraculously have not yet dislocated.

The guards undo my wrists and I crash to the floor. I lie with my arms still stretched above my head, unable to move. The door slams and everything is still. Inch by inch I slowly bring my hands down, and coil myself into a ball on the filthy stone floor. I am comforted by the silence and the prospect of two hours to get my blood flowing before they start on me again.

I try to stop my mind going to Ahmad. If I have been hanging for eight hours he must be dead by now. He is a deserter, so they have to kill him, it's only a question of how slowly they do it. The physical pain is easier to bear than what is in my head.

I divert my thoughts to my mother and my seven remaining siblings. Asad, Basim, Afrah, Khalid II, named by my mother in memorial after her third son who died in the well, Ahlam, Inas, and baby Hashim, all still traumatised from being shot at when we ran out of the city. Hassan Pilot has been mentally absent for so long now, but without me, a father substitute, what will they do? Even if I can stay alive, what will I have become by the time Abu Ghraib has finished with me? And how many years will that be?

Afrah, at only twelve, will no doubt try to fill the gaps. Despite my beaten body she brings a smile to my face. She was the first girl after four boys, and my father's unquestioned favourite. While other families celebrated the arrival of more sons, my father dreamt of having a daughter. When Afrah was born he was ecstatic.

Anything Afrah asked for he said yes to. There was no 'no' in the dictionary for Afrah. So if we wanted something, when he came home we would hover in the living room, waiting while he showered, changed and sat on the couch for a cigarette, and then we would sit Afrah next to him with clear instructions: 'I want to buy some marbles.' Or 'I want to go to the park,' and he would say yes.

My brothers and I weren't jealous, because we loved her too and she never used her special treatment against us. On the contrary, we gained considerable benefit after my father changed and started fighting with my mother. Red-faced and angry he would be swearing at Umi, when little Afrah would slip her shell-like hand into his and say, 'Calm down, calm down.' He invariably obeyed, and we, too, would want to say yes to whatever Afrah wanted.

I suddenly hear footsteps approaching my cell. Can two hours be up already? I still lie in the same position on the floor but my body, now thawing, is coming alive with pain.

The steel door swings open and I brace myself as two guards grab my hands and whip them above my head. Fire shoots through my shoulders as they haul me, not to my feet to be winched to the ceiling, but out into the corridor.

I presume there has been a change of plan and I am to be executed. It is commonly known that scores of political prisoners are randomly killed here every week. So I try to prepare myself for a miserable end, but it is hard to maintain any kind of faith inside the torture chambers of Abu Ghraib.

They drag me too fast for me to get onto my feet, so the uneven concrete floor shreds my skin. We stop, a door is unlocked and I am thrown in. Then it is slammed and locked again behind me.

I lie on the floor, trying to get my bearings, waiting terrified to see what sort of killing instrument they are going to use on me. Above me the lips on a face begin to move.

'You wouldn't happen to have a cigarette?'

I begin to focus and realise I am surrounded by a group of benign, wretched prisoners peering down at me. The torture room must have been overbooked and my interrogation delayed, so I have been fast tracked to this tiny, foul-smelling, windowless cell.

One of them hands me a tin cup of water. I take it thankfully and gulp it down. He introduces himself as Akram, which I know to mean 'most generous'. I smile and nod as he tries to help me to my feet, but my legs won't hold my weight so they prop me up against a wall.

I look around the cramped space, maybe four metres by eight, through the dim glow of a single globe hanging from a concrete ceiling. It is so high two men on each other's shoulders couldn't reach it. The prisoners are emaciated, with the remnants of putrid clothes hanging off them. Some bear the scars of recent beatings or torture. This is clearly a long-stay cell. Dante's purgatory.

My arrival seems commonplace, as the prisoners soon return to a game they are playing on the floor. Others pace, which is difficult considering the size of the cell, but Akram remains beside me. I am desperate for more water, but surmising he has already given me his share, I can hardly ask for more. Akram doesn't talk, he just sits quietly. I am grateful. There is no way of knowing how long it will be before they come back for me, but for the moment I feel comforted by his presence yet alone with my thoughts.

What will they do with Ahmad's body? Will they tell my family to come and collect it, as they often do, or will they dump it on our doorstep, another of their practices? I try to stop thinking of him. I have to accept his death and focus on staying alive, for the survival of the rest of us.

But the mind is a clever instrument. It feeds us only as much as we can take, until we are ready. And here I am, in the safest place I've been since I arrived, and there it is, like a vulture waiting to tear me apart. It suddenly all floods in, the memory of the night Ahmad came home as a deserter. I had not only supported but encouraged him not to go back to the army. My mother and I had fought. She was afraid, and wanted him to return, but I won. For one terrible moment I feel implicated in his death. I run my fingers through my hair. I want to tear it out.

Akram, sensing my distress, puts a hand lightly on my shoulder. 'The food is here,' he says softly, passing me a container the size of a sugar bowl. 'Don't look at it, just eat.'

It's too late. I have seen some dreadful grey vegetable concoction dribbled over a lump of cold claggy rice. I try not to gag as I force myself to swallow it.

Before the lights go out at eight o'clock Akram hands me a blanket stained with dried blood and urine. 'This was left by the guy you replaced.'

I don't want to think about what happened to him. I look around and see everyone spreading their blankets on the rough concrete and dirt floor. Until now it never occurred to me how all these people are going to sleep in such a small space.

I soon learn. The room takes twenty-six if everyone lies on their side, in two lines, facing the same direction, jammed together like sardines. Then there are four remaining who have to stand up all night in the small space in front of the door. When the morning comes they can lie down and sleep. When we turn over we all have to turn together, and if you need to excrete you have to do it where you lie and hope it doesn't spread onto too many other people.

After only a few minutes of lying like this on the hard uneven floor my shoulders ache, but there is nothing I can do. Then, as if an initiation for me, the door flies open and a particularly vicious-looking guard pronounces, 'There is to be no standing. Everyone must sleep.'

He begins kicking the guy closest to him in the stomach to make us shuffle back. We pack together as tight as possible. 'My job here is to disable you!' he yells between kicks. 'So when I say something, do it exactly. Don't force me to make you disabled.' The four 'standers' jam into the space we have created, three on the floor with the fourth lying on top of them. The Disabler seems satisfied and leaves.

The man who was kicked vomits blood on the man in front of him. We try to shuffle back even more to give him space, but it is not possible and no one has the courage to stand up. The stench of fear and vomit is overpowering. Pain racks my body and it is hard to breathe, yet in no time I hear the sounds of sleeping. Somehow, it seems one can adapt, but as I lie crushed between strangers, Akram's filthy hair in my face, it feels unimaginable.

The minutes become hours as the night creeps by. Life before my father changed has always been a sanctuary of contented times, to which I regularly escaped in the difficult years that followed. Submerged in this hellhole the pleasure of those days feels almost too remote to remember, but I am well practised and soon I can hear his voice and the patter of my little feet running behind him.

His tall, proud figure strides ahead, cheerfully greeting friends as he passes. On his days off, Hassan Pilot was building a new house for us, and whenever he could he took me with him. It was only a short distance away, so we walked through the bustling streets.

I would dodge behind a barrel or a box of fruit on the pavement while he made a joke that I had disappeared. Then he feigned a search, asking shopkeepers if they knew where his son could be, until I jumped from my hiding spot and ran to him. Then he'd toss me up onto his shoulders, laughing, and stride on to our half-built house.

One day a carpenter left a window ajar, which swung and bashed my four-year-old head. My mild-natured father exploded at that poor employee, but somehow I recognised the extent of his rage as a measure of his love for me. As he examined my injury I saw in his eyes a vulnerability, and then his joy that I was unhurt. In his arms in those moments I felt safe in a way that I will always remember, but will never experience again under Saddam Hussein.

The images flicker and fade like the end of an old home movie and I am left with the bleak impression of my father as I mostly knew him, post-torture, during the war with Iran. By then he was wild and undisciplined in his madness, but he still had his sense of humour and would return with his stories. But they were different now and my mother would say, 'Too black for the children.' Except for one, which he told us often and always made him laugh.

He had been with a group of commandos on a moonless winter night under fire on the Iran border. It was snowing and they were freezing. In the pitch-dark they somehow found a cave and climbed in. Hassan was so cold he couldn't sleep, but then he realised the man next to him had a blanket so he eased himself under it and snuggled in. Next morning he woke to find the man whose bed he had shared was an enemy soldier who had been dead for weeks.

Somehow, sleeping with the dead didn't amuse me, but I could always laugh at the hilarity with which he told the story. I wondered how he could sustain any humour after all he had been through, and also how, after the drinking, the violence and the psychosis took root, he was chosen as a commando in the army. Or maybe that was why they chose him.

Fearless and teetering on the edge of insanity, fuelled by rage and alcohol, he was probably perfect for the job. The commandos would sweep into occupied territory and wipe the Iranians out, so the Iraqi regular army could hold the area while the commandos moved on to their next battle. But my father was Shiite, and was being forced to kill Shiite Iranians for no reason. For this he hated Saddam.

He tried to alert his fellow soldiers, who thought they were fighting to defend their country, but when Hassan Pilot attempted to tell them otherwise they were scared of him. They thought he was secret police, who were known for confessing their opposition to the government to encourage people to say what they believed. The more my father spoke up, the more isolated he became. He was court-martialled twice for swearing at Saddam and the Baath Party, but twice they released him. Maybe his fearlessness was too valuable to the army.

At home the war was unending. The houses were draped in black flags, like rows of women in mourning, as our young men died in hideous trench warfare for no purpose. Ahmad and I kept working the markets while families wept for their sons and Saddam's oppression increased. Our cities were bombed, oil revenues dried up, and the people got angry. Without money, food and weapons from the US, which was supporting Saddam back then, the whole country could have collapsed.

To add to the strain, when my father's allotted leave of seven days came up he would stay for ten or fifteen. We knew he could be shot, but by now we were too scared of his drunken rages to tell him what to do.

We were almost relieved when he went back to the front. The stress of waiting for a knock on the door, and the rollercoaster of fear and uncertainty created by his drinking, left the family in a shambles. Strangely, he must have commanded some kind of respect in the army, because when he returned there were officers who repeatedly turned a blind eye to his flagrant disobedience.

But now in Abu Ghraib, in 1991, would that respect still reside somewhere amongst his captors? Will someone turn a blind eye to his outrages against Saddam, or will they beat him to death so as not to be reminded of their own cowardice?

I must have drifted off, because next thing I know it's morning and the Disabler and his henchmen are herding us into a small adjoining ablutions cell, where the smell is even worse than the one we are leaving. There are three toilets with no doors on the cubicles and the pans are full to overflowing. It is disgusting, but I need to empty my bowels so there is nothing for it. When my turn comes I take it.

Being surrounded by a pack of men who have been holding on all night is extremely intimidating. I'd never before had to pull down my pants and try to shit in front of anyone, let alone an audience of men yelling, 'Hurry up, you motherfucker!'

I look down at the repulsive bowl spilling its foul contents onto a floor already deep in excrement. I couldn't possibly sit on the seat without contracting some sort of hideous disease. I look at the prisoners, for whom there is only one chance a day so they are desperate for their turn. Magically I lose my desire to shit.

As I leave I observe Akram take his turn. Everyone abuses him just as much as me, so it isn't because I am new, but he is unaffected and takes the time he needs. I wonder how long it will be before it becomes normal for me too.

While we were busy in the toilets two prisoners were sent back to our cell to clean it, so when we return the smell is tolerable, or perhaps it is by comparison to the overflowing sewage. Then the first of two meals a day arrives. Half a slice of bread with an egg. Already my stomach is cramped and aching for food.

With not knowing when you are going to be taken for execution or torture, the indignities of the toilet soon become insignificant. After a week of avoiding the horror of it, my stomach is beginning to blow up, so I take my turn and soon I am calling abuse at whoever is on the pot like everyone else.

During the day paranoia takes over. They often call someone and we never see them again, others go and come back mutilated or beaten. You never know when it's going to be you, and if you're going to die. The anticipation is almost a worse torture than the event. Every approaching footstep brings terror to our hearts.

One morning the Disabler marches in and calls for Hakim. I release the breath I have been holding. It is a terrible thing but Hakim's suffering will mean one more day for me. Just to add to our misery, each one of us must live with the guilt of being glad to see our friends taken. We try to play jelga to keep our minds off Hakim, it is all in a day, but he is a friendly guy and if executed will be particularly missed.

At about midday heavy footsteps approach, the door swings open and Hakim is thrown back in. There is hardly an inch of his body that hasn't been beaten, broken or burnt. His friend Yasin rushes to his side. He looks desperately around at us but there is nothing we can do. Yasin panics. He runs to the door and screams, 'Please bring a doctor, my friend is dying, please!'

There is silence, then the door opens again. The Disabler appears with four guards. 'Who's calling?'

Yasin looks uncertain but it is too late, so he steps forward.

The Disabler regards him dispassionately. 'Okay, you want a doctor, you come with me.'

Yasin realises his mistake. He walks slowly through the door. We stand frozen as it closes behind him. Then we hear the Disabler's menacing voice coaxing Yasin, 'Come further, come further,' and then the terrible thud of boot into stomach, over and over again.

When they finish with Yasin they throw him back in next to his friend, but Hakim is already dead.

Yasin's internal organs must have been mashed by the Disabler's boot, because he haemorrhages for three days then drowns in his own blood as he lies jammed between us on the floor. There are convulsions near the end, then congealed blood spreads slowly under the men on either side of him as he grows cold and stiffens against their own wilting flesh. The Disabler has made his point, as if we didn't know, that we should never ask for anything.

It is not unusual to wake and find someone dead in the morning, but the slow death of the otherwise healthy Yasin, after his selfless act of trying to save his friend, is particularly gruelling. During the night I can't keep my mind off Ahmad, and wonder if this was how he died, alone in a cell full of strangers. Or had it been quick, maybe with the axe they used on his fingers?

Later that morning I sit with Akram, both of us looking depressed. 'What is it,' I say, 'that drives one human being to want to inflict terrible pain and suffering on another for no reason?'

Akram remains silent, but after a pause a badly scarred man to my left says quietly, 'The culture of the Baath Party, when you want to join the secret police, is to trap you in your own cycle of terror.'

I look questioningly at him. 'Were you secret police?'

He gives a sardonic smile. 'I was young and stupid. I thought I could contribute something to my country. It was before we realised

Saddam was insane,' he says, dropping his voice. 'Once you have become a member, they want to make sure you are one hundred percent with them. They choose someone who is under suspicion that they want to kill, not drug or torture, just gun down in the street. They make you believe this guy is against the government, that he deserves to die. So you drive by and you shoot him, and they film you doing it, and you suddenly realise you are on camera killing someone who has a family, a wife and kids, and a life half lived.'

The scarred man pauses and looks away. 'So you suffer and want to leave but you have to stick together with the group, with Saddam. There is blood on your hands and when Saddam's gone you are gone, because the dead man's family will kill you and possibly your family too. So that's why they have no mercy. It is not a game. They're playing for their lives.'

He nods to himself, resentment bubbling underneath. 'Saddam has them trapped and loyal to him, and they are so full of fury at being ensnared that they kill with ease, so he never has to dirty his hands.'

'But you got out,' I say naively, then regret it.

He glances around our cell then back at me, bemused. The three of us fall to staring at our shoes.

After the horrors of last night the men are already trying to find ways to move on. Jokes are being told and stories recounted. I marvel at the strength of the human spirit and how it finds a way to survive. Except when we are under torture. More than a day of it and you definitely want to die. That's part of the fear. You know you are going to want death.

I look at Akram and realise even he is smiling. The group is preparing for the new prisoner who will replace Yasin. They will take the body away when they feed us. Probably to a mass grave. We don't like to think of it.

A newcomer won't know the ropes, so when Nabil arrives one

of my cellmates starts asking us, 'What would you like for lunch?' And we reply roast chicken, lamb kebab and salad, or whatever tasty dish we have been dreaming of, until he comes to Nabil. 'Just a chicken kebab, thanks,' he answers, thinking things are not so bad after all.

When the tiny bowls of lumpy rice and putrid sauce come, we eat them quickly and then we say to Nabil, 'You want yours?' And he says no, because he's waiting for his kebab. So we eat his share and Nabil waits and waits but nothing else arrives. Slowly he realises. We all laugh and poor Nabil tries to join in, but when someone new arrives he is the first to do it to them. And so it goes around.

When the nights come and we are exhausted from a day of boredom and fear, many of us are racked with nightmares and scream into the dark. Akram cries quietly most nights, not like a man sorry for himself or missing his family, but from the very depths of his soul. The prisoners care for each other because we are in this horror together, but at the same time we all have our own suffering. The men often joke to him, 'Don't laugh too much tonight, mate.'

I try to get him to speak about it so I can comfort him but it is hard. We are all careful not to ask too many details about each other's lives, because none of us trust ourselves not to speak under torture. I discover Akram was a teacher, but that is all. He is an intelligent, sensitive man, and I imagine in the past we would have been close friends. Or perhaps not, when I think of what I became during those difficult adolescent years.

As I got into my teens, I would come home from the markets and find my father on leave from the war, drunk on the couch, my mother's face already bruised. I would put the money from the cigarettes gently into her hand then walk past him and out the door without even a hello. I would march along the street, head down, hands in my pockets, looking for someone to hit.

Underneath it all was a smouldering anger for being thrown into the parent role, and having to look after them, rather than them looking after me. My mother's two younger brothers, Karim and Kasem, were gangsters, and despite her disapproval I found myself drawn to them. To be able to say 'This is my uncle' gave me status and legitimised the violence I wanted to do.

With my thuggery endorsed by them I soon formed my own gang, and whenever I had time roamed the streets looking for trouble. I was determined not to be like my father and yet here I was, quelling my rage with violence, and believing myself to be different because it wasn't fuelled by alcohol.

Things came to a head when the inevitable happened and I failed a second time at school. Now they could force me into the army, unless I did night school, which of course I agreed to. It started at five in the afternoon, so I needed a morning job.

After two years as a labourer and a motor mechanic I passed my exams and was allowed to go back to morning school, where I began my studies in accountancy. My mother suggested that another of her brothers, a successful tailor, might need help. So not wanting to return to the markets, and knowing how afraid my mother was of having no money, I went for her.

'I don't think this is the work for you,' my uncle said, looking at me sceptically. 'But I'll give you the job because you are my nephew. You just open the shop in the afternoon, look after the workers, and write down the details of any customers.'

'Okay,' I replied, dreading the thought of spending my days here. None of my gang had anyone in their lives insisting they earn a clean living.

I headed off to meet my hooligan friends, hoping for some action. Fortuitously, another gang we had territorial issues with was showing off on the street corner where we liked to hang out and smoke cigarettes. So I was able to plunge myself into a street fight.

We gave them the beating we thought they deserved and were

about to swagger off when their leader came back for another go at me. I don't know why he chose me but perhaps I was wearing my commitment too blatantly on my sleeve. But it was just what I wanted, so I let fly with all my force, and when he went down I kicked him. His comrades ran and I had my moment of glory, but then I realised he was having trouble breathing.

I looked around at the others as they revelled in our victory, while this boy lay at my feet, turning yellow. Suddenly the better side of my nature came to the fore, and despite my friends' protests, I hailed a cab and rushed my victim to the hospital. As I sat waiting to take him home, I had to admit I didn't entirely fit the gangster mould, but at that stage I had nothing to replace it with. I was a teenager, with no other way to quell my rage.

Next afternoon I arrived early at my uncle's and opened the shop. There were fabrics everywhere so I did my best to tidy the place before the workers returned from lunch. I made them tea, customers came and went, my uncle arrived and disappeared upstairs to his office, and finally the day was at an end.

When the workers left I went up and found my uncle at his desk doing the accounts. Beside him was a bottle of arak and a half-empty glass. It was too late for him to hide it, but knowing he was aware of my circumstances at home I thought I saw shame on his face.

'I could do that for you,' I said, pointing at the books. 'I study accountancy at school.'

Uncle looked at me suspiciously. 'If you don't have enough to do, try your hand at a sewing machine.'

I quickly found a broom and made myself busy.

That night, I was lying asleep on the roof with my brothers, when I was woken by my father yelling drunken abuse at my mother downstairs. I felt my hackles rising. She made me even madder by yelling back. There was no point, he was past reason. Soon she would be calling me for help to pull him off her. She was terrified of another pregnancy and another mouth to feed. But instead there was the usual crash of a chair being thrown and the smash of a bottle against the wall. I looked at Ahmad, also wide-eyed and awake. We lay staring into the dark, powerless, waiting, listening.

Next day at work I couldn't shake my ill-temperedness. When the workers left I cleaned the shop irritably, until my uncle finally staggered out drunk, leaving me to lock up. I looked at the machines, momentarily attracted to the idea of creating something. Then I went upstairs.

There were account books open on the desk. I checked the columns of money. He seemed to be doing all right. Then I looked at the bottle of arak. I picked it up, took off the top and sniffed. It had a pleasurable, biting smell. I had never been this close to alcohol before. My father's bottles were either in his hand or hidden somewhere, and besides I had always looked at them with contempt. They were what led to him beating his wife and terrorising his kids.

Intrigued, I sipped from the bottle cautiously. It made me grimace, but then again the hot burning sensation that flooded through my body gave me a warm uplifting feeling which distracted me from my misery. I tasted it again.

That night I drank several glasses from my uncle's bottle. I found myself humming as I cleaned the shop. I decided to try to make something on a sewing machine. For at least an hour I was completely absorbed in creating a child's shirt out of colourful scraps from the bin.

My self-pity disappeared. I forgave and forgot my family. I felt like a person I was happy to be, and the soreness about our circumstances dissolved. Not for one moment did I relate this freedom of mind to why my father drank.

That night, I crept into the dark house smelling of liquor. I tripped as I went up the stairs, which made me giggle. The family were all asleep on the roof, except for my mother, who quickly closed her eyes when I looked at her. I shrugged and lay down next to Ahmad, who gave me a dozy smile and dropped back to sleep.

Next morning held none of the elation of the night before. I didn't want to get out of bed and when I did I felt utterly gloomy. My head ached, which I used as an excuse to skip morning school. When I got to the shop that afternoon I found my previous night's offering on display next to the sewing machine. I cringed. It was not quite as brilliant as I had remembered. In fact it was a hideous tangle, which everyone had now seen.

I threw the little shirt into the bin with what remained of the joy I had experienced making it. I quickly cleaned up what was left from my night of private revelry, trying to overcome the anger and resentment that had arisen in me, before the workers arrived back and wanted their tea.

The days slipped by with relative ease but I found myself looking forward to when my uncle would get drunk enough to leave and I could have the place to myself. I couldn't wait to get upstairs and have that first glass of arak to liberate me from my melancholy.

My poor uncle must have thought his own drinking had escalated, but he left so drunk each night that in the morning he had no idea how much he had consumed from the bottle the day before. So I could usually get away with enough alcohol to prime me for a night of abandon with my gangster friends, then I would go home after the family was in bed so no one would suspect my activities.

The months slipped by and I was losing my way, but nobody knew. I had a secret nightlife that justified my days. It got me up in the morning, just knowing that sense of freedom and pleasure was awaiting me at the end of my penance. For a few hours I could escape the burden of responsibility and actually have the kind of fun I thought teenagers were meant to have.

One night, which I had planned to spend out with my cousin, I hurriedly finished cleaning, pushing scraps of thread and fabric under bolts of cloth or into dark corners. I gulped down my ration of arak then took some more. I was slowly increasing my intake, which meant my risk of being caught was rising, but I didn't seem to care. I downed another glass and headed out.

My cousin waited impatiently on his motorcycle, revving it from time to time to enhance his machismo. I climbed on the back. He hit the accelerator again to let it roar before he threw it into gear and we took off. The wind was in my face and I was pumped with arak. I felt alive and free.

We had done nothing wrong but in no time the local police were on our tail. They pulled us over and began their pointless questions. They had nothing on us, they just wanted to hassle. We both hated the police so, fortified with alcohol, I resorted to where I knew my strength lay and swung a punch.

My cousin liked this course of action and weighed in too. Before long we had our share of injuries, but we beat the police so badly they took flight. Triumphant, we guessed they would be so ashamed we'd trounced them they would leave us be, but it would be prudent to get out of sight just in case.

So we rode wildly to the top of my street, where hooting and laughing, I got off and sidled home. It was already late so my family was asleep on the roof. I breathed a sigh of relief and crept inside.

When I turned on the light in the bathroom, I was a little shocked at what I saw in the mirror. I had a gash on my forehead, and blood had run into my hair, over my face and down the front of my shirt. My left eye was already purple, my knuckles were broken and bleeding, and I had lost the skin off my knee.

I filled the basin and began splashing water over my injuries when I realised I was not alone. I looked up and there in the mirror was my mother, watching me. It was not her usual steely gaze but one of smarting pain. It went through me like electricity.

'I didn't expect this of my oldest son,' she said quietly. 'Maybe I had too much faith in you.'

I felt a terrible shame creep over me. I had let her down.

'I know I've asked a lot of you,' she continued, 'but what could I do?'

I tried to hide my alcohol-smelling breath but she knew. She turned away. Mortified, I put out my hand to stop her but she looked at me with disgust.

'You're no better than your father. But at least he has a reason, so I can still love him.'

This cut me so deeply I felt dizzy. Firstly, there was her denial that I had any reason to rebel. Secondly, and more significantly, I had become the man I blamed for everything, a violent drunk. But unlike what she had done with him, she was abandoning me, cutting me loose. Outside the family I was a warrior without fear, but to lose my mother's affection left me a frightened child, regressed and alone in a hostile world.

I remembered her the day we left the mosque, trying to face the loss of the husband she loved and trying to work out what to do. She had taken the only path available to her, by giving me the role of father and provider. The truth was I was glad. I had somehow or other just slipped off the rails.

Next day I felt miserable and hung-over, but I got up early, dressed my wounds, and headed off to work with a determination to restore my mother's trust. I arrived early and swept up all the hidden deposits that had accumulated over my months of drinking my uncle's stash. If he hadn't been drunk himself, he would by now have fired me.

When the workers came back from lunch, one of the more friendly employees noticed my bruises. 'Why are you here, Ali?' he asked.

'To make money,' I responded immediately. He nodded, but then I found myself glancing at the machine where I had once tried to create a garment. I paused, because even in my befuddled mind I remembered how the few hours of crafting it had fulfilled and distracted me in a way that street fighting never had. So I said, 'I want to learn. I want to make clothes, become a professional.'

He chuckled. 'You can't do that, you're too old.'

I could only imagine he saw his craft as a sport, like skiing or horse-riding, which you needed to begin as a toddler to get one's legs, so to speak, but either way it was the bait I needed.

It fired me up. 'I'll show you one day,' I said. And I did.

Every day I would watch the tailors work. I saw how they held the fabric as it glided through the machine, how they changed the stitching, made darts, and trimmed the seams. Then when they left in the evening, I looked longingly at my uncle's bottle, but instead I would sit down at one of the machines, take the scraps from the bins, and begin practising. I was sometimes lost in the task for hours. I discovered I liked to make things and, sober, I was good at it.

One afternoon my uncle saw what I had done and was impressed. 'I have many people who want clothes for their sons and daughters. It's not worth my time, but if you like, I'll give them to you to make.'

So as my bruises faded and my shakes and bad moods diminished, I was given my own desk and sewing machine, and I began to earn more. After six or seven months I moved on to adult clothes and became better than my chuckling critic. In a day he would finish four or five pairs of pants. After one year I was finishing twenty a day, and took over his position.

I began bringing home good money. I stopped hanging around with the gang and generally cleaned up my act. This was helped by meeting and making friends with Unis. He introduced me to wrestling and I discovered a better way to get my anger out. We went every day to a wrestling club, where we met different people, talked and made friends while we were getting physically fit. It was a new social outlet.

My mother never commented but I felt a slow return of her belief in me, not to mention the growth of my own self-respect. My father could hardly live on what the army paid him so I sent him money too, which I was able to do without judging him, after my own brush with alcohol addiction.

Heavy footsteps approach our cell and I am launched back into the present. We are all holding our breath, willing them to pass, when the door is unlocked and swings open. Four guards including the Disabler appear.

They haven't been for three days, so we are expecting them. They come more frequently when something is going on outside that scares the government. Then they torture us more. Sometimes they take up to ten of us in a day. One at a time, to different places. Other times they come in with batons for a mass bashing. Afterwards there is no water to wash our wounds, which lie open, bleeding and waiting for infection.

We stand still and silent. This time the Disabler calls, 'Ali Al Jenabi.' The blood pounds in my head and I want to cry out for my mother, but instead I square my shoulders and step forward. I think of what they did to Ahmad and fury rises up to fortify me.

Flanked by the guards I am marched down the passageway to the torture room, but then I have to stand outside as if I am at a doctor's office, waiting my turn. I look into the face of the guard whose care I have been left in. He is a few years older than me with a not unkindly face. I want to ask him how he can spend his days administering hideous injuries to his Iraqi brothers, but to remind him of his inhumanity would only inflame.

But looking at him must have been enough, because he swings his baton and hits me with a blow to the head. It almost knocks me unconscious. As blood begins to run down my face the door opens and the poor unfortunate who preceded me is carried out.

It is then I see the electrodes lying on the floor and realise what I am here for. I break out in a sweat with the thought of what it did to my father. I can stand most things they can do to my body but if they fry my brain I may as well be dead. I struggle, but within a moment my guard has me in a headlock and the other three have returned to drag me in, strip me of my clothes, and tie me to a chair.

They start on the questions again but what they really want is to get on with electrocuting me so they can maintain their quota. They attach the electrodes to my back, tongue and genitals, and the current surges through my body like fire in my veins and I stiffen and shudder.

I have no idea how much time has gone by but they cooked me until I passed out, and now I am waking back in our cell. I am grateful for the familiar surroundings and the sight of Akram sitting beside me as I lie shivering on the floor. My head throbs so violently my vision blurs, and a sharp pain pulses through my limbs. The feeling of paralysis is what really scares me but Akram is reassuring.

'Better for you to stay asleep,' he says as he spreads my blanket over me. 'The numbness will go. In a few days you will be back to normal.'

'Did they get what they wanted out of you?' I ask, wondering how many goes it takes before you go crazy and tell them anything.

He clasps and unclasps his hands and for the first time I notice that Akram has no fingernails. 'They did,' he says after a pause, then goes on haltingly. 'I stayed out of politics. I taught ten- to twelve-year-olds at a respected school. We talked about many things. I was good friends with the other teachers and the children. I loved my job.'

'You don't need to tell me,' I say quickly but he seems to want to go on, perhaps to justify so many nights of soundless crying when his body shook so vigorously that neither of us could sleep.

'I'm just a normal Muslim but I wanted to improve my under-standing of my faith and to be a better teacher. There were no Islamics on our staff so I borrowed a book on Islam from the library. One day when I was walking home the secret police picked me up. I happened to have the book with me, so they took me in and beat me because they thought I must be part of some Islamic movement. Saddam had purged the Communists, now he was after the Islamics.

'When I refused to admit to something so ridiculously false they brought out their tools of trade and worked on me for so long I finally confessed. But that wasn't enough. They wanted names of others.

They tortured me until I begged them to let me die, but they wouldn't. They waited for me to revive so they could keep on with it ... until I told them all the other teachers in the school were part of an Islamic movement too.'

He pauses, hanging his head and drawing circles in the dirt with his pulpy fingers. 'So they picked up the twelve other teachers. They tortured them all, then executed six of them.'

The dormant political man inside me stirs and I understand why people give their lives to rise up against a dictator. I remember my father's voice and I wish I could tell him I am at one with him now. I want to cry out, 'Saddam is a bastard,' but if I do I endanger all the men in my cell. So I coil my legs to my body and bury my head in my knees and I think of Akram's pain and of my brother Ahmad and my own fried brain and I weep silent tears of rage.

IN A GOOD CAUSE

As dawn breaks over Abu Ghraib, the rooster begins to crow. We don't know quite where our cell is located in the jail but the roosters are the one thing we can hear clearly from the outside world. Once one starts the others follow, and as most families have at least three, when they all get going it is a cacophonous symphony of roosters.

The roosters are a major part of our lives, and the only way we can tell the time. So when they start we know it is morning, but because we are packed like twenty-six spoons covering the entire floor, we all need to rise together. So there is an early-morning period of waiting for our cellmates to be ready to get up.

At first, exacerbated by the roosters, I would wake gripped by fear that I would be taken for torture that day. But after a couple of years it lessened, as they lost interest in us and moved on to more recent victims.

So the roosters now fill a more contented role of reviving memories of when I was young, waking on the roof with my family to the sound of crowing and a blazing red sun. The giggles and the pillow-fights, and my mother's reprimands, and the promise of a hot sultry day of playing with Ahmad and my brothers.

Sometimes I write letters to them on the leg of my pants. The fabric is so thick with ingrained dirt that it makes a good canvas to engrave words on with my ragged fingernails. It might last for a week before it fades and then I write another.

When enough men have stirred we all get up and fold our tattered blankets. There was a time when I would stretch and do push-ups to stay fit, but after years of torture and starvation one tends to lose the point and I let things slip. We are a raggedy, miserable bunch and the boredom is atrophying. But maybe it is our Muslim training that helps us survive our deprivation. We don't think about sex or any of the things we have lost, we erase them from our brains in the same way we do food during Ramadan. Until after sundown of course, and then that's all we think about.

Our breakfast arrives, the same measly piece of bread and a boiled egg that we have been getting for years. They feed us just enough to keep us alive, and as it is all I have known for so long I eat it with relish. Our stomachs have shrunk and we don't feel the hunger so much any more, but we are skeletons.

We are just setting up for our first game of jelga, which we play with six stones we have managed to dig from the floor where we draw our board, when four guards intrude. To our great relief the Disabler hasn't been seen for a while, so we figure he is being used to toughen up the newcomers, or retired, or possibly beaten to death by some poor revenge-seeking prisoner who was prepared to relinquish his life and family for it.

'Pick up your things and file out,' the guards announce. 'You are being removed to another facility.'

We obediently get into line so as not to incite them to use their batons, but panic ripples through the group that we are to be sent to a new place of torture.

They march us to a muster room where we stand in line and wait. We press close to each other. We have bonded like family through our shared suffering and now we don't want to be torn apart, or sent alone to another nightmare. After an hour the governor of the jail appears with an official from the ministry and gives an obscure speech. 'We don't like you and you don't like us. We don't trust you, you don't trust us, so if in the future you have an opportunity to get out then you take it.'

We have no idea what he is talking about. Our wasted legs are ready to buckle and our anger is growing. Then, miraculously, the outside doors are opened. I am blinking into sunshine for the first time in nearly four years. They give each of us three thousand dinars and we step hesitantly into the yard. We wait to be bashed but we are not, the gates beyond are opened and we are ushered out to freedom.

The sun is hot on my back and my eyes burn with the glare. I have no idea why we are suddenly released but now we realise what the governor meant: 'We will be watching and waiting to catch you again, so leave the country if you can. We don't want you here.' But right now all any of us can think of is getting home to our families.

I shake hands, hug and say goodbye to these men with whom I have shared so much intimacy and pain. Yet even as I clasp Akram's hand I know I won't see him, or any of them, again. We were not comrades in war. There were no heroic victories or glorious moments to be shared and remembered. We were simply fellow travellers, survivors of humiliation and despair so degrading and ugly that I need to get as far away from it as possible. I need to close the book.

I wrap my arms around Akram and we hold each other tight, with no words. And then, in my rags and tatters, without looking back, I walk away from this gentle suffering man whose kindness will be forever imprinted on me.

I go to the bus station, where taxis are waiting. I show a driver my three thousand dinars and ask to be driven south to Diwaniyah. He smiles. 'That won't get you halfway there.'

It is my first realisation that I have been gone a long time. The driver closes my hand over the money. From my condition it is not hard to guess where I have been.

'It is an honour to drive you for free, my friend.' Such is the respect for the few who survive Abu Ghraib.

When I arrive at our house it is unlocked as always but no one is home. I am gripped with disappointment, but then I catch a glimpse of myself in the mirror and realise I am glad. I strip off my putrid rags and throw them in the bin. I cut my hair, shave my beard and then, as if in a dream, I step into a hot shower. I let the water cascade over my emaciated body. I scrub with soap and rinse and lather again. I can feel the filth slowly dissolving and for the first time in years I am clean.

I hear voices approaching, and the front door opening. I come out of the bedroom in clothes that now swim on me, and watch my mother for a minute before she sees I am there. She is older and thinner but still the dynamo she always was. Taking charge, sorting groceries, counting remaining food-ration coupons, and organising the younger children, who have grown so much they are almost unrecognisable to me.

Then suddenly Afrah sees me. She reaches out and grabs my mother's sleeve. 'Umi, he is home.'

My mother turns and stares. Frozen for a moment, as if I am not real. Then tears begin to run down her cheeks. I go to her and we hug and she sobs like I have never heard before.

That night we sit on the floor and eat everything my mother could prepare. They have clearly been living frugally, and despite her protests I will not let her go out and borrow money to make me a feast. Apart from anything else it will be some time before my stomach can handle normal quantities of food.

The first night out of jail is one of sadness and joy. All this time they have not known if the three of us were dead. I cannot bring myself to tell them about Ahmad, except to say there is almost no possibility he is alive. As for my father, with his legendary capacity for survival, there could still be hope. They are wary of asking probing questions, so we eat in silence punctuated by spontaneous ecstatic outbursts of hugging, laughing and weeping.

Next morning I sit on the front steps gazing at the house across the street where Intisar, through whom I discovered romantic love, lives. My neighbour, Abdul-Rafi, appears and sits beside me.

'They left,' he says with sympathy. While it was a clandestine liaison, it was still known about by all the boys in the street, apart from her brother of course, because truly romantic relationships in our culture are such a rare thing. Abdul-Rafi looks at me compassionately. 'They moved a year ago.'

I thought I had prepared myself but the disappointment sears through me. My mother hadn't told me. Perhaps she assumed with the passing of so much time my feelings would have faded, and that by now Intisar's heart would have gone elsewhere.

We had met by accident just before the Shiite uprising in 1991, when her family moved into our street. My mother had run out of cooking gas, so when we heard the gasman coming with his donkey cart I took out the empty cylinder and the old man filled it. I was carrying it back to the house when I heard a door behind me open, and I glanced around.

Two girls hurried out, one on each side of a cylinder. The donkey had begun to move on so they ran after the cart, laughing. The scarf of the younger one blew off and her long black hair unfurled and swirled around her face. She must have been only thirteen, and I was twenty, but I was riveted. She let her hair hang free and continued to laugh without inhibition. I had never seen a girl like this. I felt a rare surge of happiness and I wanted to hold her hand and laugh too. But no such thing was possible.

She and her sister stumbled back to their house with the cylinder, still giggling. I could have gone to help but when she glanced my way I was suddenly paralysed by a new feeling of self-consciousness which overwhelmed me. I backed into my house with my head spinning.

My mother, who had taken them cold water when they moved in because they had no fridge, discovered the older sister was studying accountancy like me, and offered her my help. So in the evening she came over to borrow a textbook. All night I fantasised that it would be returned with a letter in it from the younger sister, Intisar, even though she'd hardly seen me. When the older sister finally brought it back, the fantasy had become so real that I checked the whole book, feverishly searching every page, and shaking it upside down. Such is the first taste of love.

After five days of thinking of nothing but her, I came home from work hot and tired at about ten o'clock in the evening. I ate dinner, then took off my shoes and went into the courtyard garden at the side of the house to wash my socks in the trough. Since seeing Intisar, I had inexplicably been paying extra attention to my personal hygiene.

When I finished I sank wearily onto the two-seater swing. With my bare feet in the grass I propelled it into a gentle motion and lay back gazing up at the stars. As my eyes drifted from one planet to another they slowly dropped to the top of our high mud-brick wall and suddenly I saw Intisar, across the street on her upstairs balcony. She watched me unabashed then went back inside.

I sat motionless, hardly breathing, for what felt like an hour but was probably thirty seconds, until she reappeared and stood observing me again. It was a risky thing for a girl to do. Her father had died in the war with Iran, but if her brother, who was now her keeper, saw her, there could be serious consequences. I, on the other hand, was intrigued by her audacity and courage, making me even more enamoured with her.

We were too far apart to hear each other, so I pointed to her, then circled the side of my head with my finger and mouthed one word at a time. 'You … must … be … crazy.'

Her scarf was loose and slipped from her hair, which she tossed like a horse's mane, almost giving me a heart attack. 'No, not me, you,' she mouthed back, stabbing her finger in my direction as she restored her scarf.

'Why me?' I laughed. 'You are standing there.'

'I am standing here but you are sitting there watching.'

Then she must have heard someone coming, because she ducked

inside and was gone.

Next day I rushed home early from work and waited for two hours for her to reappear. At last she did and once again we mouthed, gestured and laughed, understanding each other without audible words. In my young mind it was all a miracle, but I didn't know what to do next.

Kadeen, a tailor whose machine was next to mine, had fallen in love and married without his family's consent, causing all hell to break loose. So I decided to ask him for help.

'Romeo and Juliet,' he said, smiling, when I told him of our balcony flirtation. I had heard about this story of romance and young love at school but had never been able to find an Arabic translation. I did know, however, that it finished tragically and hoped Kadeen wasn't foretelling an end to my situation.

'Write Intisar a letter,' he said, which encouraged me to dismiss these thoughts. 'But it is dangerous to let her keep it. You write half a page and tell her to write back on the bottom half and return it to you.'

I wrote and rewrote the letter in my mind all day at work, then that night I put it on paper. I professed my love and told her how pretty she was, then I asked if she was interested in having a secret relationship with me. I wrapped it around a rock and when she came out onto the balcony that night I tossed it up and quickly disappeared. Then I spent a sleepless night anticipating her reply.

Next day, as I left the house, I passed next to hers and the rock and letter dropped at my feet. I tried not to look up but couldn't help myself. I caught her smile as she vanished inside and I knew the answer. I ran all the way to work.

'She wrote back,' I whispered to Kadeen. 'She feels the same as me.'

But Kadeen was unable to help me with the central problem. I thought endlessly about marrying her when she was old enough, and wanted to ask for her hand now, but I knew I could never bring a wife into our household. My father's mental instability, violence and drunken rages, compounded by my mother fighting back or running to my grandmother with the children and leaving him to smash up the place, made it unthinkable. Neither could I go out and get our own house. It was never done, the wife always moved in with the husband until there were two or three children. Besides, I could hardly support this family, let alone another one of my own.

I tried to put aside these problems and kept exchanging letters. Sometimes I would wait for her after school, then follow until her friends let us walk on alone. Or we would see each other on the street, and while they kept guard we would hide in an alley or somewhere out of sight, where we could talk and maybe touch hands.

I was so lost in love that I paid little attention to what was happening in Kuwait but then the Shiite uprising happened and I ended up in Abu Ghraib. I knew that would be the end of it with Intisar, that I had lost my chance, so I did my best to shut her out of my mind. But in my weaker moments, especially under torture, I would let myself plummet back into my first sight of her. Then it would sometimes be weeks before I could stop reliving the moment, over and over again.

'We thought you were dead.' Abdul-Rafi breaks into my thoughts and I look away from Intisar's house.

'So did I at times,' I say, trying to forget her. 'So what's been happening in my absence?'

'It's a miserable life here. The more Saddam's power is threatened, the more brutal he becomes,' he says, instinctively lowering his voice. 'And the sanctions are killing us.'

I remember the United Nations imposing an embargo on everything except food and medicine after Saddam invaded Kuwait in 1991, but I never thought it would last this long.

'It's still in place?' I murmur, realising my mother's struggle to keep the family going must have been worse than she had admitted.

'They kept them to force Saddam to get rid of the nuclear

weapons the Americans insist we have. Of course Saddam won't comply. So everyone is suffering. Thousands of kids and babies have died,' Abdul-Rafi says, glancing over his shoulder cautiously. 'There's no food. They won't let fluoride in, in case we make bombs out of it, so the water's filthy. Disease is rife. Medicines are caught up in bureaucracy, and the dinar buys nothing. Before you went to jail one dinar would buy a hundred loaves of bread, now two dinars buy one. Apparently they're the toughest sanctions in human history.'

I recall my father's words: *Saddam will dig a big hole and bury Iraq in it.* I used to tire of his platitudes but now I see how uncanny his foresight was.

'So what are people doing about it?' I ask.

'You can go to the north.' Abdul-Rafi glances around warily again. 'People are organising there. I've got a wife and kids now, but you could go. You should, before they pick you up again. You're still dodging the army, aren't you?'

I nod. It's true I am on shaky ground, but right now all I want is to get my life back. When I mention this he laughs. 'No chance, my friend.'

His wife calls and he gets up. 'If you change your mind and want to go, I can help you.'

I return to the kitchen and sit at the table with my mother while she cooks rice and lentils for lunch. Evidently it is rare to have meat any more. 'What is being done to stop Saddam?' I ask. 'Has no one tried to assassinate him?'

My mother hisses at me to be quiet. She looks around as if the walls have ears. 'You never know who is listening. Entire households have even been betrayed by one of their own.' She stirs the lentils then sits on the chair next to me and whispers, 'He will kill the whole family of anyone who tries.'

I once suggested to my cellmates that we try to escape Abu Ghraib, and was told about the last person who attempted it. When he was caught they rounded up his wife and seven children and tortured them in front of him. I feel the same powerlessness I felt then. What a miserable submissive people we have been forced to become.

After a week of lying low, regaining my health and taking in the changes, I try to defy Abdul-Rafi and get my life back. I go to see my uncle where I used to work as a tailor and he is happy for me to return. My concentration and focus are not as good as they were but I can still turn out a pair of pants faster than anyone else.

At night I stay at home and listen to a forbidden radio station run by Iraqi dissidents in Kurdistan. They talk about the movement in the north that Abdul-Rafi had alerted me to, and interview significant people in the resistance. They encourage Iraqis to rise up, telling us that Saddam is almost finished and the end of his regime is in sight.

I imagine becoming a soldier and taking on Saddam and his army. I picture myself amongst bombs and bullets, unafraid because I am fighting to free my people. I recall the World War II movies about heroic battles that we had seen at the cinema with my father, and I imagine hordes of Iraqis mobilising, ready to give their lives. I can't get my mind off it. I try to settle in, work hard and keep my head down, but I am burning inside. I want justice for my brother, my father, and all those countless thousands lying in mass graves.

One day I finish work early and go to a teashop I used to frequent before I was in prison. The place is run-down, like much of the city, and looks as if it has changed hands.

I think I recognise the new owner, but before I can piece it together Abdul-Rafi appears and joins me. After some small talk about his family I ask him more about the north.

'Remember, the Kurds rose up in '91 like we did,' he says, looking around to make sure no one can hear. 'Well, unlike the Shiites, they escaped being quashed by Saddam's army, by fleeing to the borders and becoming refugees until things settled, then they returned. The US maybe felt guilty about abandoning *us*, because they started bringing humanitarian aid to the Kurds in the north. A no-fly zone was established so Saddam couldn't bomb them, and the United Nations created a safe haven protected by the US, the Brits and the French. Now Iraqis who want to do something about Saddam are flocking up there.'

I picture hordes of us with AK-47s hunting Saddam down but I become distracted by the new owner, who approaches with the tea. I suddenly realise who he is. He looks smaller out of his Abu Ghraib uniform, but it is unquestionably the guard who bashed me then held me down to be electrocuted.

Part of me wants to throw him to the floor and kick him to a pulp, like I saw him do many times to prisoners. But I am reluctant to reduce myself to the level of one of Saddam's guards, and I have never seen the value of revenge at an individual level. He doesn't recognise me out of my prison rags. So I hold myself in check.

Unaware, Abdul-Rafi sips his tea. It is cold so he calls for more hot water, then he continues on about Kurdistan. But I am no longer listening. I am enjoying watching our guard burn himself when he refills Abdul-Rafi's pot, then explode, throwing the pot against the wall and hurling the cup after it.

Fear builds amongst the people in the shop, but I sit quietly watching. 'Get out! All of you get out!' he yells at the bewildered customers, and bashes chairs across tables, smashing crockery on the floor as everyone scatters.

I coldly observe him turn and punch the wall with his fists, again and again until blood runs down his arms. I don't need to punish this man. He is clearly doing it himself, but I am the only one in the shop who knows what is wrong with him. I look at Abdul-Rafi, whose jaw has dropped, and pull him away.

As we walk off we can still hear the mayhem. I am glad to know that at least one of those animals has enough humanity to reprove himself, but on the other hand this unsettling event immediately revives the memories of Abu Ghraib and my own anger returns.

I can see that Abdul-Rafi is confused by the whole business. 'I thought I could go back to my old life, but I have witnessed too much of Saddam's work. He has to be got rid of. If you can help me I'll take your offer and go to the north.'

Abdul-Rafi spontaneously shakes my hand and hugs me. If he was single he would go with me, I am sure.

A few days later when I go to work I confront my uncle. 'You are not paying me enough.'

This is true, but it is not actually why I am saying it. It is because I am getting ready to leave for the north but I can't tell anyone, not even my mother. As his employee and nephew I need to make it publicly known that we had a bad falling out, so it is clear he had nothing to do with it if I get picked up. Especially as he is a Communist and hates the Baathists, for which he has already done three years in prison.

I leave my uncle's shop and head down the street, re-empowered by the thought of taking action, when suddenly in front of me I see Intisar with her friends and my heart stops. She is now seventeen years old. A woman, and more beautiful than the young girl I remember.

Clearly she is as shocked as I am. Maybe she thought I was dead, but she stares at me as I stumble gracelessly for words. I had dared to imagine this moment so many times, but not like this. While the attraction between us is still immediately palpable we are both self-conscious and don't know where to begin. We back into an alleyway amongst empty boxes from a nearby fruit shop, while her friends keep watch as they used to.

I discover she is not married and I am almost overcome with relief. We gradually find our feet with each other and talk the way we used to. The old love rekindles and for a moment I think I will marry her and to hell with everything else, but then I come back to my senses. Four years have passed and in my mind I had already let her go. In the past I have had little time to consider politics, but now I only have to think about Ahmad, and Saddam's reign of terror, to realise another fire has been lit in me.

I can't tell her where I am going, so I say what little I can, then I blurt out, 'I want to marry you,' the fear of losing her again fuelling my conviction. 'Please, if you want me, wait for me. I can't do anything now except tell you I love you.'

'I will wait,' she says softly. 'I love you too.'

Once again I must leave her with no promises. Last time I had been too ashamed to tell her why I couldn't bring her into my family. As I walk away, each step is difficult. I don't look back because I don't want to test my strength, and I pray to God that I have not just ruined my life.

A few evenings later I head off with Abdul-Rafi, telling my mother and siblings that I am going to Baghdad to get a better job and make more money. I hate lying to them, but what they don't know is easier to deny. After being gone so long it is unbearable to leave them again, but they are used to my absence now, so it hurts them less than me.

We drive north through the night to Mosul, the second largest city in Iraq, then down a dirt road through low hills to a small community of houses spread out along the Tigris River. Most of the people living here are smugglers. During the Ottoman Empire their families were merchants, who travelled the old trade routes selling their wares. But after World War I and the establishment of nation states and territorial borders, what was once legitimate trade became cross-border smuggling. This did not change their status as reputable businessmen despite it now being unlawful. So as Saddam's atrocities increase, the help of these people to cross borders continues to be considered a respectable alternative.

We pull up at a sheltered spot and Abdul-Rafi points to a small boat waiting in the predawn light beside the wide, fast-flowing river. Without switching off the engine he turns and shakes my hand.

'Good luck my friend, and remember, if you come back and they find out you have been to the north they will shoot you.'

I know this, but somehow it is more poignant now I am here.

'There are only two reasons for being in Kurdistan,' he continues. 'One, you are secret police trying to infiltrate and catch the resistance, or two, you are the resistance. They know you are not the first, so you must be the second. So *bang*.' He points his finger at my head. Then he hugs me and gestures to the boat. 'Now go, he is waiting for you. You must hurry. The sun will be rising soon.'

I thank him and get out with my small bag of belongings. He drives off in a cloud of dust and I am left standing in the silence of the crisp early morning.

I go quickly to the boat and after a brief greeting with the owner I climb in. The motor turns over and we push off. The boat is stacked high with contraband, which will be exchanged on the other side for cigarettes. I squeeze past containers of gas and petrol, cheap in Iraq but almost unobtainable in Kurdistan under the raft of sanctions and restrictions Saddam has imposed on the Kurdish people.

I join another two Iraqis sitting in the bow. As we glide through the turbulent water I feel a surge of excitement. After so many years of incarceration, where all human boundaries were removed and every fragment of my existence was in the hands of my jailers, I am taking back control of my life. I am embarking on my first step in the fight for my country's freedom.

I turn to my companions and shake hands. 'I am Ali,' I say with gusto. One of them peers at me through the dim first light and then a smile breaks on his face. 'I am Mohammad. I know you,' he says. 'We are from the same neighbourhood.'

I remember him a little but would not have imagined he would be involved in anything like this, he is from a very rich and highly respected family. But then I recall his uncle is a Communist and it all makes sense. There is an immediate feeling of camaraderie as we embrace and slap each other's back.

In twenty minutes we have reached the other shore and the three of us walk to the nearest checkpoint. As the Kurdish police check our IDs I am instantly unnerved but Mohammad reassures me. 'They hate Saddam as much as we do. They are probably glad to see us.'

So I unclench my jaw and try to relax as they load us into a small dusty jeep and we head east for Arbil, the capital of Kurdistan, which is not a country but an autonomous region of Iraq.

As the sun comes up I watch the lush green landscape turn golden, like a metaphor for my hopes.

'Wait till you see the Kurdish mountains,' one of the policemen says, breaking me out of my reverie. 'They are spectacular.'

I smile, marvelling at Kurdish pride after so many years of displacement and persecution. Always under foreign rule, their people are scattered over four countries – Iran, Syria, Turkey and Iraq – with their language the only thing holding their race together. In Saddam's early years he contributed to their cultural survival by allowing them to study in their own language, but then, afraid they were siding with the enemy during the war with Iran in the 1980s, he turned on them with genocidal force.

When we arrive at a police station on the edge of Arbil they don't seem to care we have no papers to get into Kurdistan, they just want to be sure we are not working undercover for Saddam. Although I am fresh out of Abu Ghraib and obviously on the right side of things, I don't have the proof, so I am relieved when Mohammad tells them we are together and passes the officer a piece of paper with a number for him to call.

Before long he returns and gestures for us to leave. 'We are sorry. Please, you can go.'

Outside there is a guy waiting for us. 'Your uncle sent me,' he says, shaking Mohammad's hand, then opens the door of his car for us to get in.

Relieved, we drive into Arbil. It looks like any other Iraqi city, except it is one of the oldest in the world with eight thousand years of continual occupation and an ancient fortress on a hill at its centre. We travel down busy streets, past crumbling houses of the desperately poor, colourful markets, and a handsome mosque glinting white in the morning light.

We eventually arrive at a large modern villa in a wealthy suburb. Mohammad turns to me. 'Unless you have other plans you're welcome to stay here with me.' I couldn't be happier. I never knew him well but I like him. He is a gentleman with street smarts, a good-humoured liberal thinker with *savoir faire*.

Inside, a couple of Kurdish guys show us around and offer us a room. I don't ask but clearly the house belongs to someone who is in the resistance. Mohammad, it seems, is well connected. I cannot believe I have fallen so resoundingly on my feet.

We drop our things and head out to look at the city, which feels like home except for the language and the conspicuous display of arms. Russian Kalashnikovs, the caviar of guns, seem to be carried by everyone. In Iraq they are a little more discreet, or perhaps secretive, about their weapons.

We find a kebab shop where we can sit and gaze out at the busy street. I recall those joyous childhood days with my brothers and father eating kebabs in Diwaniyah, and I yearn for them.

'So why are you here, Ali?' I turn back to see Mohammad is watching me.

'They murdered my brother Ahmad,' I say heatedly.

'I am deeply sorry. I remember you two were inseparable.' Then he adds, 'You should keep your voice down, it's not so different to Baghdad. You never know who might be sitting behind you.'

I am reluctant to let go of my first taste of liberty but I know it's true. While I might be out of Saddam's reach, they can always get to my family. I glance over my shoulder and drop my voice. 'I'm here to get rid of Saddam. Aren't you?'

'No, I never really got involved. My uncle's lost so many friends working with the Communists, who as far as I can see have gained nothing. It's not going to make any difference who you kill around him, it's Saddam you have to kill, and you're not going to do that.'

Our kebabs arrive and we eat in silence. Then Mohammad looks at me. 'I can introduce you to people. I'm sure you'll be good at it. But just don't be disappointed if it's not what you think.'

I wonder if his comment is a warning I should heed, or a reflection of his own disappointment over what happened after the Shiite uprising. Not only had the US abandoned us, but they had also lifted the no-fly zone in the south so that Saddam's military could extract their revenge. No doubt Mohammad felt betrayed like all of us, and had my father, brother and I not been put in Abu Ghraib with time to dwell on it, I may well have lost heart too.

'So what are you doing here?' I ask.

He shrugs. 'I meet my uncle. He emigrated to Germany, but he comes back to Kurdistan to work with the party. Also I trade in passports. They are cheap in Baghdad. I sell them here and make good money. I'll be leaving in a couple of weeks.'

I try to hide my disappointment. I had imagined us as comrades in arms fighting for the cause.

Since Mohammad only has a short time I decide to spend it with him, meeting people and relaxing. I am still recovering from my imprisonment, and while I am determined to put it behind me, I remain prone to the anxiety that pervaded my life in Abu Ghraib.

So we go out for breakfast and lunch, amble through the streets, sit in teashops and play dominoes and talk and talk. Some nights we stay at home and he drinks arak, or he brings back guests. There are always different groups passing through the house, so when he is out with business I meet new people.

One night, two Iraqi men befriend me very quickly. 'Come over tomorrow. We eat together, then we play cards.'

I am cautious because they are from some religious movement that

I haven't heard of, unlikely to be fundamentalist if they play cards but I can tell by their correct behaviour they are extremely conservative. This would not be a good mix with Mohammad, so I use him as an excuse. 'I am staying here with someone. I can't just leave him.'

'Bring him too,' they insist, so now I'm stuck.

I don't elaborate to Mohammad how straitlaced they are in case it dissuades him and I have to go alone, but I do say, 'Please don't do anything stupid.'

He looks at me suspiciously. 'Why would I?'

So we go, and we sit and have dinner very properly. Then they serve us tea and we start to play a game similar to poker. While they have said nothing in particular their serious religiosity is seeping through, and I suspect testing Mohammad. I am aware of him sizing up the situation, but I am unable to assess what he might be up to.

Then, when the game is in a serious moment and we all sit quietly contemplating our cards, Mohammad farts. My new friends stiffen but Mohammad sorts his cards as if nothing happened. I try not to laugh because I know they will be scandalised. In Arabic culture, if you don't know the person, farting is inexcusably insulting.

As the night goes on he does it three more times. Our hosts keep looking at each other and not saying anything. I am nervous they will do something, maybe threaten us, especially when at different times they get up and leave the room. All I can do is keep playing cards as if everything is normal. When we leave I threaten to hit Mohammad, but he laughs and laughs.

Next afternoon we run into our hosts in the street. After an uncomfortable greeting there is an awkward silence, then Mohammad says, 'Shall we come over again tonight?'

They peer at him shocked and I shift uncomfortably.

Then Mohammad adds, 'If I don't fart?' He grins and suddenly we are all laughing. It is only then they admit that when they left the room it was in order to laugh themselves.

They slap his back and shake his hand and that night, after we spend a rollicking fartless evening with them, I realise how they have loosened up, how much we now like them. Mohammad is one of those people who has that effect on people.

Two weeks pass and Mohammad has to go. With his relaxed style and generous personality it seems he has unloaded his passports with ease. He stays an extra couple of days to spend with me, then I wake up one morning and he is gone. There is a note by my pillow. 'I know you hate goodbyes. Look after yourself. Back soon. Mohammad.'

A pang of loneliness runs through me as I get up to face the day. My time with Mohammad has been not unlike it used to be with my brother. But now Mohammad has gone I must find a way to honour Ahmad by getting down to business.

There are at least a couple of thousand Iraqis in the north working with the resistance, but I find they are split between many different movements: Islamic, Democratic, Communist, and countless others. When you are new in town everyone is interested in you, but survivors of Abu Ghraib are particularly sought after.

They know we won't betray them, so are eager to snatch us up, each group trying to convince us they are the better organisation. For once, we have the power. However, I am confused that many of the discussions are about what they pay and who is behind them. I had imagined being shoulder to shoulder with freedom fighters, like Che Guevara, but am disappointed to discover they are often more like businessmen.

So I look for people I like. When I meet the People for Independent Iraq I am impressed by the way they work, and their apparent decency as human beings. They are looking for recruits to return to Iraq to collect information about people in the government. Again I am disappointed. I had expected military exercises followed by an opportunity to take on Saddam's troops. But I want to do whatever is needed to bring him down, so I agree to join.

At first they teach us how to get information, how to stake

someone out, take the right photographs, source background material, ascertain trust, and choose a team if we have to work in a unit with other people. I opt to work alone as much as possible. I am not about to put my life in the hands of someone I am not convinced is more experienced than me.

I know how the Baathists work and I have learnt from them. In the 1991 uprising, before we ran from the city, there was a brief period when the Shiites had control. The government buildings were empty so they broke in and had access to computers, videos, documents, everything. These were quickly distributed to people who were trusted, which included me, because everyone knew what Saddam's torture had done to my father.

Whenever the secret police killed someone they recorded it on film, showing how they got their information, how the person died, all their methods. So now I will take what they did to us and do it to them.

It is the end of 1994 when I get my first assignment. It is in Mosul and I am in a cell with three others. We have done practice runs, staking someone out at the railway station in Arbil, but I am nervous about going back into Iraq, and even more nervous about crossing the border with papers I have not organised myself.

We get through the checkpoint quite easily and complete our mission in a couple of days. But on our return we are stopped on the Iraqi side. They are not happy with our papers. One of our team begins to sweat and stutter. I am terrified he is going to give us away. An officer orders us all out of the car.

He is an ugly beast who reminds me of the Disabler, which triggers appalling memories, but before I do anything stupid I remind myself I am not only wanted by the army, but our papers show we have all been on business in the north. I muster a smile. 'Is there a problem, officer?'

I step forward holding out my false papers, in which I had neatly folded fifty American dollars the night before. I hope it will be enough to cover us all. He takes the papers in his thick hairy hands and stuffs the money into his pocket. 'No problem,' he says. 'You can go.'

As we travel back to Arbil in silence, I determine to manage my own border crossings in the future. In this work you can never entirely trust anyone. Often it is just the inexperience of a new recruit organising the paperwork, but we are at the front line. If anything happens it happens to us, while they are safe back in Kurdistan, and we have a bullet in our heads.

As I get more experience I start to go regularly to Mosul, the south of Iraq, and Baghdad, then back to Kurdistan with information. I get my own papers, develop contacts with smugglers, and find my own border crossings. Once I'm in Iraq I hitch a ride to Baghdad, where I call my family. Even though I have to lie, at least I can talk to them, and because the movement pays us well I can send money. I had imagined as freedom fighters we would live hand to mouth, but on the contrary, the whole of the resistance seems flush with cash.

It would appear other nations are prepared to spend up big to be rid of Saddam, even though some were once friends and supplied him arms. However, what looks like a lot of money to us is probably small fry to the major powers. What the US is paying to prop up their resistance interests for a year would probably be comparable to a day of engagement with Saddam in Kuwait.

Meanwhile Kurdistan itself is racked with poverty. After Saddam's sanctions on top of the UN embargo there is virtually no economy, infrastructure, hospitals, electricity, petrol or jobs. When I first arrived I had fantasised about bringing my whole family here while we waited for the downfall of the Baathists, but I soon realised the Kurds themselves are only just existing.

My next mission in Baghdad is to obtain secret maps and to photograph details of a secret police building. The photographs are not easy to take because the building is under constant guard, but they are much less difficult than getting the maps.

It is several days before I have a lead on someone corruptible from the inside. Then begins the tedious business of following him day after day until I can find a weakness. Eventually it becomes clear he has a woman outside his marriage and I know I've got him.

So I break into his car and wait in the back seat while he visits his mistress, and then when he comes out I threaten him the way they threatened us. I know how dangerous it is, it is no joke. Once I point a gun there is no turning back, and there is no surrender. If I slip up it will cost me my life, and if I'm lucky and can shoot one of them first, then they will shoot to kill rather than take me alive.

I play my hand well and get the maps. I strap them on my body with the photographs and then face the nerve-racking journey out of Baghdad. As I sit on the back of an open truck that has picked me up, I struggle to stave off memories of the methods Saddam uses to kill. The rumour about the giant meat grinder into which you are fed alive, feet first, has us all in perpetual fear.

Back in Arbil the sense of safety returns. After Mohammad left, I moved out of the villa into a house with people from another resistance group. One of them is also just back from Baghdad. I listen to him talk about what Saddam and the Baathists are doing, and because I have just been there I realise it is bullshit. He has found out nothing that was not in the papers or on TV. In fact he could have got it off the radio in Kurdistan instead of risking his life.

Later his boss arrives and gives him $US5000 for his endeavours. This is a lot of money. No one in Iraq has this kind of income, but all the organisations are afraid if they don't pay their recruits enough they will become double agents.

It is becoming clear that the movement is driven not by patriotism but finance, and is divided because there are so many different interests bankrolling each party. The Iranian intelligence, the American CIA, the UK, Syria, are all in there with big money, but with different agendas and propaganda, making it impossible for the groups to come together. With the continual infighting, and with so many different factions that each is too small to be effective, I wonder if they could ever become a united front.

That night I lie in bed wanting to get away from it all, but there is nowhere to go. I feel overwhelmed by the weight of responsibility for the work I am doing, yet appalled by what appear to be the driving forces behind it. They seem to have lost sight of our purpose.

I wake early in the morning and catch a bus to the mountains, and they are as breathtaking as was promised. In the distance, near the border with Iran, are colossal snow-capped granite shapes reaching high into the clouds, towering over a spectacular range that runs north and south of Kurdistan. There are deep ravines and lush valleys so vibrant with every shade of green it reminds me of a special box of pencils that enlivened my childhood with its dazzling colours.

The trees weep with vines. Crystal waters dance over polished rocks and mossy creek-beds to pure clear waterholes. I can feel myself relaxing as I climb slowly skyward. When I reach the top of the first peak I look down into a small village nestled between the mountains far below.

I sit on a log and gaze at the pretty houses, waterfalls and blossoms, coveting a life amongst such natural beauty with no Saddam Hussein. For a moment I am so transported I forget how Saddam bombed and gassed these very mountains to wipe out the Kurdish freedom fighters. Thousands were shot, died hideous deaths from gas, or plummeted from mountain cliffs as they tried to escape across the Iranian border.

In front of me is a magnificent tree carpeted in voluminous white flowers with delicate pink centres. I tell myself there is probably nothing more glorious on earth than this place, yet I am unable to enjoy it.

I am besieged by a wave of loneliness and loss – my brother, my father, my family – and now the crushing realisation that maybe Mohammad was right. We are not going to get Saddam and we are never going to be free.

When I arrive back at the house there is a message that someone was here to see me. I presume it is a member of our party wanting a report on my activities in Baghdad, but I am in no mood. I turn to leave again to avoid them, and there, on the other side of the street, is Mohammad. I can't believe my eyes. It has been many months since he left his brisk note about returning soon.

I almost sprint across and throw my arms around him.

'Come on,' Mohammad laughs. 'I'll buy you dinner.'

He takes me to a noisy restaurant where we can talk without being overheard. I can't give him any details of my work, but because he already knows why I am here, I tell him about my disappointment with the movement. 'In some cases,' I say with disgust, 'if you are too close to getting Saddam, another group will even warn him because it is not in their interest to kill him.'

Mohammad gives me a searching look. 'So have you given up yet?'

'No, I still believe it is possible,' I respond, trying to reignite my passion because without it there is nothing. 'There must be enough victims of Saddam like me up here, who could come together outside the organisations.'

'How, if you don't have money to survive? The Kurds can't help you, they can't even support themselves. There're no jobs, so how do you eat while you do this work? That's how these backers get their foot in, and you'll never know their real agendas.'

'The French managed in World War II,' I say, remembering the movies I saw with my father.

'It is not like the French Resistance, where the Nazis came from outside, with a different culture, different language. We are fighting against our own people, sometimes even same family.'

I look down at my hands and try desperately to find something to salvage my commitment.

'Anyway,' Mohammad goes on, 'you're ignoring the main problem. Saddam himself has done a very clever thing. He has made it impossible to organise against him by destroying the trust of the Iraqi people for each other. Because there is no limit to the atrocities he is capable of, Iraqis are so scared they are afraid of their own families.'

I can't help remembering one of the secret-police tapes I saw when the Shiites ransacked the government buildings during the uprising. It was of a pretty teenage girl who had fallen in love with a boy her age. They were caught together by the secret police, who agreed they would not tell her family, if she spied on her own mother, a doctor and a suspected Communist. Once they had enough information from the girl to prove it, they arrested, tortured and killed the mother.

'Any meeting you have,' Mohammad interrupts my thoughts, 'you don't know who at the table is undercover. It could be your own brother. Plenty of good Iraqis will betray you and the cause to save their children. Tell me you wouldn't, if you had to watch your family die.'

I think of Ahmad and sit quietly for a time. Then Mohammad looks at me. 'Ali, come with me to Germany.'

He takes me completely by surprise. 'I don't have a passport.'

He grins. 'I have one for you.'

'I don't have money.'

He has been carrying a small bag, which he now sits on his lap and opens. It is full of American dollars.

'Half for me, half for you. We can set up a business.'

I laugh. 'Mohammad, what are you talking about?'

'I am going with my uncle as a refugee. I am leaving Iraq. I want you to come with me.'

'But I don't want to go to Germany.'

'Why not?'

'There are too many reasons. I cannot leave my family. I want to avenge my brother, and finally, this is my country. It's the Baathists and Saddam who should have to run away, not us,' I say, remembering my father's words when we ran out of Diwaniyah from Saddam's army.

At this crucial point Ala, a friend of Mohammad's, arrives to collect a passport. He likes to talk and tells me he is going to see his family, who are farmers in the south.

'I've tried to warn him he'll be noticed in a small community,' Mohammad pipes up. 'He's been in Iran for nine years so the secret police will be dying to shoot him.'

Ala laughs. 'I'll be okay. My family have several farms, they promise me it will be easy to blend in.'

'Good luck,' I say, finding him rather naive and hard to warm to.

'So where did you find Ala?' I ask Mohammad as we watch him go.

'After being in exile so long the poor guy just needed some help to see his family.'

I shake my head at Mohammad. He is always picking up lame dogs. I can't help wondering if Ala's banishment was a result of persecution or just his own stupidity. But Mohammad has a big heart, and is always helping someone.

'I hope he doesn't cause you any trouble.'

Mohammad returns with his usual refrain, 'Why would he?'

I laugh. 'So when do you go?'

'Tomorrow.'

'So soon?' I say, feeling slapped.

'Are you sure you won't come?'

I sigh and with some difficulty shake my head.

SLEEPING WITH THE DEAD

Mohammad's whirlwind visit intensifies my loneliness and I long to be back in Iraq. Despite the danger, I go to my leader and request a mission where I can feed information to a middleman, or postman, rather than return to Kurdistan after each job. I have become a valuable member of their team, so within a few days he has it organised and I am on my way to Baghdad.

I cross near Kirkuk, wait at my usual restaurant on the highway, and soon hitch a ride to the city. My assignment is to stake out a government official but I need a job as cover, so I find a tailor in the area and try out for a position. As I can make a pair of trousers in less than an hour, the owner is delighted to have me. He pays per piece, so as long as I keep my quota up I can come and go as I wish, meaning I can take time off for my resistance work without anyone noticing.

The next problem is where to stay. I can't sleep in a hotel because every night the police check who is registered. Even though I have a good false ID it is too risky. If they start asking why I'm not in the army, I'm in trouble.

I spend my first night by the river in the cold, then the next day, almost delirious with tiredness, I trawl through mental lists of people I still know in Baghdad, and suddenly remember Saba. He was a soccer player who became a good friend when he moved to Diwaniyah with the army.

After work I go to his house and his mother opens the door. I haven't met her before but she has heard about me from Saba. She glances at my unkempt appearance but seems unfazed. 'He will be home soon. Come in,' she says. 'I will send his younger brother to find him.' Her home is warm and welcoming, and I remember with envy being part of a family.

After a long wait a teenage boy appears with dinner and I ask where his brother is.

'I couldn't find him,' he replies, looking at his feet.

'It's time I went,' I murmur, dreading the prospect of another night by the river.

'No, wait, he will come,' his mother insists, and then at about ten o'clock she puts mattresses on the floor and says, 'why don't you rest, and when he comes we will wake you.' By now I am so exhausted I don't argue. I collapse onto the mattress and within seconds I am asleep.

Early next morning I wake to my name being called.

'Wake up. Wake up. Breakfast is ready,' Saba's older brother says loudly as he presents me with fried eggs.

'Where is Saba?' I ask.

'Saba is not in Iraq. He is in Jordan.'

'But your mother said ...'

'She knew you were in trouble with the government and on the run. It was the only way she could stop you leaving. If you need to you can stay as long as you want.'

I am reminded of a relative who wouldn't even let me in his shop. 'Just let me sit and have a cup of tea, then I go,' I had said. 'No, Ali,' he had replied. 'Not even sit. Please don't bring me trouble.'

Yet Saba's family, who hardly know me, have taken me in, and when you are alone, hungry and afraid, it means a lot. All I can do is smile and nod my thanks.

With a place to live I can now settle into a routine with the tailor and my assignments from the resistance. Things go smoothly for several months. I have regular meetings with my postman from the north to hand over photos, reports, documents, and to get money for expenses for myself and the people who help with information gathering. I even go down to Diwaniyah to spend a little time with my family.

My mother is always overjoyed to see me but she is clearly suffering under the strain. I have fed her enough information about Ahmad for her to accept that he is gone, but there is still no word of my father. Between me and my brothers, who are working the markets, there is enough money, but under the sanctions there is nothing to buy. Then there is the weight of raising the seven remaining children on her own.

I return to Baghdad with increasing gloom about my mother and the apparent lack of progress in bringing down Saddam. In the morning I sleep in and miss my usual stakeout, so I go straight to work but I am restless and feel inexplicably uneasy. I am sitting at my machine making a pair of linen pants when six men with short hair and casual street clothes come into the tailor shop. I begin to sweat as it becomes clear they are on the hunt for me.

I have my false ID under the pillow on my chair and the real one in my pocket. I know this is no game, they are secret police: pit-bull terriers and ferrets. One of the ferrets puts out his hand. 'Please, your ID.' I try to think fast. I don't know if they want me for dodging the army or being in the north, but I need to hurry, they have already noted my hesitation.

My false ID gives the name I used in the north and says I've done my army training. If it's the army they are after me for, it's better to give them that. But if it's being in the north they want me for, then the real ID is better. Unless, of course, someone has informed on me. It's a Russian roulette of sorts, but the false ID is more likely to be certain death, so I reach into my pocket and deliver my real ID to the ferret.

He scans it with the savage little eyes of a scavenger and demands, 'Where are you from?'

'Diwaniyah.'

'What are you doing here?'

'I'm working for some extra money.'

'Are you a student?' If I was a student I should have papers to prove it, and I don't so I shake my head.

'Are you in the army?'

We all know that at twenty-four I should be in the army. It is becoming apparent this is why they are here. My fear that they have information about my being in the north subsides, giving me a little more latitude, so I take the risk. 'Yes, I'm in the army, but I have a few days' rest.'

'Where are your papers for a holiday?'

'I don't have papers. I just asked the officer and he said I could go.'

From his smirk I can tell I have not played my hand well.

'Okay, you come with us,' he says with the victorious tone of a schoolyard bully who has won by any means. Then he gestures in the pit-bulls to handcuff me and they parade me out in front of all my workmates.

In the past I was determined not to join the army because, like my father, I didn't want to go to Saddam's miserable wars and kill people for no purpose. Now, since they murdered my brother, I am even more resolute, but I know you don't argue with the secret police. They would love me to try to run so they could shoot me. There is nothing for it but to subdue my rage and go along with it.

They take me to a huge warehouse, where there are four, maybe five hundred men. It is like a massive waiting depot where they take all our details, separate us into groups based on which town we are from, then send us back there for processing. After three days they put me on a train with another guy.

It is steaming hot, we are handcuffed, and there is a security guard thug with us. It is looking increasingly like the game is up. Only a year since I got out of Abu Ghraib and here I am, back in another form of incarceration.

It is about eleven pm when we arrive in my home town of Diwan-iyah. We are to spend the night in a packed cell in another holding facility. I am exhausted from the gruelling trip so I put my jacket under my head and fall asleep on the concrete floor. I am woken a few hours later when the door of our cell flies open and three officers march in with a fire hose. One of them shouts an order and begins blasting water. It is so strong it almost lifts us off our feet.

The men pack into the back of the cell, crushing those behind them. Those underfoot cry out at being trampled while the ones at the front try to defend themselves with flailing arms. Then we are herded like sheep across the cell. 'Get over the other side! Move!' Now the ones who were at the front get trodden on, and the ones from the back get the full blast. Those left injured on the floor are flushed helplessly on a torrent of water into the corner. It is bedlam.

Some of the prisoners are no more than boys. There is terror in their eyes and one of the younger ones is crying. I put out my arm to protect him but the officers deliberately hose my hand away. They are enjoying themselves, dragging prisoners to their feet and throwing them back into the pack.

Then one of them yells, 'Enough!' And the hose goes off.

'What's wrong with you, are you crazy!' I scream at him, and he spits into my face, 'This is what the army is like, just getting you ready for it.' Then they march out of the cell.

Next day they take us to the local Ministry for Army Registrations. They write down our details again and photograph us. So now they have my full dossier on the record.

The next step is the Basra School for Army Training, which is in Diwaniyah, not Basra, where we begin training to kill for Saddam. If he decides to suppress the Shiites again I will have to turn a gun on my own brothers and my city.

We spend the night in the camp's prison, and it is miserable.

'We have to do something about this,' I try telling the other men, but everyone is scared. Like my father before me, they think I must be secret police because I'm daring to speak out, so they won't even talk to me. I lie awake for the rest of the night staring at the iron bars and experience my life spiralling out of control again and back into the hands of others.

In the morning I am taken to the general's office. He fixes me with stony eyes. 'You will be released for five days to organise your affairs, then you will be back in full dress with your head shaved. There will be no more running away from the army, or you will face execution.'

Then they supply me with army boots and a uniform, which they put in a plastic bag, and I am dismissed.

I leave the room with only one word in my head. All I heard was *released*. The *five days* had no traction. A window opens in my mind like a ray of morning sun. I am blinded by the thought of escape. When the jail gate is unlocked and I step out once more to freedom, I swing the plastic bag of army property around my head and hurl it back inside. Then I run, like my crazy commando father in the war.

The security guards run after me, but I run faster and as I gain distance I swear over my shoulder at them, 'You bastard motherfuckers!' These guards will never recognise me again; thousands of different faces pass through that door, and I know how the army works. Unless I am picked up for something else, they will take months or even years to track me down.

I let my resistance postman know, and then I find someone at the Ministry for the Army who, for a large amount of money, gets the dossier with all my details back. So if they find me again there will be no evidence that I have been previously inducted, and instead of shooting me, the process will just start again. It costs the resistance $US3000, but getting people out of the army is part of what they do. For once I appreciate the movement being cashed up.

At home I face a bigger problem. My mother, plagued by worries about me evading the army, especially after what happened to Ahmad, will be determined I take no more risks. Her worry is legitimate, but in all moral conscience I cannot do the dirty work for Saddam, my brother's murderer.

So the euphoria of my escape soon subsides as I prepare myself for the battle of all battles. However, when I arrive at the house it is not what I anticipate. She runs to me with tears of relief and holds me. The years of responsibility, fear and loss are taking their toll on her, and I am so disarmed that all I can do is hold her and say, 'Everything is okay, I will be starting with the army next week.'

I go into the bathroom to wash up, and stare at myself in the mirror with disbelief. I have just made my life unimaginably more complicated. I punish myself further for throwing away my uniform, but then I remember the satisfaction it gave me and smile. I know there are shops for people who want better quality than the army supplies, so next day I have to pay for a new outfit.

After five days of relative harmony with my mother I ask her to wake me at four am. I get up, shave my head and put on my new uniform. I can't look her in the eyes when she wishes me luck for my first day. I leave the house and wander down cool dark streets and along the banks of the quietly flowing river, until dawn breaks over the city.

Once the sun is up I walk to my grandmother's. 'I was on night shift at the army camp,' I say after greeting her. 'Can I come in for a rest?'

Delighted to see me she ushers me inside. I have breakfast with her then sleep until eleven. When I wake I shower and dress in my normal clothes, which I have in a small bag, and head into the city to find a new job. Even if I hadn't created this charade with my mother, I couldn't have gone back to the tailor in Baghdad without making it too easy for the army to find me.

I successfully keep up this routine for a month. I rise early, walk, eat, sleep, do what is needed for the resistance, then go to a job with Fariq, a tailor who is similar in age and political views to me. We become friends and I often sleep at his place. It is important that I don't stay anywhere too long, especially my own home.

My mother is blissfully unaware of the deception, until one morning, as I am waking at my grandmother's, I hear my uncle say to her, 'Ali is cheating on you, he's not in the army.' There is silence, then I hear my grandmother on the phone to my mother. It is clear they are onto me.

I get up slowly and prepare for a family brawl. I hate that I lied to my grandmother too. She has always been good to me. But it is like the bicycle – once my mother makes up her mind there is no way of putting my point of view. What I couldn't tell her is that joining the army is not going to make me safe. My life is now under threat from many directions.

I weather the storm of her anger but there is little I can do to allay her fears, so I have to wear her disappointment, which revives memories of earlier days when I failed to measure up for selfish reasons. This time it is to protect her, but I can't tell her that. So, like most Iraqi homes, mistrust and lies have now crept into mine too.

That night I sleep at my house to comfort my mother but, unlike her usual self, she doesn't want to talk about it. Next day I am relieved to be able to get up at a normal time to go to work. When I arrive Fariq gives me a worried look. 'There was someone here asking about you.'

I can't believe the army has been so efficient and found me already, it's more likely the secret police have discovered I have been in the north working with the resistance.

'What was he like?' I ask, my anxiety rising.

'He was driving a flash red sports car, and he had a beard.'

It doesn't sound like secret police but I can't think of anyone I know who fits the description.

'He said he would come back, so why don't you hide somewhere and watch.'

I find myself a comfortable spot opposite the shop and settle in to stake myself out. After about an hour the red car returns. Not many Iraqis have an expensive car like this, so it must be a secret-police disguise, but the guy is on his own, which is unusual. Then the door opens and he gets out. It could be anyone behind that beard but I recognise the easy gait immediately. It is Mohammad. He is meant to be in Germany but he has an uncanny ability to turn up when I most need him.

I am so overjoyed I yell his name and we rush towards each other laughing. We shake hands, slap backs, and embrace in the middle of the street like a Hollywood movie.

Fariq stands outside the shop laughing. 'Go have lunch. Spend some time with your friend.'

We go to a quiet café where we can talk. I look at him, amused. 'All this time I thought you were in Germany, but you were home driving around in a car that's certain not to attract attention! You know Saddam doesn't like anyone to have a better car than him.'

Mohammad grins mischievously and I furrow my brow.

'Did you even go to Germany?'

'Of course,' he laughs, 'but I didn't like it. My uncle was always away and I was by myself. I couldn't speak the language or get a job, I was bored, so I came back.'

'You have to be careful, Mohammad. The army got me and I'm on the run again. They or the secret police are sure to get you too if you've suddenly showed up at home.'

He grins. 'I'm not a dissident, I never went near the resistance. I was only in the north selling passports, that's nothing. I'd be scared if I had done something, but I haven't.'

'That was never a defence with Saddam,' I reply, remembering my friend Akram in Abu Ghraib. 'Just keep your head down, Mohammad, don't be dumb about it.'

'Don't worry, I'm careful. I was the one who went into hiding after the Shiite uprising. You are the one who got picked up and put in Abu Ghraib.'

It's true, neither Mohammad nor his immediate family have done anything subversive. However, Mohammad has lots of friends and by my standards he talks and jokes too much. So when I leave, with plans to meet tomorrow, I resolve not to sleep at home any more than I have to.

I decide to stay the night with my cousin, but as I pass our house I drop in to pick up some clothes. I am not surprised to find my mother in a state, there is always something. I sit her down and get her some tea. 'What is it, Umi?'

'I have heard your father is still alive.' She pauses, eyes brimming. 'But completely crazy.'

I take her hand to comfort her, but also for myself.

'They put him in a pit underground so they don't have to hear his yelling.'

I almost smile at the thought of my father not only alive but still fighting. 'It's possible he is no worse than he was, and at least he is still living,' I say with genuine amazement. 'That's *good* news, Umi.'

I realise I had given up any hope of seeing him again, and that somewhere over the last four years my mourning must have ended. I put my arm around my mother's shoulders. 'You know what he's like. He'll cope, he always does.' And I honestly believe it.

My mother remains distressed and I don't want to leave her, so I hang the risk and spend the night at home. Next morning I am sleeping on the roof when the roosters wake me out of a nightmare. I am dreaming my father's story of sleeping with the dead, except my father is the dead and I am him, sleeping next to his rotting corpse. Last night's news must have affected me more than I had thought. I fall back into a restless sleep until my mother wakes me again.

'Are you going to work? You can walk with us, I have to take Inas to be registered for school.'

'Soon,' I say, feeling dazed by my dream, and go on sleeping. She calls me again before she leaves but I am still floundering in semiconsciousness so she goes without me. I finally wake properly at about nine-thirty, have a shower, dress and leave.

When I come out the front door I notice two young guys I don't know sitting opposite. I cross the street, where another two indicate to others further along. Then I see a parked car with two people wait-ing in it and my heart begins to pound. They are everywhere. I need to think quickly but my brain is still full of images of my father and the dead.

A big black Toyota with a number plate not from this city is com-ing towards me and cruises past. When Iraq invaded Kuwait they took these special cars for the use of the government and the secret services, so it is clear this is serious and not just the army police picking me up again. This is the Mukhabarat conducting a major operation.

Fortuitously a friend is coming towards me. I don't want to get him involved, so I don't tell him what is happening but I need a moment to assess the situation and by hugging him I can look back over his shoulder and develop a strategy.

They want to pick me up without anyone knowing, in a street where everyone knows me. If my life wasn't at stake I would be laugh-ing. But to be fair, they are also worried I might have a weapon, which I do, like everyone who works for the resistance.

I realise there's a concrete barrier in the middle of the road, which will prevent them doing a U-turn. So if I can get to the other side they won't be able to chase me with the Toyota. I farewell my friend and keep walking a short distance until I get to an area I know well, then I make a dash for it across the street.

When they see me jump the barrier they get confused, which is what I was hoping for. I make this my moment to pull out my gun and shoot wildly at them. It is unlikely I will hit anyone but it throws them into panic and gives me time to disappear into the side streets. Once out of sight I run into a house where I vaguely know the people, but they have heard the gunshots and everyone starts screaming. So I dart out again. I am now in full panic myself.

Adrenaline surges through my body as I run through a maze of laneways and backstreets that I know from my youth. I arrive at the house next to where my grandmother used to live. A tenuous connec-tion but they know me like family from when I was a kid.

The door is open, so glancing over my shoulder I bend over and try to slow my breathing. It takes a dangerous few moments to get it under control but once it calms I stuff the gun in my pocket and walk in. I see the mother and daughter making bread.

'Hello, Ali. What's happening?' the woman says with a friendly smile.

'Nothing much. I just came to see you,' I reply as calmly as possible, hoping they don't notice how profusely I am sweating.

'How is your mother?'

'She is well. She says hello. Is your son home?'

'He should be back soon. Would you like to wait?'

She ushers me into the next room, gives me tea, and turns the television on. I am relieved to be left alone to assimilate what has happened. But it is hard to integrate. Here I am sipping tea and watching TV, when a few minutes ago I was being hunted by my executioners, and running so hard the rubber was almost burning off my shoes.

I use the time to decide on my next move. Fariq lives nearby. We have become good friends since I started working for him and I know he hates the government as much as I do. So I say I can't wait, check the coast is clear, and step back out into the battlefield.

The streets are unnaturally quiet, which is unnerving, and there seem to be dogs behind every garden wall. Each time they bark I jump. Even inanimate objects become a threat. Rocks and houses are watching me. Each car I see, every taxi or bus is frightening. Everything is suspicious as I skulk along the streets to Fariq's house.

When I finally arrive, Fariq and his brother hurry me inside. 'We knew you were in big trouble because we passed your street last night and saw the secret police blocking it. We found out it was you they were after but didn't know if you might be sleeping at a relative's. Anyway, we couldn't get past them to warn you.'

No wonder I had bad dreams. I can't believe I was the only one who didn't know what was going on.

'We were worried when you didn't come to work today,' Fariq

finishes with a hug. 'But you are safe here.'

Relief takes over and I collapse into a chair.

News travels fast in our community, and soon one of Fariq's friends arrives with information. Two nights ago the secret police picked up Ala, the guy I met when he collected his passport from Mohammad in Arbil. Ala had joined his family in the south as he had intended and was living on their farm when the girlfriend of one of his relatives betrayed him.

Ala was accused of living with the enemy in Iran and of having been in the north. They said he must have been working with the resistance, and wanted names. They tortured him until he gave them two: Mohammad's and mine.

Last night, knowing nothing of this, Mohammad and three friends were having a good time sitting on the riverbank, drinking arak and talking. They took little notice of a man in an ordinary car who drove past then stopped. The guy got out and put up the hood, then called to Mohammad and his friends to help him push his car.

Maybe because they had had too much alcohol, or perhaps Mohammad thought he knew him, but they went to the man's aid and started to push the car. Suddenly there was a screeching of brakes and they were surrounded by four black Toyotas. Doors flew open and secret police jumped out with guns, yelling, 'Don't move.' In a flash they were all handcuffed and thrown into the cars.

At headquarters they took Mohammad into a separate room and tortured him. Ala wouldn't have known my last name, so they couldn't have come after me this morning if they hadn't got Mohammad to talk. I try not to imagine what they must have done to him. He would be devastated he had given me away. But I know how it goes. They are professionals, they can get information from anyone.

I sit back in my chair. I don't want to hear any more. Poor Mohammad is from wealth and good breeding, he had no military or resistance training to prepare him for torture. He would not have been able to deal with it. I remember how in Abu Ghraib Akram would say, 'What makes the pain? Your mind, not your body.' We would try to practise this. Sometimes it helped, sometimes it didn't, but unlike my father I didn't lose my mind, so maybe it did.

Once they got what they wanted from Mohammad they released the other three, and as soon as they were free the news was on the street. As I thank our informants I am suddenly aware I have been so preoccupied with my own and Mohammad's plight that I forgot my family. The secret police will of course go to them to try and hunt me down.

'Fariq, I need to see my mother,' I say urgently.

'Too dangerous right now. Tomorrow we'll organise a car. No problem.'

Word is dispatched to Emir, the son of a Baathist who is high up in government. He is vigorously opposed to the Baathists, but his father is ignorant of this, so is happy to lend his official car to Emir when it is not in use. Because it is owned by the Baath Party its driver is able to go wherever he wants, even through checkpoints, without any interference. Emir enjoys the irony of transporting dissidents in it. No one wants to think of what would happen if he is caught.

I pace the floor for two days, waiting for the car. Finally it arrives and we head off with me lying behind the front seats. We go to my aunt's where we call my mother, and as I had feared, she rushes over in a dreadful state.

She and Inas had been followed to school the morning I was chased, and when she returned I was gone. Then she had heard stories of guns and shooting. That night, as she lay on the roof too distressed to sleep, she suddenly saw a boot coming over the side. From under her blanket she watched as more and more boots appeared until there were twenty men with guns surrounding her and the children.

Then the yelling started. 'Wake up, everyone, where is Ali?'

My mother leapt to her feet. 'Who is Ali?'

'Your son,' one of the police spat into her face.

'I don't know where he is.'

They pointed their weapons at the children, who were frozen in their fear. 'You need to tell us for your own sake. He has been brainwashed and is very dangerous.'

For the first time my mother realised this was about more than the army, but fortunately she didn't have to lie. 'I don't know where he is! He is a grown man, not a child!' she screamed.

They tore the house apart then locked everyone inside. After two days of getting nothing out of them they gave up and left.

I put my arms around my mother and let her sob, trying to stop my rage at the secret police for terrorising my family on my account, especially my little sisters and Hashim, who is only five. I am powerless, and it hits me that I have to either return to the loneliness of the north or remain in hiding. I don't know how I can help Mohammad by being here, but I somehow feel I can't leave until they let him go. So I return to Fariq's, assuring my mother things will be all right.

'This house is yours,' Fariq offers, disregarding the personal risk. He and his brother go to the tailor shop each morning, come back for lunch, then we have dinner together at night and pore over whatever gossip or news there has been during the day.

After a month Mohammad is still being held. I begin to feel I have put enough strain on Fariq, and despite his protests decide to move to a cousin's who had run from the army himself, and lived with us for a while when I was young. So Emir is called and I am shipped across town again in the Baath car.

My days are empty without Fariq, his brother, and our meals together. I swing between loneliness, boredom and fear. The only high points are the days when Emir comes by in the car and drops a book in a garbage bin a few doors up. Then after an hour of watching I slip out cautiously and pick it up. I never thought I would long for the sight of an official Baath car.

One book he brings me is a love story translated from English. It describes how the hero kisses the girl, how he takes her clothes off, how she smells. In Iraq we are not allowed to read a book like this. Emir must have got it from the black market, or perhaps he stole it from his father, whose needs no doubt are met by the party machine.

The book is both erotically stirring and deeply depressing, as a torrent of vivid memories of Intisar tumble back. I lie for hours replacing the girl in the book with her, reflecting on how much of my life has been lost to imprisonment in one form or another by this regime. No matter how many times I read it, while it fills my day, it fills none of the gaps of what I have missed.

Against my better judgement I ask Emir, via the garbage bin, if he can get hold of *Romeo and Juliet*. I'm glad I don't have to say it to his face in case he thinks I've lost it. Within a week a well-thumbed copy arrives and I read it hungrily, remembering the thrilling sensations evoked by my own balcony scene and the exhilaration of that first naive love. I think of what I could have had, and as I close the book at the end I weep quietly on my bed.

The nights are the worst. Any sound or voice I hear outside ramps up my anxiety. I sit at the window watching, smoking cigarettes and straining to hear the slightest sound. Maybe they are poised to jump. Any minute. Often I won't fall asleep until dawn. Sometimes I get into an almost delirious state and think I see Mohammad waiting for me on the other side of the street.

There is, however, a tender moment in my mornings, which helps revive me for the day. My cousin is blessed with a sweet wife who, once the sun has risen and I am finally asleep, soundlessly checks how many cigarettes I have left. Then she goes to the shop, buys more, and refills the packet before I wake. It is such a loving act that I wish I had the courage to tell her, quite apart from my gratitude for the cigarettes, how sustaining this gesture is.

One day I discover my cousin and his sweet wife have begun to have trouble. It seems he has a girlfriend. Such is the irony of life. It's been nearly six months and there is no news on Mohammad's release, but I am not sure how much longer I can hide without losing my mind. When he gets out he is unlikely to stay in Diwaniyah, so I decide to go to Baghdad. I can meet him there.

I put grey dye though my hair and the beard I have grown while in hiding. It elevates my age considerably. I gaze into the mirror and wonder where I'll be if and when I reach the age I look. I hug my cousin and thank his wife for caring for me. I can tell she understands how much her small act of generosity meant. As I step out into the street I hope I will one day be able to pass on her kindheartedness.

I keep my head down and hurry to the train station. I buy a ticket to Baghdad but my luck is out. The train is old and chugs along, stopping at every station, where a new lot of police keep getting on. They work their way through the carriages, unabashedly collecting bribes from any young men they can find who should be in the army.

While my disguise makes me look too old for the army, it also makes me look much older than the photo on my ID. So trying not to panic when they appear, I get up casually and go into the next carriage. Then I keep jumping ahead of them. When the train stops I get off and walk down the platform to the back of the train and board again. Maybe they see me pass the window, but with grey hair and my shoulders slumped I look like an old man, and old men, I discover, attract very little attention. It is a harrowing journey, but I become increasingly competent at my subterfuge.

When I get to Baghdad I find a public phone to let my mother know I have arrived. Our family's phone is bugged, so I use our usual code to call her at my aunt's, then I wait smoking cigarettes to give her time to get there. She calls back almost immediately, panting, so she must have run all the way from our house.

'Ali.' She breathes heavily, sounding extremely upset. I am not unduly worried because it is not unusual.

'What is it, Umi?'

'It's Mohammad.'

'Have they let him go?' I ask, elated. 'I knew as soon as I left they would release him.'

'No, they shot him in the head.'

She begins to cry with fear, panic and empathetic pain. A wave of nausea passes over me. The receiver slips from my hand. I watch a man on the other side of the street kick his dog. Two men stall their car and get out and push. A little boy drops his kebab and his mother scolds him. It all passes before me in slow soundless motion.

And my friend Mohammad is dead. A bullet through his head.

I vomit in the gutter, then wipe my mouth and walk back to the phone, where my mother is still crying as she talks.

'This big general who planned to kill Saddam was caught. You must have heard.'

I had heard, it was big news, but I am not thinking about any big general. I am thinking about my friend, but there is no way to stop my mother. 'So Saddam decides to clean up everything against his government. He kills the general, and everyone around him and anyone in the resistance in one big hit. They say Mohammad had been in the north so they killed him. And Ala, they shot him too.'

I want my mother to cease.

'Mohammad's parents are completely distraught. I've just been to visit them. He had nothing to do with anything and they have murdered him.'

'I have to go, Umi.'

My body has taken over. I can speak no more. I cannot help my mother, not now, not this time. I hang up the phone and stand calmly in the vortex of a storm of grief so great I don't know if I can manage it.

I walk through the streets in a daze, with no concern of being picked up or seen. My hands deep in my pockets, through bustling shops and restaurants with diners on the footpath, eating, talking, laughing, and empty dark streets, and lanes with dogs behind walls, and cats in dangerous alleys, and kids out too late. I walk, feeling everything and nothing, until the city is quiet and everybody has gone to bed.

By now I just want to sleep, so I head for a bus station. It is empty and dark but I want to be left alone so I lie under a food vender's trolley that has been locked up for the night. After an hour of fitful sleep I get up and move on, but there is nowhere to go and I am too tired to think. Bleary-eyed, I know something terrible has happened but I don't exactly remember what it is.

I wander through the markets, so vibrant by day but desolate at night. I recall the good times and the bad in the Diwaniyah markets with Ahmad, and I feel my grief for him will never end. And then it hits me with full force. Mohammad is dead. My mother saw his body. He is dead. Why him? Why not me? Why have I been chosen to survive? Why didn't I die in Abu Ghraib? Most people did. Why have the good been killed?

I have very little faith left after Abu Ghraib but for some unconscious reason, as the sun rises and a clear melodious voice making its pledge to Allah rings out over Baghdad, I find myself stumbling towards a mosque. When I arrive I go to the bathroom and discover the back of my T-shirt is black with a thick layer of cooking oil and dirt from under the trolley at the bus station.

I usually hate to be unclean but today I come back out and kneel with the filth on my back. Normally I would be afraid of the clerics, who could call the secret police, but today my heart breaks for my friend Mohammad. As I kneel alone the call to prayer wafts gently over the city and I weep. I weep for Mohammad, and my brother, and my father, and finally for my guilt for still living.

REFUGEES IN OUR OWN LAND

I must have knelt for several hours in my shattered state, before the slow realisation of my situation creeps up on me. With the general's attempt on Saddam's life our leader's paranoia has clearly escalated. There will be a concerted campaign to capture anyone who has escaped him, so doubtless they will be on my trail soon.

I stagger to my feet and back out onto the street. Then I head to the station where I catch a train to Mosul, where my old friend Unis lives. He had helped shepherd me through a crucial period once before, guiding me away from gang life and into wrestling. We had spent many hours laughing and joking at our misadventures in the ring.

I am exhausted, and it is mostly a blur, but after another journey of walking the carriages ahead of the police, I arrive to find the same old Unis, just as he had always been, easygoing, gentle, and honest, with a firm grip on reality.

'So, I hear you are in trouble,' he says calmly.

I tell him about Mohammad, and Ala. How their families had been called to the police station and the bodies handed over with no explanation. 'They are heartbroken and enraged, but they just have to bury their sons and say nothing.'

We sit silently for a moment then I ask him, 'Can you help me get into Kurdistan, Unis?' With the current upheaval I am afraid to use any of my old contacts.

'You should stay here, Ali,' he replies, and I see the disappointment in his eyes. 'You can work with me in my business. My brother is a colonel in the army, so you are safe in my house.'

'Thank you, Unis, but if I could be safe I would go home to my city where I long to be.'

That night I call my aunt to get a message to my mother. But my mother is already there and close to hysteria. After what happened to Mohammad she is afraid the police will pick up my brothers, Asad and Basim.

I calm her down but knowing nothing will allay her fears, I tell her to send them to me in Mosul and I will take them with me to the north. It is the first time I have mentioned the north to her but by now she has realised I am up to my neck in trouble, so accepts without comment that I would be trying to get out of the country.

I have my doubts Asad and Basim will come. They are still teenagers, and teenagers are self-occupied, out of touch with the real world, and will not want to leave their friends. At their age I was roaming the streets with my gang.

Sure enough, on the day they are supposed to arrive, they don't turn up. I don't want to call again, because if something has happened everyone's phones will be tapped and we could all get caught. I wait for two more days with no sign of them. I am increasingly annoyed. The longer I stay in one place, the more dangerous it becomes and I suspect I am on borrowed time.

On the third day I say to Unis, 'Let's go. You can send them later.'

Unis agrees, so we set off in his car for a small country town where we meet Harith, the smuggler, who is to my relief still waiting for us.

'Why do you want to go to the north?' he asks, looking at me doubtfully. 'There is plenty of army in this area, sometimes they catch the people and they take their money, sometimes they take the people. We can't guarantee.'

'I'll take my chances,' I reply, thinking this is a rather bad start to things.

Unis doesn't want to leave until I am safely across the Tigris, but I am concerned that if my brothers have turned up after all, no one will be there. We hug, both knowing it is a final embrace, and as I watch him drive away I think of him, and Mohammad, and all the other friends I will never see again.

That night I set off to leave Iraq for the last time. It is very dark and we are about one kilometre from the river. I am ready to make a dash for it, with Harith showing the way, when I discover there is a whole train of donkeys, loaded to the hilt with cans of oil, gas and petrol. As they wind their way through the rough hilly country, I can see how slow it is going, and what a prime target we are for the army.

Frustrated I turn to Harith. 'Are any of these donkeys yours?'

'No, today I just take money and bring back cigarettes.'

'That's good. Do you know the way?'

'I know it exactly, like I see you now.'

'If we make it to the river will we find the boat waiting?'

'Yeah, the boat is already there.'

He is beginning to tire of my questions and I am beginning to wonder how bright he is.

'Okay,' I say, 'so can we move faster?'

'Like what?'

'Can you run?'

'Yeah.'

'Okay, run and I will follow you!'

So we run, but he runs so slowly I am on his heels. 'Faster,' I say, ready to explode. 'Faster!'

'What about the army?'

'Don't worry about the army. If we go fast enough they will miss us when they shoot!'

So we run, gasping and sucking at the cold night as our feet fly across uneven ground, expecting at any minute a bullet in the chest. But tonight I am running to my freedom, and apart from leaving everything I have ever loved and known I am elated by the prospect of escaping Saddam for good.

When we get to the river a small boat is indeed waiting. We double over, trying to get our breath. Harith is laughing. He shakes his head and I stuff some extra money in his hand. He slaps my back and wishes me luck as I climb into the boat and we head off into the night.

I clutch a cheap bag containing my few remaining possessions. I'm not sure why but I let my hand slip over the side with it and hang in the water. As I listen to the waves shlucking against the plastic I look back to where I once belonged, then slowly, one finger at a time, I release the bag and let it slip away.

In Arbil I go to the house I previously shared with some other resistance workers, which has a small spare room where I can sleep. Once I'm settled I phone Unis in Mosul for news of my brothers.

'Thank God you called,' he exclaims with uncustomary alarm. 'They've been picked up by the army and handed over to the police.'

My stomach turns.

'They arrived a few hours after we left, and instead of waiting they found a smuggler on their own, which was really stupid.'

'They're only teenagers,' I say, trying to quell my fury at their disastrous mistake.

I hang up full of dread. With my father still in Abu Ghraib voicing his hatred of Saddam, me already known to be in the resistance, and now two of my brothers caught trying to get into the north, there is no way my family will not be seen as a target for retribution.

I call my aunt and soon have my mother on the phone. She is a mess. Her worst fears have been realised, now she has lost two more of her children. I am close to panic myself but I manage to pacify her enough to get her to listen to me.

'Umi, you have to pack up your most important things. Only what you can carry. I cannot come and help but I am going to send someone to collect you. You have to leave Diwaniyah. You must leave Iraq. I am sorry, Umi, but all your lives are now in danger.'

I speak slowly and gently, but she cries throughout my speech and I wonder if she is hearing anything. She loves the home my father built for her, it is where her children were born. She has never been anywhere but Diwaniyah. It is her life and her community. She spends part of every day with my grandmother or other relatives, who all live there. I don't know if this is going to be the point at which my mother, always the tower of strength, can't take it any more.

'Umi, do you hear me? Do you understand what I am saying?'

I can feel her nodding through her tears, so I go on. 'You only have a few days. Can you do it?'

'Yes, Ali,' she eventually whispers. 'Don't worry, I do it.'

With some relief I hang up the phone then I face the enormity of it all. The children will have to leave their schools, their friends, their cousins and their home forever. And they will have to leave Iraq, where their brothers and father will be rotting in Saddam's jail, and become refugees. It has become a tragedy of gigantic proportions.

That night I dredge up my old resistance contacts and plug back into the network. From inside the movement it is not hard to find a smuggler who knows all the checkpoints, how to deal with police, where to get the paperwork, and who to pay. And a woman with young children is no threat to anyone, making it easier. Before long I find a guy I know is a professional. I pay him to make six new IDs, and to take these by car to Diwaniyah, where he will collect the rest of the family and bring them here to me in Arbil.

Next day I go to the resistance headquarters to let them know I am back. They are aware of my circumstances because I have remained in contact through my postman while I was in hiding. Each week he would put his book in the garbage bin, like Emir. I would collect it when the coast was clear, read his notes, and return it to the bin.

They are pleased to see me back but seem disconcertingly uninterested in my plight. It is true they have looked after me but now that it is impossible for me to return to Iraq I need to be able to contribute in some other way, but they are not open to redefining my role. Despite the suicidal nature of it, they have missions they want me to return to Baghdad to pursue.

'Are you out of your mind?' I explode. 'I am being hunted by the Mukhabarat. Two of my brothers have just been picked up by the police, and my friend Mohammad has been executed because of my connections with you.' I look around at them savagely. 'The rest of my family are escaping and on their way here as I speak. So who is going to take care of them for me if I am killed! You?' I conclude by banging my hand on the table and they look startled.

'Okay,' the boss finally says. 'But if you don't go we will need the details of the people helping you in Baghdad, so we can deal direct.'

I look at them incredulous. 'So they can meet the same fate as Mohammad?'

I storm out. I have had enough. They are all talk. In my time with them I have not been aware of any action they've taken against Saddam. Who knows if all that information I risked my life to get has ever been used. I have no stomach for them any more. I am finished. It is over. Mohammad's words finally come home to me: *Just don't be disappointed if it's not what you think ... it's Saddam you have to kill and you're not going to do that.*

Thus the inglorious end to my career with the resistance. Now I must turn my focus to saving what is left of my family.

In the time it takes the police to send Asad and Basim to Baghdad to be tried, my smuggler has brought the rest of my family to Arbil. We soon hear that the court has given my brothers seven years each.

In a final blow to completely break my mother's heart, they will be separated. Asad will go to Abu Ghraib, then in two years, when Basim is older, he will join him. By then, supposing they survive, they will be so hardened by fear and loneliness they will be strangers.

Like all our reunions, when my family arrive there is both exhilaration and sadness. As much as we try to relish the taste of freedom, the shadow of Asad and Basim's incarceration hangs over us. Fortunately the children are caught up in the adventure of the journey, so the loss has not yet fully hit them.

But the euphoria of escape quickly loses its shine as the reality of Kurdistan sets in. It is not a place you go to live, it is a stepping-off stone to somewhere else. Ninety percent of the people have no job and no money. As I no longer work for the resistance I have no income either, and with the expense of bringing the family here, no savings. So we have to decide quickly what to do next.

In the golden era, when Iraqis left home for education or holidays, they went to Europe and returned with captivating stories of ancient cities, castles, autumn leaves and snowfields. It is where I had imagined we would go first. My mother is beyond making any further decisions, so we set off for Turkey as the first step to Europe. I don't know why I think we can cross the border without passports or papers, but we have so few options that we may as well at least try to smuggle ourselves in.

We leave Arbil in a minibus and go north to Duhok, and then to Zakho where we catch a taxi to the border. After the anticipation it is hard not to be disappointed to find ourselves in a barren rocky landscape with nothing but mountains ahead of us. However, we are not alone. There are nearly a dozen other Iraqi families in the same situation and more arriving. We gather together and head off into the rugged terrain, but before long we are seen by the Turkish militia, who tell us they will shoot us if we try to enter Turkey.

One of the more informed members of the group demands to speak to the UN, and within an hour we see a cloud of dust approaching. They arrive in army vehicles with American, French and British soldiers. But their response is cool. 'You cannot cross the border, and we can't help you because you are in your own country. Kurdistan is still part of Iraq. So you have to back up.'

We argue, but we soon find ourselves being returned to Duhok, where we are herded into a large refugee camp. It is mostly tents but the UN has begun to make it more permanent by putting up buildings. This brings out the ugly side of the Kurds. They don't want us to stay, they don't believe we belong here.

With no school or stimulation the children become quiet, afraid they are stuck here forever. My mother is not well at the best of times, but now, having no tea, no sugar, and watery soup every day starts to take its toll, and the constraints of living in a tent under a military guard wear thin. When the Kurdish guards try to provoke us we start to hate everyone, the Kurds, the Americans, the Iraqis, all of them, and the deep humiliation of being a refugee in your own country begins to sink in.

During the winter it is so cold that every day I have to find wood to make a fire for us to sleep beside. Once the summer sets in, the heat becomes unbearable and we fester in our own sweat with no relief.

To lie around bored and with no purpose is debilitating, leaving us too much time to think. So restless nights and nightmares become regular for us all, as we relive our various traumas from previous years.

By the middle of 1996 we have given up any dreams of Europe, so when we hear of agents who work with the Syrian secret police and will take you across the border to Syria for around $US300 per person, we decide to try it. This time the right way, at least as right as it gets.

My mother suggests we call my Uncle Kasem, who lives in America. I had helped him escape before I went into Abu Ghraib, and by now he might have made some money. It is not hard to get out of the camp by day, so I go to Duhok and find a public phone outside a small shop. I call and ask him to ring me back, because I don't have enough to pay for the call. Then I pace, and wait, but nothing.

I begin to worry that maybe he's broke or can't borrow it. I don't worry that he is offended, in our culture we believe money is like a car. It takes us from one place to another, but it is not the end of the journey. Particularly within our own family or tribe, borrowing money, if someone has it, is not such a big deal. It's just that with the devastation of Iraq and so many of us on the run, very few have any to give.

I am about to go home when the guy who owns the shop comes out.

'Why are you hanging around?' he asks.

'I'm waiting for my uncle to call me back.'

'How can he? This phone is run by satellite and the numbers are rented out to different international suppliers, so he can't find out where you are calling from.'

I call my uncle again and he says, 'You give me a headache. This number is a big ship in the middle of the Atlantic Ocean.'

I laugh. After a few moments he laughs too, and we are off to a better start. Maybe he had heard of our plight from family but to my relief, because I have to pay for the call, he asks no questions and agrees to send $US3000, more than we could have hoped for.

So I find an agent who, to our amazement, says he will take us tomorrow. We are all excited, but the next day he takes another family. I see the disappointment on the faces of my mother and the children, all packed up and ready to escape this misery, and I fly at him. 'Not only did you promise us, but instead you take the family of a bitch who has given everyone endless trouble in the camp with her selfishness.'

He coolly gives our money back and says he will take us another time, but I can see I have blown it, and now we will pay. I try and comfort my siblings. 'Don't worry, we will go next time,' I say weakly, in the face of their distress. We had built up so much hope for Syria, with the possibility of being able to stay in an Arabic culture, work, eat similar food and remain near our homeland, where our father and brothers are still imprisoned.

Early next morning I slip out of the camp and travel to the border near Faysh Khabur, to see what else I can arrange. But instead I discover that the agent has put our name on a list that prohibits us from crossing. So now, because of a few angry words, we are blocked forever from going to Syria.

In desperation I decide to see if I can swim the Tigris River. I team up with an Iraqi guy I have made friends with in the camp. When we get there the water is so strong, if you put a donkey in it, it would take the donkey. I am not scared but it is teeming rain, which makes it even more sinister, and my companion is so afraid that he won't let me go on my own. When I attempt it he starts crying, so I give up and back we go to the camp.

My fuse is getting so short that when the Kurdish police start taunting us to entertain themselves, I begin to crack. Whenever they want to give us an order, they command that we bring the women too.

'Just tell us and we'll tell them, you motherfucker,' I retort, knowing quite well they just want to show the women their muscle while we, their men, are so impotent. They threaten me but I am so worked up I snap, 'You are as bad as Saddam's people, you Kurdish bastards,' forgetting the consequences.

I march off to our tent but sure enough, within a short time the Kurdish police arrive and take me away. The look of despair on my siblings' faces as they are left fatherless again haunts me in the underground jail I am thrown into. There is another guy already there, not that we can see each other. It is pitch-dark, and we can't stand up because the ceiling is only about a metre high. As we crawl around in the blackness it smells and feels like it has been used as a garbage tip.

At night it is so cold we think we will freeze to death. The other guy has managed to keep his cigarettes and matches, so we roll paper from the rubbish into a ball and light it. But there is more debris on the floor than we thought, so flames soon lick around the walls and acrid smoke threatens to suffocate us. Fortunately it seeps into the room above and the guards, presumably not wanting to explain how we burnt to death, drag us out coughing and retching.

They punish us with threats of torture, bringing their snarling dogs so close to my face their saliva flies into my eyes as they strain on their leashes to savage me.

After the letdown over Syria, the taunting of the Kurdish guards, then being back in prison again, I have spiralled into a hole as black as the underground cell I am in. So I tell them I don't care what they do to me. Because of this, and a curious response from the dogs, they back off.

When I was four or five I had a dog that I adored. But for some reason that no one ever explained to me, it became ferocious and began to bite people. So the dog was taken away, presumably to its death and I was seriously conflicted. I loved the dog but was also afraid of it. Consequently I must have projected the same perplexed response to my attacker dogs, who, reading my combination of curiosity, love and fear, got confused themselves and turned away.

So I am left to stew in my own misery. But I soon begin to think of my family, stuck in the wretched refugee camp that I brought them to, and a small survival flame must have rekindled, because I gird up again, like my mother, for another round.

When my cellmate is released I manage to get a message out to Umi. I tell her how to find a resistance friend I made in Duhok. He has a contact in the Kurdish militia who may be able to help me.

Due to his diligence, within a couple of days I am free. But before they let me go an officer snarls, 'You must leave Duhok.'

'Okay, I will go to Arbil,' I say, relieved, only to find myself caught in the complex web of Kurdish politics.

'You can't go to Arbil,' he retorts. 'Arbil is controlled by the PUK. You can only stay in territory controlled by the KDP.'

I sigh. The Kurds are as bad as the Arabs. Instead of gaining maximum strength by uniting against Saddam, they divide themselves into two political camps: the PUK, the Patriotic Union of Kurdistan, and the KDP, the Kurdistan Democratic Party. And then, like the Iraqi resistance, they dissipate their power by being at each other's throats.

'Arbil is the only place I know,' I say impatiently.

'If you go to Arbil or we catch you in Duhok again, we will send you back to Saddam. You must find somewhere else not controlled by the PUK.'

The officer pushes a written agreement under my nose to sign. I stare at him. I may as well be back in Iraq if I am going to be under the threat of being dealt with by Saddam again. I think I might go crazy or hit someone if I don't get out of here, so I quickly pick up the pen, sign it and walk out. There are so many people after me anyway, the KDP peshmerga are hardly the first in line.

I go straight back to the refugee camp and find my family huddled in their tent. Their future already in doubt, they had no idea what they would do if I didn't return. I hug and reassure the children that I will always come back to them, which is a foolish lie because anything could happen to me, but I ache at the sight of their distress and I am running out of ideas.

We head for Arbil and we find a house to rent. It is a big city and if we lie low I am unlikely to be noticed. I immediately go to the markets and put the rest of my uncle's money to work, exchanging dollar to dinar, dinar to dollar, with each conversion making a profit, and soon I am earning enough to set us up. We get a fridge, a couch, a TV to entertain the children, and my mother begins to cook food we like again. The nightmare of the refugee camp slowly subsides and we decide things are not so bad after all.

The only problem is that I am constantly looking over my shoulder for the peshmerga in case someone recognises me. Also, it is impossible to find out what is happening between the Baathists and the north. I know from my work with the resistance that what we hear on the radio or TV is mostly propaganda. For all we know an invasion could be imminent. Maybe Saddam is waiting to pounce. The tiger and the chicken. The danger is still there, it seems, so long as we are on Iraqi soil.

HEJIRA

We keep meeting people who say Iran is our only prospect for escape, but it is hard to consider because the war with Iran was the source of so much misery for us. Not only my father's seven years at the front, when he was so mentally ill, but also the death of two of my mother's brothers, especially the colonel.

He had helped us locate my father when he was being tortured in 1980, and was there for our family during that terrible time. He was an intelligent, generous man of great integrity and became a powerful role model for me. Early in the war his tank was so incinerated by the Iranians that it melted the metal doors shut, creating its own crematorium and tomb for him and his men. Our grief was intensified by the arrival of a coffin holding three bags of sand to symbolise his body.

Not only do Iraqis not cremate their dead, we must bury the body immediately, otherwise the spirit cannot rest. So when the coffin turned up and we opened it to find no body, we knew his soul would wander in torment for eternity. Or worse, we began to think maybe he was still alive and captured in Iran, which kept Umi and my grandmother in a state of doubt and longing for many painful years. It never healed, but gradually with time and other misfortunes, it was put aside.

Despite these unhappy memories, now that Turkey and Syria are no longer options and Iran is the only border left with Kurdistan, I have to consider it. But it is going to be hard to get over the mountains with a smuggler. The children are really too young for such a treacherous journey, and my mother cannot walk very well. When they put us in Abu Ghraib, I later discovered she had tried to find us, and instead was incarcerated and beaten so badly that the baby she was carrying died, and remained dead inside her womb until she was let go many days later. Since then her strength and invincibility have never been quite the same.

While I am searching for information on the best way to get to Iran, I meet Haddad, an Iraqi man, with his wife and children. They are from the south, so I am as pleased as them to meet someone from the same region.

We immediately get on and over the next few weeks we drink tea and talk often. He has no work and they are obviously struggling. Haddad thinks he can make money if he sets up a mixed business stall with cigarettes and drinks. I help him by paying for the stock to get him started. But it fails.

His children are going hungry, so I suggest he comes and works with me exchanging money at the markets. I give him US dollars to buy for dinars, back and forth, and we work so well together that I stop collecting the money from him every hour. Then one morning when I am going to be late I give him all the money so he can get started early. When I arrive he is nowhere to be seen. He has gone.

I am devastated by this act of betrayal. Without money my exchange business is destroyed, our livelihood has gone and our chances of escaping to Iran are stymied. Suddenly all our prospects have evaporated again.

I am on the verge of panic when I meet Abdul-Haqq, whose name means 'servant of the truth'. He works with the Islamic Party. This would normally not impress me, but under our present circumstances, when he says he can help us go to Iran for free, I listen. He is a warm, friendly guy who has a big beard, which in our culture indicates that he practises his religion, and tends to suggest he is honest.

'I work with a charity,' Abdul-Haqq explains. 'We collect money from rich people in the Islamic movement in the south, and use it to bring families north to be smuggled across the border.'

It is hard not to see this opportunity, with what little faith I have, as a gift from God.

I invite Abdul-Haqq to meet my family and they are impressed with him too, so we decide to take the leap.

'Look,' I stress as he leaves, 'my mother is not strong, and there are five young children.'

'There won't be any problem,' he says reassuringly and we shake hands.

We begin to replace our fantasies about Europe and Syria with the possibility of a new life in Iran, and as an added bonus we will still be close to home if Saddam falls. So when in three days Abdul-Haqq says he is ready to go, we go.

We leave everything behind. All the furniture, the appliances and household goods I have worked so hard to get. My mother's plates, pots and pans, and cooking utensils. The mats and bedding, and the brightly coloured cushions from the markets that we sat on to eat our meals. Anything we can't carry is left for the neighbours to keep. My siblings are not particularly attached to most of it, but I see the anguish on my mother's face as she shuts the door on another home.

And so we go to Sulaymaniyah, a large city at the base of the mountains near the Iranian border. Then we wait and our excitement begins to fade. We discover Abdul-Haqq won't actually know how much money has been collected until it is time to leave, so if there isn't enough he can't send everyone. It also becomes apparent that what city or party you come from affects your position in the queue. There are two other Islamic families waiting and both are from towns close to where the donors live. There are no benefactors in Diwaniyah, it seems.

That night the decision is made. There is only enough money to take two families, and as the other two have better credentials than us, we are to be left behind. My mother becomes hysterical.

'Why did you bring us all this way?' she screams at Abdul-Haqq. 'We had a home. Now we've lost our lease and given everything away. We have nothing. We will have to stay in a hotel with money we don't have, or sleep on the streets. How could you do this? You promised us.'

They offer us nothing. Not even accommodation if we wait until the next time and subject ourselves to the same lottery.

Early in the morning the other families leave. We are left sitting in a line along the gutter in the street, all seven of us. Umi and me, Afrah, Khalid, Ahlam, Inas and little Hashim, who plays with a single marble in the dust while he waits as I decide what to do next. The others become increasingly hot and irritable as the sun rises in the sky, and my mother continually looks at me, asking, 'What are we going to do?'

'Give me a break, Umi,' I finally fly at her. 'Just give me a minute to think, and stop whingeing. What do you think I am, a magician?'

The children giggle.

I am still bleeding from losing all our money to Haddad, and despite Abdul-Haqq apologising and claiming he had believed there would be enough for three families to go, I want to kill him. I am so worked up I am beginning to question everything I have done, when Afrah interrupts my spiralling descent.

'It's not your fault,' she says warmly. 'He seemed nice and we all wanted to go.'

After a moment I smile gratefully. Through Afrah I can always put things into perspective and think things through.

I endeavour to restore some kind of balance to my beliefs by remembering how often kindness has been bestowed on me. Lifting Hashim up onto my knee, like my father used to do when he told us stories, I begin, 'When I was in Baghdad and desperate for somewhere to sleep, I found a scrap of paper in my pocket with directions to a bakery where my friend Mahdi had said he worked.

But when I got there it was closed.

'I asked an old man selling cigarettes on the street, "Is Mahdi coming back?"

'"Yes, he sleeps here and he has to prepare the bread for tomorrow."

'It was getting dark when finally a small bus pulled up and a guy got off.

'"Here he comes," the old man said. I thanked him and went towards the bus to greet Mahdi. But when I got close I could see it wasn't him.

'But he grabbed me and gave me a big hug. "Just come with me," he said. "We talk later."'

'What did you do?' Hashim gasps.

'I was unsure what to do, but he was my last chance for a place to stay so I went along with it. He unlocked the bakery and we ate and drank tea, but each time I tried to say something he wouldn't let me. Then he lay out bedding for me, and in the morning he made breakfast. Then, putting some bread in my bag, he smiled. "And now I have to get to work."

'"I am a complete stranger to you," I said. "Why did you take me in?"

'"I am Mahdi. Just not the one you were looking for. But you were waiting with your little bag. It was obvious you have no place to sleep and nowhere to hide. I don't want to know your problem, but I do want you to know you are welcome and can come here any time."'

When I finish the story everyone, even my mother, is smiling.

'Okay,' I say, revived by their cheerful faces. 'Let's catch a bus back to Arbil and find another house.' I help them to their feet and hoist Hashim onto my shoulders. 'This is just a small setback. None of us is dead.'

Back in Arbil we manage to find a place to rent, with promise of payment later. But it remains empty apart from the few things we borrow from the neighbours.

One night a few weeks later I wake up to a massive explosion. It is four o'clock in the morning. I lie still on the hard floor, my head on my jacket for a pillow, telling myself this is not Saddam's army. But there is no fooling myself, they are coming. We have faced war many times so we know how it sounds. It is not the random blasts of insurgents, it is rapid and regular, like music. It has rhythm. If there are ten tanks they shoot one at a time with exact intervals.

By the time I reach the roof the southern sky is lit up like a carnival. I stand there watching the lights and a cold shiver passes over me as I realise Saddam is on my heels again.

At six o'clock the bombing stops, and there is a terrible quiet. Nobody knows what is happening, everyone is scared. Out on the street I see some Arabic people and ask what they think we should do.

'Do nothing,' they all agree. 'Nothing is going to happen. Each time he does this he backs off. He's not going to take over the city while the UN are here.'

It is possible Saddam just wants to show his muscle and scare the resistance, but there has never been anything consistent about his strategies, and sure enough, by nine o'clock they start bombing again, and continue to pound the city until four in the afternoon. By now I can hear the rumble of the tanks and there is no question he wants to take Arbil.

The children have suffered a lot but never a bombing like this, so they are terrified. In the uncertainty I have stayed longer than I should, but now that the army is so close I can't possibly make my escape with all of them. I reassure them that the army just wants to show its strength and will not be looking for women and children, although in truth I know of many stories of Saddam's army shooting the entire families of freedom fighters.

But the house is small and unnoticeable, and as always I have no choice. I am no use to them dead, which I will be if the army catches me. 'I will be back for you, just stay inside and lock the door.'

I hug them and take off, trying to wipe the memory of their ter-rified faces from my mind as I run through the streets. I get to the Arabic centre, where people are panicking. They have already run from Saddam to the safety of the north and now they are cornered again.

A bomb lands nearby. The ground erupts, buildings crumble, bro-ken electricity lines crackle and snake amongst the rubble. People are running in all directions, even the police are trying to get away. So we begin to run and don't stop until the bombs are well behind us.

By the time we get outside the city we are a group of about twenty. We decide to walk to a town several kilometres away. We go as fast as we can but it is hot, and soon Saddam's tanks appear behind us as they surround Arbil. We run into a Kurdish guy who tells us a checkpoint up ahead is held by the PUK, so we decide to make a run for it.

Over the past year, relations between the PUK and the KDP have descended into a state of virtual civil war, and now Massoud Barzani, the leader of the KDP, has asked Saddam Hussein to intervene, no doubt with a deal to take the PUK's half of Kurdistan and leave the other half for him. Saddam's first goal is clearly the PUK stronghold of Arbil. So we figure our best bet is to be with the PUK, because at least we know they are fighting against, and not for, Saddam's army. At the moment, that is.

We've only gone a short distance when the tanks begin to swing their guns around and the army starts trying to hit the checkpoint we are running towards. The PUK fire back and we are stuck in the mid-dle of their crossfire. We stumble across a dry irrigation canal and dive into it.

About a kilometre away, through open farmland, is a small village. It is nestled at the foot of a mountain, which will offer us an escape if we can make it there. We leave our cover in groups of two or three and scatter across the fields, ducking and weaving over rough ground with bullets whistling overhead. They say when you are close to death you feel your heart come into your mouth, and I feel it. I don't know if it is from the heat or the speed I am running, but my heart is actually thumping in my mouth in the same rhythm that my feet are pounding the earth.

I make it to the village, but as the remains of the group arrive in dribs and drabs we discover seven have been killed. 'Keep running,' I yell to the twelve still left. 'We have to get to the mountains.'

But suddenly we are drawn to a halt. In front of us are KDP peshmerga with their Kalashnikovs pointing at our faces. They march us out to the checkpoint they have now captured and lock us up. It becomes clear they are preparing to hand us over to Saddam's army, so once again I am left to contemplate a miserable end at the hands of his torturers.

During the night we hear an Iraqi resistance group arrive and argue with the peshmerga. I can by now speak enough Kurdish to understand they are trying to persuade them to release us, but knowing the ineptitude of our movement I hold little hope. To my amazement, and their credit, next morning we are kicked out, reawakening my belief in the resistance.

Once out, I look for someone to ask about what is happening in Arbil. 'The army has control,' a Kurdish guy says nervously, 'and it doesn't look like they are going to pull out. But at the moment it is quiet, no rampaging or killings.'

Having experienced Saddam's methods after the Shiite uprising, I know I have to get my family out during the calm before the storm. And I don't trust he will stop at Arbil, so I plan to go back to Sulaymaniyah and try to get across the mountains. I have saved a little money for a smuggler by trading with the tiny bit of cash remaining after Haddad, so despite my concerns, it seems like our only option.

I manage to convince the guy to take my relatively new clothes for a pair of worn baggy Kurdish pants, a shirt and turban. I catch a minibus back to Arbil looking like a Kurd, and as I had hoped we are waved through the checkpoints. In Arbil everything is quiet, but I am unnerved by the eeriness of the empty streets.

When I reach the house I find my mother and the five children huddled together in a corner, like everyone else in the city. When I open the door Umi clutches the little ones to her, then they realise it is me and I become their comic relief as they fall about laughing at my ill-fitting Kurdish outfit.

I urge them to hurry as we gather up our meagre belongings. I relinquish my disguise because I realise there is no point if I am travelling with my mother. Most Kurdish women will wear the scarf, but that is all. My mother wears her scarf and long black hijab. You know from a hundred kilometres away that she is Arabic, but she would rather die than take off her traditional clothes.

At other times we have laughed at her stubbornness, but under the present circumstances I am furious. 'You are putting all our lives at risk,' I shout at her. 'No one would try to get past Saddam's army dressed like that.' But she won't give in, and from experience I know there is no point fighting her, and after all, many times her obstinacy has aided our survival.

As it happens, miraculously we see no military as we rush hand in hand through the streets to the bus depot. Even more incredibly, there are no checkpoints where they are stopping buses and pulling people off. Maybe our luck is turning.

As soon as we arrive in Sulaymaniyah I begin searching for a smuggler. Conscious of our last betrayal, I am perhaps overly cautious, but then I meet an old Kurdish guy who grew up in Baghdad but was deported when Saddam came to power. He knows about dispossession and his hatred of Saddam runs deep. I believe I am in good hands when he says he has someone in his family that I can trust to smuggle us.

When we meet his relative and the poor guy sees the number of children and the small amount of money I have to offer he is reluctant, but my mother can be very charming at her best and she surprises me by winning his sympathies. Eventually he says we will go tonight at two am.

It is only ten o'clock, so we sit at a table on the pavement at a kebab shop while we wait. There is a dreadful disquiet hanging over the city. Everybody is nervous. The word is that Saddam's army is on the move again but no one knows what city he plans to take next. By midnight news is spreading that the KDP or Saddam is heading this way and people begin coming out onto the streets. Then someone shouts from a window.

'It's on TV. Saddam's army is coming to take Sulaymaniyah. They will be here soon.'

A wave of fear goes through the people around us and we huddle together, wanting to go before the chaos that is unfolding takes over. But it is another two hours before we are due to leave.

Suddenly, as we sit nervously waiting, a young man runs through the crowd yelling, 'Chemical Ali is coming. Saddam said it himself on the news!'

Now there is mass panic. Hundreds of frightened people begin to pour out of their houses with whatever they can carry. We watch as the trickle becomes a flood and soon there are thousands abandoning their homes and fleeing the city. Within hours Sulaymaniyah will be empty. Such is their fear of Saddam and his ruthless cousin, Chemical Ali, who in 1988 had brutally gassed nearby Halabja, killing five thousand Kurdish men, women and children. Another seven thousand died in the bombing that followed.

We are on the verge of panic ourselves when our smuggler appears in the mayhem. He smiles good-humouredly and returns our money. 'You don't need to pay me. Now everyone is going. You just have to join them and you can go by road.'

I thank him profusely for returning our fee, he could easily have disappeared leaving us with nothing, and with some trepidation we join the exodus.

I look down the road at the convoy of desperate people in flight. It is cold and dark, with the headlights of cars in the middle and people on the sides carrying their possessions on their backs, or pushing trolleys. Children clutch at their mothers' skirts, crying, and fright-ened dogs and goats strain at their leashes. You can smell the fear.

I knew it would be a few days' walk to the border this way, but now I find out it is more like four or five days' march. After two days of walk-ing and sleeping on the side of the road my mother looks exhausted. We have brought food but I am afraid we don't have enough. I am working myself into a state of anxiety when I see a truck nudging by.

Because of my mother's clothes we are obviously Arabic, and maybe an Arab did something good for the driver once, or perhaps it is the look on my face when I run beside his window begging, 'Can you take us? Please, can you?' but either way he stops.

'Just family?' he asks.

'Yes,' I say with conviction.

'I don't want any trouble.'

'We are just running from Saddam, like you.'

He looks at us for a moment with kind eyes, then gestures to the back where his own family sit. 'Get in.'

The relief is so great I could kiss his feet.

They put the children on their knees and squeeze us in. As we drive slowly past endless lines of people I feel guilty to be the ones rid-ing, but it is time we got a break.

When we arrive at the border we are daunted by what we see. Thousands of people are already here, with the Iranian army and secret police standing and watching at the gate, not letting people in.

The refugees are mostly Kurdish, then we see a cluster of six or seven Arabic families. We hurry towards them but they are from the Islamic Party and when we try to join them they ask us to go away.

I had always found the Islamics' extremist views difficult, and then there was the betrayal in Sulaymaniyah after disbanding our home in Arbil, and now this. A small slight, but it leaves us all feeling embit-tered. When the children ask I try to contain my distaste. 'They don't want to risk their chances, or share their possible good fortune.' I never could understand why people remain divided even when we are all in the same boat.

So we stand separately, and after a long wait the gates open and the officer in charge comes through in a jeep. He cruises slowly amongst the people, discussing individual groups with his officers. We try not to be irked when he stops in front of the Islamics and invites them in. It seems unfair, considering their snub to us, but they have been ruthlessly repressed by Saddam, and Iran has an Islamic regime, so it is in fact reasonable.

When the jeep reaches us the officer looks at my mother in her Arabic clothes, surrounded by five children. 'Who are these people?' he asks his cohorts.

Iranians see the Arabs as being under more threat than the Kurds, who at least are meant to have UN protection at the moment. So it looks like we might be saved by my mother's maddening refusal to take off her costume.

I have been standing talking with an Iraqi guy while we wait. His name is Wahid and he speaks enough Farsi to interpret for me. He nudges me and whispers, 'Stand back. If they see just a woman with children they will be sympathetic. If they see you are with them they won't let them in.'

There's no way of knowing if Wahid is right or not, but in that split second I have to make a choice. I don't want to be separated from them, but neither do I want to cripple their chances of getting in. So I step away.

'They don't seem to belong to anyone, sir,' the officer's deputy says. 'They are just family.'

The officer beckons my mother to come forward. She glances around for me and I try to indicate with the smallest gesture that she should do what he says without me. Trusting that I am right, she gathers her strength and approaches the officer cautiously.

Through an interpreter he asks, 'Who are you?'

She is about to look around to me again for help but realises just in time not to. One thing you can trust about my mother is that the survival of her children will always come first. If I am there she defers to me, but without me she is still capable of being a powerful force.

She looks the officer in the face and turns on her charm. 'We are Shiite Iraqis. We are running away from Saddam. He has my husband and two sons in his prisons and murdered another. We ran to the north and now Saddam bombs the north. We want to come to Iran, where there is safety for us. We just want to find peace.'

The officer looks at her longer than he needs to, then says, 'Do you belong to any party?'

'No,' my mother is quick to reply.

He turns to his deputy, 'Okay, let them come in.'

My mother hurries towards the gates, her eyes fixed in front of her, her arms around the children. I know she is telling them not to look back, but little Hashim can't help himself. He turns to see me one more time and stumbles. Afrah grasps his hand to stop him falling, but as she does she catches my eye for a second and I can see hers are full of tears. I want to call out that everything will be all right, but instead I have to look away as if I don't even know them.

'You did the right thing,' Wahid whispers, and he is probably right. But if I never see them again this moment will haunt me for the rest of my life.

My mother and the children are bundled into an army vehicle and I watch forlornly as they are driven off. Then the guards open the gates and the army surrounds the thousands of us who are left. We are mostly men but there are some women and children as well. We walk for several kilometres until we reach a site where they have set up a huge makeshift refugee camp and herd us into it. The camp revives abysmal memories of my impotence and failure in Duhok.

I try to count my blessings. I am now technically on Iranian soil, and so long as Saddam doesn't invade Iran again, I have escaped him. And my family are on their way to a new life. I hope they are heading for Qom, the holy city where most Iraqi Shiites go and where we had discussed settling, but the little money we have is in my pocket and I have visions of my mother, hungry and cold, sleeping on the street with five kids.

I immediately start looking at how I can escape, but I have trouble finding anyone else who wants to come. Now that the people are off Iraqi soil, most of them want to wait to see what happens before they abandon home and country. Not to speak of the camp being heavily guarded. Also, the surrounding terrain is mountainous, and the closest village is many kilometres along roads that are infested with checkpoints.

I share a small tent with Wahid, but after about a month he manages to get his wife and three-year-old daughter smuggled out of Iraq to join him. I say I will move but Wahid insists I stay, so we all bunk in together. The tent is so narrow that the only way we can sleep is if the three adults lie lengthways and his daughter lies across the bottom of the bed. By now it is getting extremely cold and we have no blankets. Wahid and his wife get body heat from each other, but I have to leave a space, and his daughter suffers most at our feet.

There are dead trees around, so I find an old four-gallon oil drum, dig holes in the sides, and put some wood in it. Then at night I make a fire outside, and when it has stopped smoking and burnt down to hot coals, I put it inside the tent next to the daughter. We all sleep comfortably for a few hours until the fire is out, then I get up and collect more wood, and set it ablaze again.

Back in the stultifying boredom of a refugee camp, it is hard to keep my mind off whether my family has made it to Qom or are destitute. I have heard nothing about Basim and Asad since they were sentenced. My father is still in jail, and like my mother with her brother the colonel, because I never saw Ahmad's dead body, I am stalked at night by the possibility he is still alive somewhere. In the mornings I wake with the image of him fingerless and bloodied in my jacket. I had lent it to him to keep warm that night, before they took us.

So I try to plan a strategy to break out and get on my way again. I have been in the camp for nearly two months when one moonless night I successfully get past the armed guards. But the rugged mountains are so difficult to navigate, even by day, that I am forced to follow the roads. I am soon arrested, because it is impossible to get around the checkpoints without a guide. They take me to Sanandaj and lock me up for two weeks, then send me back to the camp.

Shortly after, I try once more, but I am picked up again and given another stretch in prison. However, I am getting to know the territory and statistically am due for a win, so after a month back in the camp I try again. Before I leave, Wahid gets a message from contacts he has in Iran. My family has been seen in Kermanshah, a busy city a hundred and fifty kilometres from the border. I leave with renewed vigour.

Extraordinarily, with the help of a few dollars and a Kurdish guy with a donkey, I make it to Kermanshah. It is a beautiful city surrounded by snow-capped mountains, but it still carries the scars from extensive bombing by Saddam during the war. I hear there is a camp with Iraqi families in it and hurry to the address. It is not like the camp at the border, there are no guards and it is clean and orderly. There are small buildings rather than tents, and my excitement grows as I go from one to the next.

I am finally directed to their dwelling. The door is ajar so I slowly open it, but it is empty. They have left. The pleasure I had anticipated bringing by my sudden appearance evaporates and I plunge into despair. I momentarily forget I am on the run and without caution walk aimlessly along the street. It is not long before I am asked to show my ID and I am caught again.

This time I am to be deported. At the border they push me through the gate and say, 'Go.' But no one seems to expect me to stay there. Although we fought each other for eight years on this frontier, few soldiers on either side did so willingly, and now those Iraqis who end up back here have in common a hatred of Saddam.

I know my way around so well by now that it doesn't take me long to smuggle myself back over the border and into the refugee camp. But I am exhausted and unprepared for Wahid's news when I arrive.

'The camp is to be demolished and everyone sent back to Sulaymaniyah. Can you help us get out of here?' he asks tentatively.

'It's not hard to get out of the camp,' I say, panic rising. 'It's getting through this border zone that's the problem. It's riddled with army and checkpoints, and almost impossible to get across the mountains without help.'

'Someone in the camp has made contact with a smuggler who knows a route,' Wahid comes back quickly. 'If there are a few of us we might be able to afford him.'

I have had so little success on my own that I agree, and reluctantly pay up the last of my money, fearing how desperately my family might be needing it.

We escape from the camp one night just as they begin to dismantle it, and the smuggler, Wahid, his wife, daughter, another couple and I, are well gone into the mountains before sunrise. It has been nearly six miserable months of incarceration there, so we are glad to see it gone, but it is an arduous journey ahead and I understand the reluctance of many to attempt it.

We have warm clothes but once we get high up on the ranges it is like being in a refrigerator, and the woman from the other couple is seven months pregnant. We are all worried that the baby may not survive. I am so cold I feel like I have been stabbed in the stomach with a knife and when I shit it is like water. There is occasional relief when we come down from the icy peaks to sleep in villages, or to be picked up by a vehicle until we near another checkpoint, but then it's back into the ranges.

It takes us three days but eventually we begin to descend and come out of the mountains. Our bodies start to thaw and there is a moment of joy when the baby confirms it is alive by kicking. We are finally far enough inside Iran that there are no more checkpoints, so we can catch a normal bus to Qom.

It is March 1997 when we arrive in Qom. We wish each other luck, and I tell the man with the pregnant wife that I will contact him if I can find a place to live. Then I start to search for my family in the Iraqi community, but with little success.

I am becoming desperate when I bump into some people from Diwaniyah. The woman lights up when she sees me, so I can tell she has good news.

'Yes, they are here,' she says with delight, 'but I don't know where they live. Your brother Hashim goes to school with my son, so you can find him there.'

She gives me the address and I get a taxi, excited by the thought of Hashim's little face on seeing me. But when we arrive at the school we only find her son. Hashim didn't come to class today. When the taxi driver, who is half Iraqi and speaks Arabic, sees the disappointment on my face he suggests we ask the teacher if we can take the little boy to show us where the house is. Fortunately she knows the driver, so is prepared to trust us to take the child, who directs us to where my family is staying.

It is a dingy basement below a place where students live. We knock loudly but there is no one home. The taxi driver takes pity on me. 'We'll take the boy back to school, have some lunch, then I'll bring you back.' He is good company and it will help to pass the time, so we eat together then return to the house.

I knock again but there is still no answer. I look around, becoming irrationally angry, when suddenly I see my mother coming down the street. Then I see Hashim running behind her. He is about to take her hand when he sees me, and stops. He doesn't know what to do. He is crying and smiling. It brings tears to my own eyes. After a moment he runs and throws his wiry little body at me and I wrestle him to the ground. I look up at my mother, who weeps with joy and relief as I stand up and put my arms around her.

They had waited for me for over two months and then they set off for Qom, two days before I came looking for them. When they arrived some students heard about their plight and gave them their cellar to live in. She was able to buy food with money they were given by Iranian authorities in Kermanshah, then when it ran out she went to the Iraqi resistance. But if you don't speak the language, have no job and little money, you are always afraid about what is going to happen, so she has hardly slept.

The cellar is little more than a roof over our heads. It is damp, cold and cramped for a family of six, let alone seven of us. I want to get them out of there quickly, but I have no money. I have one Iraqi friend in Qom, who is distinguished by having had an ear chopped off by Saddam's torturers. He lives in a much larger basement, so he and his friends let us have it until we get settled. Wahid has found a place but I tell the pregnant couple they can join us, so for now everyone is accommodated.

Being an Iraqi with no visa, only the worst jobs are on offer to me, but I discover a builder I know from Iraq and within a few days Khalid and I start working for him. The hours are from eight until four but the builder lets me leave at three, so I can get on my borrowed bicycle and ride to a job I have with a tailor until one in the morning.

With this breakneck schedule we begin to make good money and can rent a house. Once we get set up with a fridge, TV and furniture, Khalid stays on at the building site and I quit there, and start living a normal life just working for the tailor.

After nearly two years in an educational wilderness, my sisters Ahlam and Inas have not only been able to finally go back to school, but to an Arabic school, where they easily fit in. All we have to pay for is the bus to take them there. They are quickly picking up Farsi, a difficult language quite unlike Arabic, and becoming normal kids again.

Then another small pleasure comes our way. Afrah has met an Iraqi guy who escaped to Saudi Arabia, then on to Australia, where he now has citizenship. He is in Iran on business, and in no time they are married. Now he is going to take his new wife, our precious Afrah, back with him. We know nothing about Australia except it is a democracy on the other side of the world with strange animals. It occurs to me that I should have considered it as a place for us to go before, but it is so far away and even though Afrah encourages me, once she settles and stops writing regularly, the idea disappears.

And at the moment Iran is good to us, and we begin to relax. While we will always be foreigners, they mostly treat us like one of them, and the freedom I experience as a result of feeling safe is unimaginable. We have money and food, and even my mother begins to perk up. She cooks big meals, we get healthy, make friends and become part of a community. So long as we can keep our memories at bay, we are close to being a happy family. So I decide I am going to stay here until the demise of Saddam and then we will go home.

I cannot help pondering the strange irony that my father must have killed so many Iranians in Saddam's useless war, yet Iran is the place to give his wife and children back their lives. I am sickened by the thought of what it must have done to the psyche of Iraqis, being forced to fight and kill a people they had no issue with.

So now that my family is out of danger and verging on happiness, I allow myself to think about my own future. Over the years, no matter how I have tried to discard the memory of Intisar, the magic of our balcony romance is indelibly imprinted on my soul. I have spent many miserable nights putting myself to sleep replaying it in my head, and many daylight hours wondering if she is still waiting for me.

While I am now safe, getting in touch with someone in Iraq is not. There are no phones to Iraq and sending in a messenger is dangerous. If the Iraqi secret police discover a letter from Iran they will torture the recipient until they find out if there is any secret information in it. Iran is their number one enemy, so they don't trust anyone coming from Iran, living in Iran, or bringing anything in from Iran. To make it even more perilous, messengers work for both sides, they have to, because it is the only way to cross back and forth. So you can never trust which side they will come down on if they are caught.

Through my job at the tailor, I meet an Iraqi woman working in a small clothes market, who crosses the border with her business. I get to know her as a good person, so when she offers to take something to Iraq, I give her a letter. I am careful to make it as much like regular family news as possible. Sufficient to let Intisar know I am alive and still wanting her, but not enough to identify me or incriminate anyone.

A letter comes back swiftly. Sweetly written and with no blame, it assures me she is still waiting. I let myself wallow in a mixture of bliss and longing as I read and reread it. Three more times the woman takes letters back and forth for me, and I am ready to ask Intisar to come to Iran to marry me when my mother intervenes.

'It is too much to handle,' she says with dread. 'If you marry, that will be it. You will settle down, have children, and try to build something here for yourself. Then you will be stuck, and if you are stuck we are all stuck with you, and we don't want to stay forever in Iran.'

I feel like a child again, but as with the bicycle, the decision has been lodged in her brain and there will be no changing it. She rightly thinks that although the Iranians treat us well, we will always be second-class citizens, and perhaps I have been blinded to this by the pleasure of some semblance of a normal life again.

'Everyone is looking for another place to go,' she says, working herself into a state. 'It is not somewhere you settle, we will always be insecure.'

I storm out of the house. She has jolted me into realising marriage is an impossible dream so long as I have my family in tow, but this time it seems really unfair. Alone, I could be far away in another country, getting married, having my own kids. I am not the father of these children, I didn't bring them into the world, so why do I have to care for them?

I know I am being irrational but I am enraged. All that time in jail I thought I had lost my opportunity with Intisar, and now when I get a second chance, once again, because of my family, I can't take it.

'Better we leave Iran now,' my mother cries later that night, 'before it goes any further.'

Eventually I buckle under the strength of her opinion. I send one final letter to Intisar. I think my heart will break. What would have been a marriage proposal becomes yet another farewell. She has already waited seven years for me, turning her focus to study and becoming a teacher. There have been other marriage proposals, and I try not to imagine how she has managed her family's wrath for resisting them. Her devotion to me is more than I could have hoped for, but at what price for her? I go back to the building site and working two jobs. I let go my dreams of a domestic life, and Iran becomes just another escape route.

CLUTCHING AT STRAWS

I talk with the guys at work and discover they are all thinking about where to go. It seems the majority are of my mother's view, that Iran is only temporary. Up to fifty people a week are evidently leaving our community, and the general consensus is that the best option is through Turkey to Germany or Sweden. I can't believe I am back to where I was two years ago, trying to get into Turkey, but maybe it will be easier from here than from Kurdistan.

When I have made enough money to leave for my mother, and talked Khalid into filling my shoes, three of us from work meet with a Kurdish smuggler and make a deal. Before long we are in a taxi heading north to Tehran. On arrival we join another five men and take a bus to another town, where we are put in a small covered ute.

Late the following afternoon we arrive at a farmhouse close to the mountains and join up with another ten men.

'Turkey is behind this range,' the smuggler says, pointing up at towering snow-capped peaks. 'Tomorrow we will cross them.'

We clamber out of the ute, hoping he knows what he is doing. They look treacherous and uncrossable to us.

We wake as the sun is rising and walk to the foot of the mountains, where a tractor with an old wooden trailer waits to take us up the first slopes. After a few hours the driver stops.

'This is as far as I can go, now you will have to walk.'

We get off reluctantly and look up at the arduous trek ahead. This will be climbing, not walking, and the higher we go, the colder it will be. We are all beginning to realise we are faced with a terrible problem. It was hot in Qom, so none of us thought to bring winter clothes. T-shirts and jeans are all most of us have.

As it gets dark, the snow comes with the wind, and the cold sets in. It cuts through what little clothing we have like blades of ice and we are defenceless. We start eating our small ration of chocolate but nothing helps. The snow is like sleet, lacerating our eyes and face. We are travelling blind, with perilous ravines on either side of us.

Worse, we fear being trapped by the Turkish army. If they don't know who you are, especially at night, they kill you. We could be the Kurdish peshmerga, so they don't take any chances, they surround you and they shoot. There are many stories of such massacres of Iraqis on this route.

Next day we find the landscape has plateaued and is drivable again, so they put us in an open truck. We drive through the day and on into the night, and arrive cold and sore at the bottom of another mountain. There is a guy waiting for us. He sums us up, then points with his stick. 'See that light? My job is to get you past it, so we have to go in a circle, and there is a river to cross.' He doesn't elaborate, but we have no choice but to trudge unwillingly after him into the uninviting gloom.

It is about two-thirty in the morning when we reach the river. There are sharp stones, so I leave my shoes on but almost pass out from ice water swirling around my torso. On the other side we begin running with no time to empty our shoes, we must reach the road where we are to be picked up at four.

We make it but the bus is not there. Our feet are numb and our faces blue. We are shuddering so violently it is hard to keep moving, but if we don't we will snap-freeze very quickly.

Ihsan, a guy I know from Qom, begins swearing at God, Saddam, and everyone else he can think of, then he yells at us through chattering teeth. 'Let's keep going. It is better than dying here.' One of the others stutters back, 'If the army sees us they'll shoot us.'

'The army!' he bellows, challenging the night with his fists. 'Come out, you bastards, wherever you are. Come out, you murderers, come and kill us now.' Nobody tries to stop him. We are all so cold we think we are going to die anyway, so we are happy to hand over to anyone who will do the job more swiftly.

It is another hour before we hear the distant roar of an engine and at last the ice-covered bus appears out of a howling squall. We sit shivering in our seats as it takes us to a large house where another group of about forty Iraqi men, women and children are waiting. They give us hot tea and we gulp it down feverishly.

Then they bundle the whole lot of us onto a large covered truck. We are packed in and can't see out, which makes the whole thing more frightening. When the truck goes down a hill or slope we imagine we are plummeting into a chasm. The road is extremely rough so we are bouncing on hard wooden seats, and because of the four cups of tea I drank I am desperate to pee.

At first I think I am the only one but then I realise everyone in our group is in the same situation. We begin to tap on the back of the cabin but the driver ignores us. We knock harder until the men are kicking and banging so loudly that he finally yells back, 'I am told not to stop, now what is the problem?'

'We have to pee!'

'Go in the back. It will run out.'

So we struggle to the back corner of the truck, jam-packed with men, women and children, and try to pee. I wait my turn as Ihsan, who must have had six cups of tea, kneels and opens his pants, but he has held on for so long nothing will come. As he stoops and sways, clinging to the tailboard of the truck, the physical pain in his bladder is so great he begins to cry like a baby.

Each in our turn goes through the same agony. I can't help wondering if the smugglers and our hosts had not deliberately done this for their own amusement. Maybe I have seen too much of Saddam's practices but I will never know if the humiliation and pain inflicted by that simple gesture of giving us tea was intended.

At six o'clock in the morning the truck finally stops and they open the back. We clamber down, every inch of our bodies aching.

'No more walking or trucks, from here more comfortable,' the smuggler says, looking pleased with himself and pointing to a bus. 'Now you are inside the country you can get normal transport.'

After two days of buses we arrive in Istanbul, the largest city in Turkey, which straddles the two continents of Asia and Europe. It is a cultural and ethnic melting pot with thousands of beautifully mosaiced shrines and mosques, churches, synagogues, palaces, castles and towers. It has a population of over twelve million and is the perfect place to hide. As we drive through the bustling streets I realise we are at last truly on our way to Europe.

This time when we disembark our smuggler leaves us, so now we are on our own. My friend without an ear, who gave me his basement in Qom, knows someone in Istanbul who has organised a flat for us. Our original group of eighteen all move in together for the first night. We are exhausted from the enormous physical toll of our journey, so some sleep, but the rest of us stay awake talking about our futures, too energised by the possibilities of what lies ahead.

One of the younger men wants to go out. We caution him to wait until we have slept and acclimatised a little, but he is restless and won't listen. We forget about him after he leaves but are relieved when he returns at around ten in the evening.

Half an hour later, most of us are asleep when there is a loud knock on the door. Terrified, we all jump to our feet. A few minutes later they pound with their fists and we freeze. It has to be the police, but it is too late, we are on the top floor and there is no way out. So I open the door before they bash it down, and six Turkish police with guns march in.

I feel sick to my stomach. I have had less than a day of freedom in

Istanbul, and it is over already. Suspecting we could be Kurdish militia, they take us straight to the army headquarters. They check our IDs and return waving them at us. 'These are false.' As if we didn't know.

They leave us locked in a room while they work out their next move. I turn to the guy who had left the apartment against our advice. I grab him by the collar, lift him off his feet and shove him backwards.

'What happened when you went out? What the fuck did you do?'

The others crowd around me, all wanting to kill him.

'I ran into this Kuwaiti guy I knew and we got into a fight,' he whimpers. 'The police broke it up and must have followed me.'

I slam him hard against the wall. 'Why didn't you tell us when you got back? We could have got away before they came if we'd known.'

He begins to get the enormity of what he has done and starts to blubber apologies.

'You fucking idiot,' I bark, thinking of the number of times I have outwitted police, only to be delivered into their hands by this jerk.

The army interrogators seem to have worked out that we are not peshmerga, and when we unanimously say we are from Iran and on our way to Europe they seem happy to buy it. Soon we are on a bus driving back across Turkey. After two days we reach an army camp, where we are surrounded by soldiers and marched to the border. When we arrive they say, 'This is Turkey, that is Iran, go and do not come back.' That is it. Once again, in one small gesture, my dreams of a future are gone.

We are now faced with crossing the mountains back into Iran without enough clothing, but worse, without a guide. When the sun sets it is soon pitch-dark and the temperature is below freezing. With no shelter to spend the night, there is nothing for it but to push on. We don't know where we are going and we can't see each other, so we hold hands to avoid getting left behind or falling off a cliff. After a few fraught hours we stop. We have done nothing but argue. One saying left, one saying right. I finally yell at them, 'Even if we freeze to death let's wait until the morning.'

Using my prison experience, we pack together on a tiny plateau of icy mud with our arms around each other, maintaining what little warmth remains in our frozen bodies. A skinny guy is crying that his twelve-year-old son is turning blue, so we put him in the middle of a fat guy and me. With his body wedged between us, and the fat guy's breath on his neck, despite the filthy sludge that we are sleeping in, he survives.

When the sun comes up we begin to thaw and soon find a small river we can follow. Even the cold seems less intense once we have a direction. After several days we leave the mountains and in the distance we see a small village. We are desperate for food, so we decide to wait until dark to go in, but as soon as we do every dog in the district barks and in no time we are surrounded by local police. By the morning we have been loaded into a covered truck for deportation to Iraq.

At the border they call us one at a time into a room in a small rustic hut where they take our money. We all carry US currency because we can exchange it in any country, the only downside being that everyone wants it. Some of our group had sold everything and had thousands of American dollars to start their new lives. They were told they would be sent to court, where it would be decided if they got their money back, but we all know they will never see it again.

For those with not enough to matter, like me and Mustafa, another Iraqi, who only has $US150, there is no court. Next morning they come for the two of us and we are to be deported to Sulaymaniyah. At least it is not Duhok, or directly into Saddam's hands. I should be grateful.

The Kurdish militia seem disinterested when we are handed over in Sulaymaniyah. All they ask for is our names and then they let us go. I am ready to head back to Iran and my family as fast as I can, but Mustafa likes alcohol and wants to get as much drinking done as he can while he is here.

Then there is the problem of paying for a smuggler. I now know that while it is not difficult to get across the border into Iran, it remains impossible to get any further on your own. I had hidden fifty American dollars and some Iraqi dinars in my shoe, but it is hardly going to be enough to live on.

At first I remain patient but on the third night Mustafa staggers into our tiny hotel room singing. It is three o'clock in the morning, and he wakes me up to ask for money to keep drinking. His alcohol breath and maddening behaviour remind me of my wayward youth and I am unable to contain my fury. 'What are you doing? I hardly have enough left for us to eat!'

'No alcohol in Iran,' he says with a hiccup, 'so we have got to drink as much as possible before we leave.' He leers at me and I have to stop myself from hitting him.

'Are you out of your mind?' I yell, but as I watch him stagger around with a ridiculous smile on his face, I remember that complete abandonment of any responsibility and the glorious sense of freedom that alcohol brings. For a moment I wish I could say, 'To hell with it all,' and join him. But instead I grab Mustafa and throw him on the bed.

I cover him with a blanket, but he flings it off and tries to struggle back onto his feet. I raise my fist to him and he slowly shrinks back down. Then I restore the blanket and command with one hand still clenched, 'Sleep!' and he quickly shuts his eyes. Within minutes he has fallen into a deep drunken slumber and snores so loudly that I give up on any chance of further rest and sit at the window waiting for the sun to rise over the city.

I must have dozed off because the call to prayer begins to waft mournfully out from the mosques and my eyes snap open to see Mustafa sitting, head hanging low, on the edge of the bed. I go to the bathroom and get him a glass of discoloured water from a rusty tap in our cheap hotel. He gulps it down and looks at me. He is not about to apologise but he is clearly full of remorse.

'Do you still have the $us50?'

I stare back at him, wishing I had never told him what was in my shoe.

'Yesterday, before I was too drunk,' he says sheepishly, 'I met a smuggler who can take us to Qom.'

'Even if we get ourselves across the border, $US50 will hardly get us around one checkpoint and there are at least five or six before we would be out of the woods,' I say sceptically.

'If we give him your $US50 up front, he is prepared to trust us to pay him $US150 when we get to Qom. I have someone there who will lend us the money for him when we arrive.'

I look at Mustafa, wondering what sort of smuggler would make that kind of risky deal. There is no way of knowing what condition Mustafa was actually in when he made it, so I am understandably uneasy. 'Is he any good? I mean, why would we trust him?'

Mustafa shrugs. 'Do we have any choice?'

I want to shout at him, 'If we had gone immediately, and not had to pay for three days of drinking, hotels and food, we may have had more options,' but I don't, because I know the price of blame, and I just want to get back to my family. Besides, I identify with Mustafa's need to salve the pain.

The smuggler, Fadi, is friendly enough. A tough, swarthy Kurdish Iranian in his forties. We meet him in a small village on the Iraq side of the border. Considering how Fadi came our way, I am slow to trust that he knows what he is doing and am already wary when he says, 'Tomorrow we go by car and then by bus.'

I had assumed we would be going the same way as when I finally escaped from the border camp in '97.

'Isn't it safer through the mountains?' I say, trying not to show my irritation.

'I always go on the road,' he replies casually.

'Great,' I say and glare at Mustafa. 'I appreciate your deal,' I tell Fadi, 'but it's worth nothing if you can't get us there.'

'Don't worry.' He waves his hands dismissively. 'You get there.'

I feel as vulnerable as I used to with the resistance, when they would organise our papers then leave it to us to get ourselves out of trouble.

Next day a car arrives to pick us up. As we approach the border Fadi turns to us in the back seat. 'When we get there you say nothing. Even if they ask you something you don't say anything. You ignore them.'

With the prospect of another jail term or deportation looming ahead of me, I join Mustafa in nodding compliantly.

A bull-headed guard leans into the car and looks us over. I am waiting to be dragged out, when he exchanges a few words I don't understand with Fadi and waves us on. I put my head back on the seat and breathe again. Despite my pounding heart, that certainly was easy.

At the first checkpoint the same thing happens and I begin to feel a little embarrassed that I doubted Fadi. He is smarter than I had given him credit for, and whatever deals he has in place with the authorities are being respected. My confidence in him has grown to such an extent that I settle into my seat and fall asleep.

I am woken with a jolt by Fadi issuing new instructions. 'We eat and sleep here in Marivan, then tomorrow we go by local bus.' I don't know what had tempted me into becoming so complacent; of course this dream ride couldn't last. Now the nightmare begins. Fadi sees my face and laughs reassuringly. 'No problem, you will get to Qom.'

But I doubt it.

Next morning, before we leave to catch the bus, Fadi says, 'We'll have to get off the bus to get around the checkpoints. The driver will find a way to let you off and on without the passengers knowing, or they might tell the police as we pass through.'

I stare at him, astounded. 'How?'

'Don't worry, we will work it out,' he says, again waving his hands.

I am now having serious qualms, but I am comforted by the fact that he said *we*, so at least we're not expected to work it out by ourselves.

When we get on the bus the driver takes no particular notice of us so I begin to worry that while Fadi shone on the previous leg, the deal with the driver may not have been as convincing. Mustafa and I sit together, with Fadi across the aisle. After a couple of hours we are approaching another checkpoint, and I become uneasy.

Then I notice the driver making a show of finding he has run out of cigarettes. He throws the empty packet on the floor and shortly after pulls over into a roadside café. As he gets out he calls down the bus, 'Anyone need cigarettes or anything else, you can get it here.'

Fadi gets up and we follow with a group of other passengers. Some go into the café, use the toilet or stand outside and smoke. It is not difficult for us to sidle off. Then it is a mad dash behind Fadi to get to the pick-up point faster than the bus. We run like maniacs along rough, stony donkey tracks until we see the road again, then sprint towards a bus stop where people are waiting to get on.

The bus is filling up, so it is easier not to be noticed when, later that day, it stops and the driver announces he thinks he has a problem with a tyre. As he gets off to check it, Fadi pushes us out ahead of him and when no one is looking we sneak off.

Fadi knows the fastest route around the checkpoint but we have to really run to keep up with him. The poor bus driver must have thought we wouldn't make it and have actually changed a tyre, because we end up waiting for him. But this gives him a reason to stop again, to check if the new one needs tightening.

And so it goes. Holes in the road, engine problems that require regular attention, and tyres that need checking. Nobody seems to be paying the slightest attention. They talk with each other, play with their kids, read and sleep. Despite myself, I begin to think this is a pretty professional setup.

It is night when we approach the city of Sanandaj. When the bus stops to let some passengers off Fadi nudges us. 'You go with him.' We are near the exit and we see an old man getting off. I now trust Fadi enough to do whatever he says, so we follow the order. But as soon as this guy hits the ground he takes off like a hare. I thought I was fast but he is something else.

'Wait, you motherfucker,' I swear, but he won't. Mustafa is close to passing out after his three days on the bottle. But when he yells, 'You're killing us, you crazy idiot,' the old man calls back over his shoulder, 'They have dinner in the city, then the bus will go. If we are not there they will leave without you.' I must admit, as I gasp for breath and clutch my chest, Fadi certainly has a dedicated team.

After several kilometres up and down uneven hilly country we make it into the city and to our relief the old man grabs a taxi to the restaurant. We collapse into the back seat and try to get our breath back. The old man is hardly panting. When we arrive he beams, 'We made it.' I look into the restaurant and indeed the other passengers are still eating. 'Thank God,' I sigh and pat his back gratefully.

We don't know when we will eat again so we are gulping down chicken and rice when Fadi joins us and whispers, 'Okay. Let's go.'

'Where?' I sigh incredulously.

'You must hurry,' he urges.

Mustafa looks as if he is going to faint.

We drag ourselves into another taxi and while Fadi directs the driver we try to psyche ourselves up for another lap. On the edge of town we get out and Fadi points to the lights from a highway nearly a kilometre away. 'We have to get to that road before the bus does, so come on.'

For the fifth time we begin to run. Fortunately it is downhill but it is so dark we can see almost nothing. We are running full pelt when we plunge into a hedge with sharp thorns. Then as we tumble over it and into the dry soil on the other side the dust is salty so burns our cuts and we howl like beaten dogs.

When we finally get to the road, we don't know if our bus has gone or not. We wait and wait but there is no sign of it. So when a different bus comes, Fadi pushes us onto it. I am alarmed because I know there is another checkpoint, which is meant to be impassable, and Fadi has no deal with this new driver.

Everyone on this bus is asleep so we stand up the front, with Fadi hanging over the driver. I can't hear what he is saying but suddenly Fadi is pointing and making him go faster. I peer into the traffic and there ahead of us is our bus.

Our original driver must have been going slow and watching for us, because when he sees us, he pulls over and we get back onto our bus. Everyone is awake, even the kids, sitting up watching us with huge smiles on their faces, glad we have made it. So much for our subterfuge.

Mustafa and I nod and smile back. We are deeply touched that they are on our side. I feel their warm embrace, and for a moment that deep wound of loss for my country, my little city of Diwaniyah, my home, opens like a bleeding flower. They make room for us to sit, and exhausted, we both fall asleep until we reach the last checkpoint. It is as I had heard, up in the mountains with no other way around.

I have no idea what Fadi has planned but I have come to trust he has thought of everything. He passes Mustafa a container and says, 'When we stop, put this water in the radiator.'

Then he gives me a wet cloth and a bucket. 'And you can climb up on the front of the bus and clean the window.'

Knowing that not just the driver but the whole busload are with us makes everything easier. We do what Fadi says and as the police march around the bus, checking the passengers, not once do they even notice us. So miraculously we pass through with no problems, and this time as we get back on the bus and set off everyone claps us, and we are at last on our way to Qom.

When we arrive Mustafa gets the money we owe from his friend and we pay Fadi. I wish I had some more to give him extra. I had misjudged him. He is wily, diligent, clever and professional. Getting us here seemed to matter to him more than the money.

'Thank you,' I say, shaking his hand with admiration and respect.

'You are some smuggler.'

He grins and goes on his way, but I won't forget him.

I have been gone so long my family assumed they would soon be preparing to join me in Germany or Sweden. They are of course disappointed, but I am glad to be back in Qom. I get my job back and am soon living a normal life again, but unfortunately, it doesn't feel the same. Maybe I'm paying more attention to our circumstances now, but the atmosphere feels unsettled. Things are relatively calm at the moment, but the tide could easily turn against us.

So, although I have only been back from my Turkey debacle for a couple of weeks, when I meet an Iraqi guy who is living happily in Australia I am all ears. He has come to Iran to marry, and can't wait to take his bride back to his good life in Sydney.

'What is Australia like?' I ask tentatively. Caught up in her new life, Afrah has not told me a lot about it, or perhaps I haven't asked.

Because Australia is so far away from our homeland, since she left we haven't really considered it as a destination, any more than we have considered Iceland. But now I listen when he describes a carefree existence with good food, plenty of work, business opportunities, and leisure time to go to movies and magnificent beaches. He concludes by saying, 'There is already an Iraqi community there. It is a good place, the people are friendly and you are safe and free.'

'How can we get there?' I ask with a sudden new rush of interest.

'I have some forms for the United Nations. I will give you one. You just fill it in. The UN office for this area is in Pakistan, so send it there.'

'How could it be that simple?'

He shrugs. 'It was a while ago now, but that's all I did.'

I am amazed. I get the form from him, but some of it is in English. He helps us translate, we each get our photo taken, then after the family has sat up for several nights trying to answer all the questions, it is eventually completed and we post it off.

This time we are really full of hope. At last we have found the right way to do things. Why have we never been told before? It is liberating to feel we are following the correct procedure and it makes me realise the toll it has taken to be always on the wrong side of the law. What's more, we know it works, we have two examples now, Afrah's husband and this guy. We are excited and begin a new dream of a friendly democracy with safety, freedom and kangaroos.

We wait for six or seven months and hear nothing. Slowly our excitement fades, and about that time we hear there have been border meetings between Saddam's people and Iranian officials. Even Saddam's son has been here meeting a chief agent from the Iranian secret police. Fear is growing that they could become friendly again and work together to force us all to go back to Iraq.

I panic and decide to try to get into Pakistan, so I can go to the UN and see what has happened to our application. I join a group of seven other Iraqis who have organised a smuggler and we set off on a bus for the long dusty journey south-east to the Pakistani border.

Before we reach it we find ourselves in Zahedan, one of the poorest and dirtiest cities in Iran, with a fertile drug mafia. One guy gets ill immediately from the water. We don't have facilities to boil it, so within a few days we all have bad diarrhoea and are dehydrated. The mosquitoes are bad and malaria is rife. So when by chance we meet an Iraqi coming back from Pakistan, I ask him if he knows anything about the UN and if we should continue our journey.

'I have been there for eleven months trying to get to Australia through the UN but it is hopeless,' he says dolefully. 'Unless you have the money to pay a smuggler to help you go by airplane, forget going to Australia.'

'We've sent in the forms the way you are meant to. Maybe they prefer you don't go to them in person,' I say with a glimmer of hope. 'They've ignored us so far but —'

'Forget it, you will never hear,' he cuts in, with bitterness in his voice. 'And even if you do it's like a lottery. You tell them you are an educated guy. I have this, this …' He gestures as if displaying his records of achievement. 'Then the next day they take someone who is uneducated and dumb. Then you tell them you are stupid and they take the educated guy. I know two brothers who had exactly the same background, one is accepted and one is not.' He throws his hands in the air. 'You will never get there if you try to do it the right way, my friend.'

My heart sinks. It had all seemed too easy. Within a few more days the whole group agrees to return to Qom.

Back on the bus I stare out the window at the endless, desolate landscape as I realise there are no more borders to cross, no more doors to open. But then, by some strange synchronicity, a few days after I get back to Qom, a letter arrives from the UN. With a rush of hope I finger the envelope, afraid to open it. Despite all I have heard I can't help clinging to the possibility that we are the lucky ones, that at last our ship has come in.

The house is quiet. Khalid is at work on the building site, the children are at school, and my mother, almost breathless with anticipation, sits beside me. The idea of joining Afrah and being there for her first grandchild has enhanced her fantasy of Australia, and opening this letter will either delight or dash her. As always, the chance of a good or bad life is in the hands of others, through no fault of our own. The frustration and anger I feel at this gives me the courage to tear the envelope open, but then I wish I had not.

The letter is dated 14 July 1999. The UN deems our plight is not sufficiently serious for us to qualify as refugees, and refuses the whole family. By their criteria we have not suffered enough.

Thus another road is closed.

I return to work at the tailor's. Escape to somewhere safe is impossible. My opportunity for marriage to the woman I want is gone. I am powerless over our future now and I am all worn out. I have failed so many times. I just want to be left alone to do my job, to earn enough money for us to live, and to sleep. But my mother won't let me. The dream has taken hold in her brain, and she is not letting go. We must find another way.

At the tailor's I have become friendly with a guy whose name is Siraj. His background is Iranian but he grew up in Iraq. When Saddam deported the Iranians from Iraq in 1973 Siraj became stateless, so he is always looking for somewhere to go. After the UN's rejection I am so dispirited that he takes me under his wing, and in light of my mother's determination, I let him.

I tell him I have no passport, no papers, nothing to go anywhere, but he says it's no problem, he will organise it all for me. And he does. I thought he was joking but he's not.

Siraj knows of a smuggler who has the connections to arrange the journey all the way through to Australia. My mother has got the bit between her teeth and is determined that I go first, then she and my siblings can follow. Khalid will support them. Resigned to her immovability I finally give in.

I give Siraj a photo and in a few days I have a brand-new Iraqi passport with correct names and dates. It is legitimate in every way except it is homemade in Iran. Because I came in illegally I also need official exit documents to get out by plane. Siraj has a friend with the police who will give me the papers, but they won't get me back in. And to enter again with a smuggler, I would, somehow, have to get into another bordering country. So if I can't move my family to somewhere safe from the outside, I may never see them again.

Then we get good news. There is an amnesty and Basim is being let out of jail early. Poor Asad, who they think is more political and dangerous to the regime, is to remain in Abu Ghraib, but at least by hearing this we know he is alive. Aware we need to get Basim out of Iraq quickly, I manage to contact the smuggler who brought Umi and the children to Arbil. As our family home now stands empty, I assume Basim will go to our grandmother's, so I ask the guy to collect Basim from there. He is so efficient he picks Basim up just as he finishes his first home-cooked meal.

Within a week he has brought him all the way to Qom. I hug Basim with relief and watch my mother's jubilance at having her son back in the nest, but now with his return I find it is even harder to leave.

I have very little money left after Turkey and Pakistan, and now Basim's smuggler, so I have to borrow everything for my tickets and smuggler's fees to Australia. All I can leave my mother is $US50, but she uncharacteristically brushes it aside.

I have to catch my plane to Malaysia at dawn in Tehran, so before we go to bed the previous night I say goodbye to everyone. I hate goodbyes so much I know I won't be able to leave if I do it in the morning. One at a time I hug them. My sisters Ahlam and Inas, who I have raised and loved like my own children. Basim, who has had a hideous four years in prison, and Hashim, who says nothing. For most of his life all his other brothers have been imprisoned, except for Khalid, who now has to take over supporting the family although he is only fifteen. I hug him and tell him to take care of everyone for me, and my mother cries as usual.

That night I lie in bed listening to them sleeping, and pray that something will happen before the morning to cancel my trip. I recognise the rhythms of their breathing and try to lock the different sounds of each one into my memory.

Beside me little Hashim struggles to stay awake, his face turned to me, eyes fluttering closed then snapping open, afraid I have gone already. I slip my arm under his small body and holding him to me I whisper that everything will be all right. He rests his hand, all scratched and scabby from playing in the street, against my face and drifts off into a gentle sleep.

In the morning my mother has broken the pact and is up and

waiting to say goodbye again. She wants to kiss and hug me but I can't. 'No, just let me go,' I say and I leave. I wish she hadn't done it because now I have the image of her distress imprinted on my mind.

When I arrive I am nervous because all this is new to me, it is the first time I have been on an airplane. I meet up with Siraj, who has his wife and two children with him, and some other couples. We go through customs and it goes so smoothly I feel foolish for being apprehensive.

I strap into my seat and by the time we have lifted off I am exhilarated. It is like seeing the earth from the moon. First Tehran, then the mountains, and soon the deserts of Afghanistan and Pakistan. I wish we were going to fly over Iraq so I could wave goodbye to Saddam, but then my happiness leaches away as I think of my father and my brother Asad still down there at his mercy.

Through the tiny porthole window I gaze into wispy clouds where I think I see the yearning faces of Hassan Pilot's children, my children, left behind in an unsafe world. They stare wet-eyed back at me, and I wonder if I will ever see them or the Middle East again and where on earth I will end up on this journey to the other side of the world.

PART TWO

INDONESIA

1999 — 2003

SEIZE THE DAY

We are all uneasy when we arrive at the Kuala Lumpur airport, but once again there are no problems. They stamp our passports, giving us fourteen days in Malaysia. Outside, a guy is waiting to take us to a hotel.

The first thing that hits us is the heat. It is not the dry heat we are used to, it is more like being wrapped in a thick steaming blanket of humidity. Then we discover we can't eat the food. We use similar ingredients in Iraq but they cook them another way, so the spices, sauces and textures all taste different, and the smell makes us want to be sick.

I had tried to stop my mother from packing nearly fifty cans of tuna and chickpeas in my suitcase. Now, as is so often the case with her and me, I will be forever grateful. This also helps my budget, which I am constantly worried about. I am on the other side of the world with virtually no money except for the smugglers' fees, which we have to pay as we go along, and from one day to another we never know what new situations might occur.

To take my mind off my financial concerns I wander through the city, soaking up the sights and sounds. I have heard about Kuala Lumpur's Petronas Twin Towers but when I come upon them it is breathtaking. The dazzling building glows like phosphorus in the night, circles of light reaching into the sky, joined by a suspended bridge at the forty-first floor.

I sit by the water fountains at its feet and gaze up at its sparkling exterior, soaring into the heavens. I have never seen a real skyscraper before, let alone the highest in the world. In the face of this magnificent sight I am suddenly overwhelmed by sadness for my country, decimated by Saddam with his wars, sanctions and destruction. I want to cry out, 'You live with such beauty, why do we have none,' knowing it will be generations before Iraq finds any splendour in its cities again.

After a week we are ready to set off to Indonesia. The smuggler has organised a Malaysian guy to collect our visas from the Indonesian embassy. 'When you get to Jakarta put $US50 in your passports before you hand it over to Immigration,' he tells us.

We don't know if he is joking. Normally I can read these types of situations but we are in a new culture. He was talking through an interpreter and I could not read his face. So we sit on the plane stewing.

When we arrive in Jakarta we hang back, letting others pass us as they hurry to the queue. But lingering will soon draw attention to us, we already stand out because of the women's Arabic clothes. So an older man, more courageous than I, decides to take the gamble. We stand frozen as the officer takes the passport. When he sees the money he looks over at the rest of us and gestures for us to move to the side.

We step out of the queue, letting others pass while we stand there paralysed. There is no way of assessing if they want to arrest us or take the money, if we should leave it in the passports or take it out. Before we can make a decision an officer strides out, collects all our passports and disappears with them into an office.

We are left glancing over our shoulders, afraid any minute the police will arrive, when suddenly the door opens and the officer marches back out. He presents the older guy with the passports all neatly stacked together, then gestures for us to pass through. All he says is what must have been 'Go' in Indonesian.

When we get outside we find the money gone but our visas

stamped for one month. If it runs out we can apply for another, but hopefully we will all be in Australia long before then.

A minibus is waiting for us and takes us to a hotel in the middle of Jakarta, a huge teeming city bristling with skyscrapers, shopping malls, apartments and slums. The most populous city in South-East Asia, with the thickest haze of pollution hanging over it that I have ever seen.

At the hotel we meet up with other groups who have recently arrived. The single men bunk in together to save money, four or five to a room. I share with Malik, a good-humoured, friendly guy in his mid-twenties who came on the same plane, and two others. After a day of waiting around, the smuggler, Omeid, who is to take us on the final leg to Australia, appears. He is an Iraqi in his thirties and has a scraggy beard, is unwashed, and smells.

We are keen to know the details of the voyage, the time of our departure, and what we have to pay. He tells us that within two weeks we will leave for Christmas Island, which we learn is part of Australia. It is December 1999 and I muse that we will arrive in time for our first Christian Christmas on an island called Christmas. We enquire again about the money but he seems in no hurry, which is unusual from what I know of smugglers. Apart from Fadi who took Mustafa and me to Qom, it tends to be the first thing on their minds.

'I only have a thousand American dollars, is that enough?' I eventually ask.

He replies with a dismissive gesture. 'Everyone will get on, don't worry.'

I notice others in the group becoming stressed that they will be left behind because Omeid hasn't yet let them pay. Some argue with him, and he certainly seems to be accepting money from a few of them, but no one will discuss what went on.

After a week, Omeid comes one morning with buses and tells us we are moving to Bogor.

'I thought the boat was leaving soon,' I speak up.

'Yes, but we can't go until we have enough people to fill it,' he responds, and there is nothing we can do.

Bogor is a pretty tourist town, nestled beneath rolling hills covered in tea plantations about an hour and a half's drive from Jakarta. Known as the City of Rain, it is famous for its cool climate, and the historical President's Palace surrounded by parklands and wild deer. When we arrive other asylum seekers are already there in rented houses, which they call villas, scattered around the lush hillsides on the edge of the city.

We squeeze as many people as possible into each place to reduce the cost, and there are markets nearby with fresh produce, so we buy cheaply and cook the food we like. Bogor's transient population is from many different cultures, so it is easy for us to blend in. It is a beautiful place, but we are unable to enjoy it because we are using up the little money we have, and many of us still haven't paid Omeid. We are restless, worried and just want to get going.

Omeid keeps gathering passengers, then after a few weeks when he has over one hundred people, he comes with the news that we are on our way. As we pack our meagre belongings, a calm descends over our group. We are excited our day has come, yet full of trepidation about the voyage ahead. Then strangely, just before we get on the bus, Omeid asks me for my money. I give it to him, relieved that I am definitely on the boat, but I remain confused as to why it is so last-minute.

They load us into four buses and we go back through Jakarta and on out to an isolated beach. It is dark by the time we arrive but a large yellow moon is rising, and we are shocked to see about two hundred or more people gathered on the foreshore. We thought it was just our group that was going. My stomach is churning, but all that matters now is that in a few days we will be in Australia.

As we clamber across the sand to join the others we see a number of small boats transporting people out to where we are told the large boat is anchored. Depending on how many children, they take ten to fifteen people on each one, then return for another load. It is a slow process, made strangely surreal because it is too dark to see where they are being ferried to, so the passengers just disappear into the night.

Each time a boat comes back there is a rush to get on. I stand back but begin to realise only the ones who shove are being successful. Siraj and his family are already on the main vessel so when the next small boat pulls up, contrary to my nature, I push forward with everyone else. Then I hear Omeid, who is helping control the crowd, call, 'Ali. Don't worry, everyone will go, let the women and children and families get on first. The boat is big, it takes four hundred people, you don't have to hurry, just wait.'

Somewhat relieved I step back and sit on the sand a short distance away with Malik and a group of other single men. Along the beach, in snatches of moonlight, I notice an authoritative-looking Indonesian, who clearly commands the respect of a group of officials around him, watching the proceedings.

'That's Zaqi,' Malik says. 'Someone said he's a big operator, runs a smuggling business even though he works for a government ministry.'

I look at Malik questioningly.

'It's not illegal in Indonesia. Look around you. Half the establishment are here.'

I glance over my shoulder and see a group of about thirty official-looking men, some in police or navy uniforms. 'What are they doing?'

He shrugs.

After about half an hour we see some activity further down the beach. Flashlights slice the darkness, then hone in on hands and faces. We realise people are giving Omeid money. We don't know what is going on. Maybe they had refused to pay until the last minute. We don't worry too much because the small boats are still shuttling passengers out to the larger vessel, and there are plenty of people queuing in the shallows, so we continue to wait our turn.

Then, as the moon appears from behind clouds, I see one of the boats returning fully loaded. When its bow runs up on the sand the Indonesians assisting Omeid force the people to get out. Voices are raised and women are crying, then in the convergence of several beams of torchlight we see people fighting. As the moon begins to disappear again we suddenly hear the sound of the big boat opening its throttle, and as I strain into the night I can see its faint outline gliding off into the distance.

There are screams from the shore and shouting, but it is too late. The boat has left, our money and our hopes for the future with it.

I feel my blood rising until I am a volcano inside. I think of my mother and the children waiting in Iran. Omeid agreed to a price. It was a deal. I should be on that boat. I'm not because Omeid, a fellow Iraqi who knows only too well what we are running from, betrayed us, his own people.

I leap to my feet. 'I am going to kill that motherfucker,' I yell and I mean it. Malik bounds after me. We look to the other men but they glance away sheepishly, afraid of losing their chances of getting on another boat. Flashlights fly around the beach as the smugglers round up the fifty or so remaining people and herd them back onto the buses. Zaqi and his men have miraculously disappeared.

We storm along the water's edge in the dark, shouting for Omeid to come out and face us. But fortunately for Omeid he is nowhere to be found, he is obviously very skilled in knowing when to exit. Eventually we give up. There is no point remaining on an empty beach in some obscure location hours from anywhere. So seething, we get back on the bus.

The hardest thing for everyone is that we have never done this before, so none of us know what is going on until it happens. But once we share our stories it becomes clear. By refusing to give us a price Omeid had us all on edge. Then he promised a guy free passage if he spread it around he'd paid $US3000. So people were offering Omeid $US2000 and he would say $US2500 as a special price for them. He didn't take my $US1000 in case I told the others they had been overcharged.

And so it went. Bargaining with people at their most vulnerable. So the panic took hold and like the Islamics at the border to Iran, people became so afraid of losing what good fortune they might have secured, they shared what they knew with no one.

At the beach, Omeid was looking for a second bite. Once the boat began to fill up, he only let those who paid extra get on. The rest of us were just pawns in his game to make himself rich. There were enough bus drivers waiting patiently to make it clear Omeid knew plenty of us wouldn't be getting on the boat. But by having us there we created the necessary pressure to force up the bidding. We were all just part of Omeid's human auction.

The bus drops us at a hotel in Jakarta. People immediately begin calling Omeid, leaving messages demanding he come and see us, but he doesn't respond. We wait for three days, with our frustration and anger increasing. Most of us have lost everything, our hopes for our families joining us destroyed.

On the third night, Omeid finally arrives with two Indonesian guards in his wake. This just amplifies our rage. He stands there with his thugs and no remorse. After years of built-up fury from injustice, I erupt like the street fighter of my youth and fly at him with both arms swinging. I have never felt such satisfaction as when my first punch hits his jaw and nearly breaks it. Malik is beside me, and blood and saliva fly as we beat Omeid and his guards so badly the other Iraqis begin to take pity on them.

Then a bizarre situation occurs. The Iraqis are so desperate they become the protectors of their enemy. They know they can't get their money back and they have no more, so they want to keep him alive and sympathetic to them, so he will put them on his next boat, or the one after, or the one after that. They will play his game with him, and take whatever he serves, because they are impotent. They have no rights. They are refugees. If they are patient and do what they are told it might be less painful than fighting for what is right. This is what Saddam has done to our people.

So about fifteen of them pull Malik and me off Omeid and drag him into another room with his bleeding guards. But we are not finished with Omeid yet, so they lock the door and won't let us in. On top of everything else they are scared the hotel will call the police. Then more of their hopes will be dashed.

Omeid must have, quite rightly, thought we were going to kill him, because he is suddenly penitent and ready to negotiate. So the door is opened and the Iraqis allow us in, but not until they are standing like a human shield between us and him. I shake my head in disbelief, then with eyes still wild with adrenaline I bark, 'Omeid, give our money back.'

'I can't return the money,' he splutters. 'We will take you on the next boat for whatever you paid.'

I feel my blood rising again. Our opportunity is gone. No one knows when there will be another boat. Omeid is a smuggler, not an airline that flies at the same time every week. I know he can't sail until he has enough people, and I can't imagine all the other requirements that must have to be in place.

'When will that be?' one of the group interjects.

'Maybe in a few months,' he replies sheepishly.

'And how will we live for those few months?' I keep my voice low and steady but I raise my fists again. 'Just return the money, you motherfucker.'

Omeid knows despite the barrier of people I will reach him. He cuts a cowardly figure as he and his thugs recoil.

'You don't understand. I am just the middleman. I have big Indonesian bosses behind me and I have to do what they say.'

I remember Zaqi standing sentinel on the beach and I don't doubt this is true, but in our current predicament I have little sympathy. 'I wonder if they know how much profit you pocket?'

Omeid doesn't respond.

'Give the money back to everyone or I swear we will kill you.'

I am glad to have Malik behind me because I am not sure I can go another round, but I suspect Omeid is not sure he can survive another beating either, so he reaches tentatively into his pocket and pulls out a huge roll of notes and a grubby notebook where he records his takings. With trembling hands he slowly redistributes the money and I can see how the people relax and glow. They have got back control of their lives and for a moment they are no longer powerless victims. It is Omeid and his useless bodyguards who have to slink away.

So we are free to plan our next move. Someone has the phone number of a Pakistani smuggler who works out of Bali and who, they have heard, has a boat ready to leave for Australia. We decide to go there and see.

We call him and he agrees to meet us. So we organise a bus for the whole fifty of us and, with a new injection of excitement, head off for the long drive across Java towards Bali. Our money is back in our pockets, the bus costs less than hotel rooms for the night, and the possibility of still getting to Australia is ahead of us.

It is a warm, sultry night and I drift in and out of sleep as we drive through small villages and paddy fields lit up in a mosaic of silver panels in the moonlight. Next morning I am woken by the bus cutting its engine and I look out to see we are on a ferry, crossing Bali Strait.

Soon we arrive in the capital, Denpasar, and Malik and I meet the Pakastani. After Omeid, everyone is very cautious, so having witnessed our abilities they nominate us to check him out. He is nice enough but we both feel uneasy about him. Like Omeid, he avoids certain questions and we instinctively don't trust him. When we go back and tell the group, they are disappointed but don't argue. However, the mood becomes sullen as we all face the bleak question of what to do next.

The Balinese air is thick with the sweet smell of incense, lush tropical plants, and the hypnotic beat of gamelan drums. There are splendid Hindu temples and ancient statues, blue waters and white sandy beaches, but once again we are unable to appreciate any of it.

After a couple of days in a cheap hotel, becoming increasingly depressed, we get a call from an Egyptian guy called Abu Quassey. He works for Zaqi, the big Indonesian boss. Zaqi has evidently fired Omeid for losing all our business, and replaced him with Abu Quassey. Omeid was meant to hold onto us by not returning our money until there were enough people for another boat.

While Zaqi did not like losing money, he disliked even more the bad name he would get if we were to go with another smuggler. And a good name is everything in this business. So Zaqi has given Abu Quassey the job of getting us back, and of course we don't let on how easily he could do that. We play hard to get, but the offer of free accommodation and food if we return to Jakarta swings it.

I am not happy about returning to the same operation that has already betrayed us, but Omeid has gone and I have little else to suggest. The people, especially those with children, are beginning to despair.

We return through the night and I gaze out the window. In the distance I see the glow of molten lava flowing down the side of a volcano, and am struck with awe at its beauty. I think of how little of the world I have experienced because most of my adult life has been spent in hiding, on the run, or in prison. And I could have been in Australia by now if Omeid had been a decent human being.

We go back to Bogor, where we meet Abu Quassey. He is tougher than Omeid and just as unlikeable. He doesn't play the game that Omeid did but he tries to get $US2000 out of each of us. I give him $US800, saying, 'I don't have any more left.' He accepts it. He seems to have a healthy respect for Malik and me because of the Omeid incident.

The weeks drag by while we wait for enough people to fill another boat. Zaqi keeps dropping in to reassure us he will pay for everything until we go. He is nervous. If we find another alternative he will lose the money he is spending on us, and his reputation will end up in tatters anyway.

About this time, Resa comes into our lives. He is an Iraqi who works for Omeid, and had come to the hotel the night after we beat up Omeid, to apologise for what had happened on the beach. We didn't blame him, it wasn't his fault, he just worked for them, but we thought him rather stupid to be involved with such a nasty outfit. The whole operation was run by Indonesians, so as Resa and Omeid were the only Iraqis, we understood his desire to befriend us. But I sensed he was driven less by remorse than fear of what we might do to him, so he was playing it safe by becoming our ally.

Now that we are back from Bali, Resa comes to the villa in Bogor with a message from Omeid for Malik and me. We don't have phones, so it is the only way to make contact.

Omeid is now in hiding from Zaqi and, having no income, is trying to set up on his own. We are not interested in hearing anything about Omeid, but Resa insists: 'He wants you and Malik to work for him. You can clearly look after yourselves and he needs partners. And protection from Zaqi.'

Malik and I start laughing. 'He has to be joking. Are you crazy?'

Resa shrugs. 'Maybe you should keep your options open, in case Zaqi's next boat never happens.'

I look at him with alarm.

Resa dials Omeid on his mobile phone and passes it to me. I flare at the sound of Omeid's voice. He could have begun by apologising for what he did to us and the fifty others left behind, but he doesn't. Instead he simpers about himself.

'Zaqi wants revenge on me for giving back your money.'

I sense he is somehow trying to put the blame on us. It is questionable if Omeid has any moral boundaries at all. I bristle with contempt.

'Having wanted to kill you myself, I don't really care what Zaqi does to you.' I hang up and hand the phone to Resa.

Omeid rings back, and Resa holds it out to me. When I don't take it he shoves it into my hand, and Omeid's whiny voice is in my ear again.

'Resa says you need money to get your family to Australia. I will help you get them there.'

I hesitate.

'Working for me you will earn enough to bring them from Iran to Indonesia. Then each time I send a boat to Australia, I put one of your family on it for free.'

I stand stock still staring at the floor. I suddenly see a light on the horizon of my essentially black world. I have previously had no idea of how to get them here, let alone any further. But now a door is opening, with the only problem being the extent to which I despise the opener.

I force myself to adopt a conciliatory tone. 'What would you want us to do?'

'Talk to people, they respect you.'

I feel my hackles rising at the thought of having to suggest anyone travel on his boats, but Omeid jumps in. 'We will set a price. Without Zaqi it will be different. Not like what happened to you. And you could protect me from Zaqi if there is any trouble,' he adds hopefully.

I doubt if I would do that, I would prefer to cause the demise of them both, but getting my family to Australia is more pressing, and he has just presented a way I can do it.

I spend several sleepless nights coming to terms with going against my principles and aligning myself with such a low-life, but considering my situation I have to weigh up the benefits. And in this dog-eat-dog world, by working from the inside I may yet be able to get even with Omeid. After a couple more calls with him, I am finally persuaded by Resa and Malik to go along with it. They, of course, will be on the payroll too.

Once Omeid has an agreement with us, he leaves for Malaysia to gather up new arrivals, and Resa moves into our villa in Bogor. This may not have been such a good idea because the next thing we know Abu Quassey comes knocking on our door.

'Is Resa here?' he says politely when I answer it.

When I see four Indonesian heavies behind him I realise Resa's attempts to play both sides may not be working for him. I haven't particularly warmed to him, but I am inclined to favour the underdog so I look at Abu Quassey innocently. 'Okay, just wait here.'

I go back inside. 'These people are coming to take Resa,' I say to my seven housemates.

Resa looks at us, wide-eyed and scared. None of them know him well, but while he may not be too smart, Resa is Iraqi and has become one of us. Besides, they don't like the Egyptian, so they are quite happy to stand behind me.

Aware that my decisions have led me back into the world of gangsters and thugs that I tried so hard to escape, I go back out and in my toughest voice say, 'He is not coming out, and only one of you can come in.'

They back down when they see the small army behind me, and I usher Abu Quassey in. He tries to convince Resa to stay with Zaqi and not to go with Omeid. Not, I suspect, that Abu Quassey has any time for him, he is just hungry for people and if Resa takes me and my roommates away from Zaqi, that's eight less fees for him.

After Abu Quassey leaves, Resa is unnerved by this close call, especially as he lied and had denied he was working for Omeid. So he goes back to Jakarta, where he can live in relative anonymity, but it is not long before he sends word that he wants to meet. We don't know if we are being summoned to do something for Omeid or to babysit Resa, but we are so bored from waiting around that we will go anywhere.

We meet at a Chinese restaurant recommended by his girlfriend

Francesca. She is no beauty but she is clearly devoted to Resa and he seems equally enthralled. She is Chinese, speaks several languages, and works in a travel agency that helps Omeid's business. She knows the menu and orders for us. By necessity I have grown accustomed to the smell of Asian food and am finally able to eat it, but I only have to think of my mother's lamb biryani to set off a craving.

While we are eating, Resa's mobile rings but he doesn't answer it. Instead he puts it on the table with a laugh. 'Whenever Omeid goes to Malaysia he leaves his phone with me.'

I can see he is scared, and would like to escape this mess but he can't find a way out.

'There is some trouble going on,' he says. 'How can I contact you?'

'We can't afford a phone,' I reply cautiously.

Resa slides Omeid's phone across the table. I suspect this is the point at which he tries to use me to facilitate his exit.

'Now you are working with us, you keep this one.'

This is the phone that co-ordinates Omeid's venture. People call it when they are looking for a smuggler, when they first arrive and are waiting to be collected from bus stations and airports, or if they are in trouble. It was the hub of Zaqi and Omeid's operation before they split. Resa wants to dump the phone and the responsibilities that go with it. I am indifferent. I am not afraid of these men, I just don't like them. So I take the phone.

Malik and I return to Bogor and I forget about it because it never rings. Until Resa calls. He wants us back in Jakarta. Omeid is now on the island of Lombok, to the east of Bali, where there are good beaches for boat departures. He wants Malik and Resa to meet him there and me to remain in Jakarta, in case there are any arrivals or problems to fix.

I am more than happy not to have to deal direct with Omeid. The only thing that concerns me is that I have virtually no money. Abu Quassey still has my $US800, which I have left with him in case his boat should eventuate, but this is not the time to tell him I want my money back because I am staying to work with Omeid.

Before they leave, Resa gives me the key to his room in a big old colonial house full of Chinese and Indonesians. I impress on him again, 'Don't take too long, I am almost broke.'

'Don't worry. Omeid will pay us and we'll send you your share,' he says casually.

So I sleep in Resa's studio with the phone beside me and wait for the money to come or something to happen. After about a week I only have a few hundred rupiah left. I call Resa and he says he is sending me money via Western Union. I am relieved and wait but hear nothing. After another three days I try Resa again, but his phone is off or out of range. By now I have no money left at all. I stave off panic, drink water, and sleep to ward off the memories of Abu Ghraib, where starvation racked my body for nearly four years.

As the days go by I lie on the bed conserving energy, and listening to the sounds of the big house and its occupants. I can't speak Chinese or Indonesian so it is pointless trying to get to know them. Besides, I am hardly in the mood. I have become Omeid's sport again.

One night I am so hungry I wait until everyone is asleep, then I go to the fridge in the big communal kitchen and take some of the other people's food. I quaff it down, then go back to my room and sleep again. But it is a fitful, wretched sleep as I toss and turn to the rhythm of my father's words: *Don't lie, don't swear, don't steal.*

During this time, I begin to receive phone calls from Iraqis in Iran, or on their way to Indonesia. At first I say, 'Sorry, I'm not Omeid.' But as I grow hungrier and thinner, when somebody says, 'Hello Omeid,' I neglect to correct them. And when they say, 'I want to come to Australia. What's the deal?' I start to tell them details about what to do, from my own limited experience. Finally one day, when my stomach is cramping and I am craving cigarettes, someone says, 'Hello Omeid,' and I say, 'Yeah, that's me.'

As I talk I realise I know a bit about how it goes. As well as my work with the resistance, I have been smuggled many times, and of course I made the journey here myself. This inspires confidence in the caller, and I suspect they would have preferred to talk to me than Omeid, if they had known I wasn't him.

Then I get a call from the guy in Malaysia who smuggles Omeid's people to Indonesia. I thought he was going to ask me what the hell I'd been doing, but he doesn't.

'Thirty people have arrived for Omeid,' is all he says.

'Okay,' I reply, not sure what he wants me to do about it.

'They don't have passports so I am sending them overland through Sumatra. When they get to Jakarta in a day or two they will call you to meet them and take them to a hotel.'

I say okay, hang up and go back to waiting.

That night, completely out of the blue, Resa and Malik arrive back from Lombok. Apart from the occasional guilt-ridden midnight foray into my housemates' food stashes, I have had almost nothing to eat or smoke for more than two weeks.

I glare at them both. 'What the fuck is going on?' I say, tight-lipped and ill-tempered.

Malik is shocked at how thin I look. 'We sent you money,' he exclaims, clouding over as he looks at Resa. 'Didn't you?'

'I sent it to Francesca to give you. Maybe she took it.'

I find it unlikely. In our brief meeting at the Chinese restaurant Francesca seemed open and friendly. More likely, Resa is playing games with us that he learnt from Omeid. Either way I am almost too angry to speak.

'Just give me some money and go to hell.'

But Resa has nothing, so Malik digs in his pocket and pulls out his own pay. He divides it in half and hands me $us300.

With money in my hand, I can think only of food. We go to a nearby restaurant and I order half the menu, but my stomach has shrunk so much I have to cancel most of it. Malik and Resa watch me uneasily. Once I have eaten I look up and break the silence.

'So Resa, how is the business? How is Omeid?'

'Everything is okay,' he says confidently. 'The boat is almost ready to go. Once it gets to Australia, Omeid will pay us a share of the profit.'

'That's good news,' I say sceptically. 'So what do we do now?'

'You stay here, and when people arrive from Malaysia you just take them to a hotel, then send them to Surabaya by train.'

We walk to Resa's place with him and I pick up my things, then Malik and I head off to the Matraman Hotel to get a room. We amble down streets with gleaming glass towers, and into alleys where single globes light busy family restaurants. As I watch mangy, short-tailed cats scavenge under tables, I ask Malik what's going on.

'It's all bullshit. There are more than two hundred people in Lombok, just waiting. They are so despairing that every few days Omeid takes them to the beach, pretending they are about to leave just to shut them up, then he brings them back to the hotel with some lie about why they didn't go. The police keep trying to get cash out of them and they don't know what to do. Omeid's got all their money so they're stuck. It's awful.'

'I might have known,' I mutter angrily, then walk on silently. I need time to think, but when we reach the Matraman I find everything is coming to a head. Abu Quassey's boat is leaving Jakarta for Christmas Island later tonight. He is rallying the people he has in this hotel and has been looking for us.

I thought I had made my decision to stay with Omeid, but after what I have just heard, and faced with Abu Quassey actually leaving, I am again confused. Only a few hours into recovery from near starvation, I don't want to deal with the choice being presented to me. I just want to find somewhere comfortable to sleep.

We go to reception and get a room. As we climb the stairs I try to think it through. Abu Quassey has my $us800, so I can still go to Australia and then work out how to make the money to bring my family once I am there. Alternatively, I can go down the new road promised by a man I cannot trust and whose principles I spurn, but whose offer is more likely to expedite getting my family to safety.

As I struggle with my dilemma Malik looks at me. 'Are you going to go?'

'I don't know.'

'Resa says when you arrive in Australia by boat they lock you up in a detention centre, which is like a jail. Sometimes for years.'

We knew there was detention, but not that it was a jail. We thought it was more like the house in Bogor, where you stayed for a couple of months. But we didn't really think about it. It had always been the way that the men go first, then send for their families. We were so used to the escape being the main game that we seldom contemplated what would happen on arrival, we just dealt with it once we got there. We were always heading into the unknown and every place was different, so there was little point speculating. We knew we had the right to seek asylum from persecution, and we knew Australia was a democracy, committed to human rights. After what we had been through, a few months in detention would be more than worth it.

I lie on my bed, stewing over the decision. I can't stop the feeling that I missed my chance on that first boat. I was still naive then and determined. But now I know too much. My hands are getting dirty and my optimism fading. I am fast becoming part of an underworld of liars and cheats, and the pressure to bring my family out of Iran is increasing. In 1997 and '98, when we were first there, Iran was going through a period of increasing freedom after the election of liberal-thinking Khatami as president. However, things are closing down again, with the clerics regaining control, and now in 2000 the future for Iraqis in Iran is become increasingly insecure.

My mind keeps returning to the calls on Omeid's phone from desperate Iraqis, their families torn apart, trying to escape Saddam like I had. I begin to think if you empathise with these people's plight, refuse to play games, and really want to help them, the job wouldn't be too hard.

At first it seems like a ridiculous thought but it soon takes hold. There is no reason why I couldn't do Omeid's job better than him. The joke is I have in my hand the phone that is central to his business, and have already been liaising with both the refugees and Omeid's associate in Malaysia.

I have my own contacts in Iran. In fact by the second week of enforced hunger and nicotine withdrawals, I had started giving them to Iraqis so they could get their passports, tickets and other papers. I am trained in accountancy, I would get decent people to work with me, I would be honest and upfront with everyone, and with any profit I would fly my family here and then get them to Australia on my own safe boats for free.

There is no law in Indonesia against people smuggling. It is just another business, one which provides a path to asylum for refugees who have no other options. So I will do it myself the way it should be done. I will not only save my family, I will save other Iraqis, and everyone I help escape will feel like a personal victory over Saddam.

I sit at the window, chain-smoking as I watch the people climbing onto Abu Quassey's bus. I wish I could share my plan with my mother and siblings. I wish I could tell Intisar. I can feel myself reclaiming my life again. I am back at the helm.

By morning it is clear I made the right decision. Abu Quassey is back in the hotel with the people, and I realise he is doing what Omeid did in Lombok, just moving them around to keep them quiet. I am both disgusted and uplifted.

Malik and I go to our favourite coffee shop in the Atrium Mall for breakfast. It is two stories up on the bridge between the shops, and looks down over the open area around the entrance to the mall. We like to watch the Indonesian girls as they come and go. They are strikingly beautiful, and mostly friendly. It is easy to meet them, you just have to chat, buy them a drink, and some of them will go with you and have sex if you want. Coming from the strict segregation of our culture this is a new and exciting prospect for us, but the image of Intisar still lingers in my mind so I just observe.

While we are eating, Omeid's phone rings. I still haven't told Resa or Malik about the thirty Iraqis, who at this moment are on their way through Sumatra. I answer it to a nervous male voice.

'We will soon be in Jakarta. We will call you when we get to the bus station.'

This is my moment. I can still just be Omeid's agent, or I can step up. 'Welcome,' I respond decisively. 'I will meet you there.'

'What's going on?' Malik says, looking over the rim of his coffee cup. 'You're up to something, aren't you?'

I grin broadly and pay the bill, then look at what is left of the $US300 Malik gave me. I think of Omeid's greasy clothes and how he smelt, and I remember wondering how you could trust a man who cared so little about himself.

'We are going to buy some decent clothes,' I say.

Malik is happy to shop, so we spend the next several hours indulging in the luxury of buying some nice jeans, T-shirts and running shoes. We take off our old clothes and put on our new outfits. We make a handsome pair as we step back out into the mall.

We return to the coffee shop and I can't take my eyes off Omeid's phone, which sits on the table like a pot that won't boil. Malik is still not sure what is happening but as usual is happy to go along. But I am restless and twitchy from nerves and too much caffeine. In Iraq we drink thick black coffee but only once or twice a week. In Indonesia I have discovered cappuccino, which I can't stop drinking and am now addicted.

When the phone rings I almost jump out of my chair.

'We have arrived,' a man says.

'Okay, stay where you are. I will be there shortly.' He gives me the name of the bus station and I hang up. Malik looks at me questioningly. 'Drink up. Let's go,' I say, paying the bill.

I haven't told him yet of my decision, it is still too fragile to risk him pouring cold water on it. But the rush of adrenaline that accompanies my taking charge gives me a strength that inspires him to follow.

We take a taxi across this massive city of nine million. The fares are so cheap, it is hard to know how taxi drivers make a living. One of the pleasures of having money in my pocket is that I can tip them. A thousand rupiahs, which is about ten American cents, will feed their whole family for a day.

The bus terminal is a large asphalt area surrounded by open food stalls, with vehicles of all shapes, colours and sizes randomly roaring in and out. The air is thick with noise from broken exhausts and spluttering engines. Swarms of people clamber on and off buses but it is not hard to spot my group. They are poor to middle-class Iraqis, huddled together, the women in black hijab. I greet them, introducing myself as Ali. They don't realise it is me they have been talking to all along, but it is fortunate I didn't say I was Omeid as some of them recognise me from Iran.

I have to get them out of here before the police appear and start asking for ID, so I rent one of the smaller buses and load them on. They do whatever I say, they are scared and don't know what is going on. They just want someone to save them. I remember how it feels.

I show the driver a card from a hotel where I have made a deal. If I take seven rooms, they will give me mine plus meals for no extra. I won't utilise it now as it would be unwise for me to be on the same premises if the police are called. Also, I don't want to get involved in their disaffections and personal battles. I need to remain objective.

The bus revs its engine, and blowing black smoke, rattles off towards the skyscrapers in Jakarta, down roads lined with colourful food stalls, barefoot children and poverty. Malik and I get in a taxi and follow them.

'Does Omeid know these people are coming?' Malik enquires, looking at me.

'If you remember, no one was answering the phone. I couldn't even ask Resa where the money you sent had gone, let alone tell him that thirty people were on their way.'

I am more snappy than I meant to be, it wasn't Malik's fault, but it prevents any further enquiry.

At the hotel I help seven of the people to register in the rooms I have reserved and tell them to go ahead with the luggage. I only know a couple of Indonesian words, but because the Iraqis don't know any they think I speak the language, which I am hoping will raise my stakes. Then I go back to the others who I have left outside.

'Come in a couple at a time, as if you are visitors.' I recall how we had done it when I first arrived. 'This way you can split the cost of each room between four or five of you.'

Once in the safety of their hotel rooms they want to ask me a million questions about what is going to happen next. And more importantly they want to meet Omeid, the smuggler who they have been told will take them to Australia.

I remember how it felt walking into the unknown. They have not only left their previous lives behind, but most of them are survivors of unspeakable traumas. I need to give them space to get adjusted; this is not the time to tell them the man they want to cross an ocean with is a crook.

I give them directions to where they can change their money or locate a phone, how to find a supermarket with food they will be able to eat, and that we will talk tomorrow. I am exhausted already by the strength of their need.

Malik and I catch a taxi west of the city centre to Sinbad's, one of the few Arabic restaurants in Jakarta. The walls are panelled in dark wood, there is deep red carpet on the floor, and I am comforted by the smells of home. We order kebuli laham and reeyas, and while I savour the anticipation of Iraqi food I can feel Malik waiting for an explanation.

The time has come to fess up, so I plunge in. 'I'm not going to just hand these people over to Omeid, I will give them a choice. If they want they can go with him. But I'm going to tell them the truth.'

I watch and wait as Malik tears at a piece of flat bread, chews it thoroughly, then replies, 'All right.'

I feel a surge of relief. I need Malik on my side, we have become good friends and he is the only one I trust. But even though he despises Omeid, I'm not sure if he will want the responsibility of what I have in mind.

'So what are you going to do if they don't go with Omeid?' he asks.

'I'm going to send them to Australia myself.'

He looks at me incredulously. 'How?'

'I don't know. That's what we have to figure out.'

'We?'

'It's not that big a deal. We just have to work out how it's done,' I say reassuringly, trying to pass it off. 'If Resa joins us, he's worked in the business with Omeid. We already have thirty people, we buy a boat and send them. How hard can it be?'

Malik stares at me in silence, then to my relief he nods. 'Okay.'

'Is that all?'

'What more do you want? I don't know how to do it but I am with you.'

I laugh and shake his hand. It was in this spirit we had confronted Omeid and got our money back, forging an unspoken bond.

When I call Resa he is glad for a reason to get away from Omeid. Not, I suspect, because he has any scruples about Omeid's ethics, but simply that he thinks we are the stronger team, and he would rather not have us as his enemy. He says he was in the Iraq Navy and has learnt a lot from Omeid. In fact he rather unnecessarily oversells his usefulness. The truth is I am happy to have anyone who knows anything about the job.

That night I lie in bed not sleeping. Now Malik and Resa are on board my idea has become viable, so how do I convince these people to come with me? Do I reassure them it is not greed but concern for their welfare that motivates me? But then that is not entirely true.

I need the money. However, the fact that they are the means by which I can get my family to safety does not detract from my desire to protect them. I want them to make it to Australia without being fucked over, and I don't want Omeid's filthy hands in the pot stealing their money.

Next morning Malik and I sit down with all thirty adults and their children crammed into one hotel room and I ask, 'So you want to go to Australia?'

'Yes,' someone says, 'it is all organised with Omeid. He said we make final arrangements when we get here. He said that there would be no problems. We thought you worked with him.'

'Have you paid him yet?' I ask, knowing what the answer will be.

'He said we would work that out when we got here.'

I nod. Omeid's promise to change was clearly, as Malik puts it, bullshit.

'Okay, look. It is not as simple as he has made it sound. You can go with Omeid if you like, but I can tell you he will cheat on you. I don't want to say too much, but Omeid is not that good, people are still stuck here who should have gone long ago.'

I glance around the room and see their faces falling as disappointment takes over. They are used to it, this is how it so often goes. I decide to avoid further letdown by sparing them the details of what happened to Malik and me.

'I know it is hard for you to change plans, but if you like I will get you to Australia.'

I look around at the circle of frightened faces and blunder on, imparting all I can from my limited experience, and addressing my own credentials.

'I am not going to tell you I am a good guy, a tough guy, you need to ask that of the ones who knew me in Iran. But at least you have met us,' I gesture to Malik, 'and I will tell you everything I can, and it will all be above board.'

I pause, waiting for a reaction, but they remain mute.

'We will leave you to think about it for a little while. But if you say yes I will need the money straight away.' It would not be long before Omeid found out what was going on and then things could get very messy.

'How much will it be?' an old man barks from the back.

'Each one of you gives me one thousand US,' I decide on the fly. 'No games, everyone the same, so you all know where you stand. If you have more than that, you help someone who doesn't have enough. Or if someone is waiting for money to be transferred from family or friends, you lend it to him. You help each other.'

They look uncertain. Caring for community has been all but eradicated from our once generous culture, making sharing limited resources a life-and-death decision. Preserving immediate family is now the primal drive, and as much as they often dare to hope for.

Then a timid voice comes from amongst the crowd. 'How much for the children?'

I look around at small hands clutching their mothers' robes, their innocent faces, wide-eyed and afraid, and I think about my sisters and my brothers.

'They don't pay.'

Malik elbows me. 'There goes your profit.'

But it is too late.

A woman next to us with two little girls smiles appreciatively through tears. 'Thank you,' she whispers.

I nod and look away. I could be brought to tears myself by the thought of Hashim as he slept in my arms that last night in Iran, and how I left him without a final farewell.

'When would we go?' the old man demands.

'The sooner we get more people, the sooner you can go. If you have friends coming from Malaysia, that would help. As soon as there are sixty, not including the children, I can send you.'

At this point I am guessing, because I have no idea what size boat we can get, or even how to get it, but I do know, at $US1000 per person, we will need more than thirty passengers. Quite apart from Omeid's auction on the beach, I also know that plenty of money must have gone to the authorities who stood watching, and I am yet to find out how all that works.

Malik and I leave the hotel while they make their decision. I am too nervous to sit still so we walk the streets. After an hour we go back, and as we climb the stairs a number of them are waiting with money to procure a special deal to secure safety for their families.

'Please, if you have something to say, say it here in front of us all,' I declare once we are back in the room. 'If you come with me there are to be no secrets, no special deals. I have told you what you pay, and everyone will be treated the same.'

There is a moment of silence, then a man my father's age stands up and looks around at the group. 'That's good,' he says, nodding.

Maybe because I have spoken from the heart and genuinely want the best for these people, they believe me enough to trust me. Or maybe, like me with Abu Quassey, after the bad news about Omeid, they would go with anyone. After your first experience of disillusionment, you tend to become more reckless. Either way, the man goes on to state with certainty, 'We decided we will come with you.' And suddenly everyone is smiling.

'Okay,' I say, smiling back. 'If we have a deal, go to your rooms and put your money together and I will come around and collect it. But remember, help each other. Iraq is behind you, but you still have a long way to go and you need one another.'

MY OWN MASTER

When Malik and I go to collect the money, some of them don't have it. I have been in their situation myself so I understand, but I can't send anyone if there is not sufficient to buy a boat.

'So what are you going to do?' I say, looking around at the fifteen or so who don't have enough.

'I have $US700 and my cousin in Germany will send me the rest,' one says.

'Okay,' I say, 'give it to me and I put your name down, but you will have to pay the rest, otherwise you're not going.'

Another has a brother in Iran, and so it goes.

We leave the hotel and walk trancelike onto the busy street. I am both terrified and exhilarated by taking control. I just have to keep my sights on why I am doing it, which at the moment is not hard. I am constantly worried about what is happening to my family. They have no phone, so to call them I have to contact their neighbour, and they get my mother to come.

Since things in Iran have been tightening up politically, the Iraqi community has been fragmenting, because everyone is leaving. My mother is terrified she will be left behind. Now that she has set her mind on Australia she just wants to get there. She doesn't know how I am going to do it, but she is past being rational. Our phone calls are an unpleasant, guilt-ridden business as I try to reassure her I will get her there somehow, but her unhappiness always drags me down.

The small bag I carry is bulging with about eighteen or nineteen thousand American dollars. More cash than I have ever seen, let alone held in my own hands. Hands which are now sweating. Malik skips along beside me like a truanting kid.

'Can you imagine what we could do with all that?' he asks.

I nod and walk swiftly. With this kind of money I could purchase the necessary passports and paperwork for my whole family, fly them all out of Iran to Australia with ease and follow them, instead of the nightmare that lies ahead. Malik is a good reliable friend, yet I know he would consider keeping this money if he could think of a way to do it.

'Where are you taking it?' he asks when I don't answer.

'To a safety box in the hotel.'

Silence. I know what is coming.

'Can we keep some of it?'

I look at him warily and laugh. 'No.'

'There's so much. Why not just a bit?'

'No,' I say more firmly, already dizzy with the enormity of what we have done, and wishing he wasn't making the job harder. 'What if tomorrow they change their minds and want their money back, and we are the ones who took it?'

'Okay,' he conciliates, but I can tell it might be different if he was carrying it alone.

Forewarned, when I ask for a safety deposit box at the hotel I insist that under no circumstances is anyone other than me to open it. The receptionist agrees and gives me the only key.

Now we wait and I begin to realise it's not as easy as I thought. I don't know how real smugglers get their passengers. Apart from Omeid's phone, we have very little access to arrivals. We can't buy a boat until we get enough people to pay for it. Nor can we calculate what size boat we need until we know how many people we have, and we can't keep the people waiting too long, because it is costing money no one has. I've heard about a book called *Catch 22* and I suspect I am living it.

The money sitting in the safety deposit box haunts us in different ways. Malik and Resa just want to spend it. I, on the other hand, am afraid we will somehow lose it and I will be left with the responsibility of all these people's lives on my hands. To curtail my anxiety I sometimes go to a place I found called Dunia Fantasi, a large fun park near the sea, with an aquarium and a big dipper, which I ride trying to recapture the childhood I never had.

Malik is happy spending most of his time hanging out and chasing women, and Resa is cementing his bond with Francesca. It is during these times I miss Intisar. I know it is impossible she would still be waiting for me. By now her family would have forced her into a loveless marriage. I manage to keep this unhappy image at bay, like I did in Abu Ghraib, by fantasising about seeing her again. Over and over I would picture the joy in her eyes, her smile, her shiny black hair swinging free as she took off her scarf for me.

One night Resa calls. 'Ali, we're going to an Indonesian club tonight. Come with us.'

I don't know anything about clubs in Jakarta, so I have no idea what they even look like, but I once went to one in Iraq with my uncle, where there was alcohol, which only reminded me of my father's tirades, and my own painful flirtations with the bottle.

'No, I don't think I'm interested.'

'It's Francesca's birthday. We want you to come.'

I tell him I can't, but he keeps trying to convince me, until he wears me down and in the end I give in.

Even from the outside it is not what I expected. It is off a mall and up an elevator. When the doors open there is no loud music or flashing lights. It is a very large, softly lit room with people sitting at tables, eating, listening to the music, or on the floor dancing. There is an outside garden area with a barbeque and a long table of food and drinks under the stars. I am disarmed and somewhat enchanted.

Resa waves and I join him at a table where he sits with Francesca. From what I can see, Resa and I are the only Arabic people. I have been in Indonesia for two months now but have not yet begun to grasp the language. Francesca is fluent in Chinese, Indonesian and English. Resa, on the other hand, is far less assured in Indonesian than he let on to us, but he does speak good English.

All around us people are dancing and singing, and I remember what it was like back in Iraq before Saddam took my father. I begin to smile involuntarily, and realise how long it has been since I have had this feeling. I order a Coke and sit back and relax. Resa is talking with Francesca, so I look around the room, absorbing the atmosphere.

My gaze is drawn to a girl who sits at a table with her two girl-friends. I seldom see Indonesian girls who are not attractive but she is exceptional. Her hair is cut short in a bob and she wears a blood-red T-shirt and tight jeans. I find myself studying her, when suddenly she looks up and catches my eye. I quickly turn away, but can't help myself from looking back again. When I do she is still looking at me.

'She likes you.' Resa nudges me.

'What's the point, when I can't speak her language?' I reply, try-ing to be dismissive, but despite my resolve I glance her way one more time. From the way she and her girlfriends look in my direction I can tell they are talking about me.

Then one of the girls gets up and comes over. She begins speaking in Indonesian and I can't understand a word she is saying. So she tells Francesca who passes it on in English to Resa, who tells me in Arabic.

'Her friend wants to come and sit with you, what do you say?' Resa grins.

'Okay,' is all I can think to say.

The next thing I know the beautiful girl comes and sits beside me at our table, and then quite unselfconsciously holds my hand. This is unfamiliar territory for me, but it is a small sweet hand and I am enjoying holding it. Sadly she breaks this glorious moment by starting to talk to me in Indonesian and I am at sea again.

So I direct her to Francesca, and Resa comes back to me. 'She says she likes you and would like to see you again.'

'Tell her I like her too,' I say, feeling the warmth of her soft hand in mine.

'She's gorgeous, and from a good family,' Resa says, with almost too much enthusiasm. I detect a little jealousy. Perhaps he is not as ready to settle down with Francesca as I had thought.

'Good luck to me,' I say, grinning.

'Her name is Eni.'

I smile at her and point to myself. 'Ali.'

She smiles back and keeps talking, but sometimes I think Resa is not translating everything she says. I can tell he wants to talk to her himself, but can't because Francesca is next to him. I suspect he has decided if he can't have her he would rather I didn't, because after a while he tires of being the translator.

'Let's go,' he says out of the blue. 'Let's go to another place for dinner.'

I am annoyed with Resa, always putting himself first, but I don't have a lot invested so I agree. My failed relationship with Intisar is still coiled in my heart, so while I am happy to play, my interest is rarely engaged for long.

Eni and her group have decided to leave too, so we walk out together, but as I say goodbye she grabs my hand and writes her phone number on it. I smile and thank her but then she wants my number too, so I write it on her delicate hand and find myself wanting to hold it longer. She lets it linger before backing away to catch up with her friends. But as we walk off I hear her calling and ask Resa what she said.

'She's just saying goodbye again,' he replies offhandedly.

It sounded like more than that to me but I'm not about to take Resa on over something so trivial.

We go to Sinbad's for a big Arabic meal and laugh and talk until midnight, then Resa and Francesca drive me back to my hotel in a green van owned by her. I go to bed relaxed and happy, but then at about two am the phone rings. As always, in response to any late-night intrusion, I am bolt upright. But it is not Saddam's police, it is Eni.

Neither of us can understand anything the other is saying but we discover we both know a few words in English, which I learnt in its most basic form at school. I had only mastered a few adjectives and nouns, but we are able to communicate that we are attracted to each other, which is very titillating.

Afterwards I lie awake feeling a long-dormant part of myself igniting. It is the first time I have felt anything emotional towards the countless appealing Indonesian women who surround us every day. I put Intisar out of my mind as an impossible fantasy, and drift into a contented state dreaming of countless intimate acts with Eni.

When I wake the next morning the euphoria still lingers, and I am open to any means by which I can hold onto it. I remember seeing people on the street selling quarto pages printed with a selection of words in English, Arabic and Indonesian. It is the most fundamental of dictionaries but I rush out and buy one, and with its help I manage to work out how to tell Eni in Indonesian that I would like to see her.

When she says she can't, I realise how much I have been looking forward to being with her again. We don't have enough words to get into an explanation, so I am forced to go back to Francesca and Resa.

I know Francesca likes going to lunch, so I call to ask her. She is delighted but Resa is so easy about it that I am beginning to think he is preparing to leave her. I hope I am wrong, because we need her help at the travel agency, but I am not about to ask him. With my main purpose in mind I diplomatically ask Francesca to make a phone call before we go, and once again she talks to Eni then tells Resa, who reluctantly translates for me.

'She can't come,' is all he says, which of course I already know.

Again and again I return to Francesca to make my phone calls, and take her to lunch as payment. Lost in the first flush of this verbally sensual affair I don't take into account how Francesca is dealing with translating my amorous missives, until one day she takes my hand while we are talking and I realise she is developing a crush on me. The price of these phone calls seems to be escalating so next time I say firmly through Resa, 'Look, I want to see this girl.'

Francesca seems to do more talking than necessary to make this point to Eni, but Resa's interpretation is adamant.

'She can't see you, why don't you understand? She says don't call her again, she doesn't want to talk to you.'

It is a long way back to my hotel but I walk it. I am tired of my life without a family, state or home. I am not a complicated man. I am not yet thirty and I just want to be with my mother and siblings, and have a wife and children of my own. By the time I reach my hotel I am exhausted enough to sleep but the phone rings and it is Eni.

'Why are you calling?' I say gruffly in a combination of English, Arabic and Indonesian. 'You said you don't want to talk to me.'

She understands enough to tell me she did not say that. She manages to reveal that on the night we met at the club she had invited me to come with her to another place. So Resa had deliberately mistranslated. It would seem he wants her for himself, and Francesca has feelings towards me, leaving both of them with their own reasons for trying to stop the liaison.

'Okay,' I say. 'We can do this on our own.'

I get my five-page dictionary and we begin. One at a time we work words out. 'Slow, slow,' I tell Eni. 'I am listening to the sounds.'

I write each word down in Arabic and then translate it into Bahasa. Then I get another word and start to make a sentence. Once I have worked out what she has said I craft a response, which she tells me how to say properly in Indonesian.

The phone call takes many hours but we giggle and laugh as we go. There is something very personal about the experience, and I sense an intimacy and warmth developing between us.

By the time we hang up I have several properly constructed sentences in Indonesian in my mind. It is much simpler than Arabic or English. I can feel another world opening for me. Each day I go out and practise on the street, then at night I look forward to our long flirtatious language lessons on the telephone.

Soon I take the plunge and construct a sentence that asks her to lunch. There is a pause and her reticence confuses me. All the signals are that she wants a relationship. She says goodbye but then she calls back. She gives me the name of a restaurant where I can meet her on Sunday. Then our familiarity returns as she tries to help me work out how to write down the address.

The night before I wash my shirt and in the morning I iron it. I catch a taxi and show the driver the address I have written. I am clearly not a native so he drives me around the city for thirty minutes before I realise the restaurant is just around the corner from my hotel. I am angry when I have to pay, but then I smile at him because I got the girl.

I buy her lunch, which I can't afford but I don't care, I am so happy to be with her. She is bright and chirpy as she struggles to understand my stumbling Bahasa and I think she is enjoying herself, but then as we finish eating she glances at her watch and shortly after says she has to go. I walk home trying to overcome my disappointment at her sudden departure, but the next night she goes back to calling me the same as she had before, so I remain confused.

A few days later my phone rings and it is one of our thirty refugees. 'Ali, twenty-seven Iraqis have just arrived in our hotel. We have already talked with them and told them about you. Can you meet them?'

'Okay,' I say, thinking it is unlikely they will have come here without another smuggler in mind. But as they would bring our number to nearly sixty in one hit, I need to get over there quickly.

I put thoughts of Eni aside and go and find Malik, who is sunning himself by a small drab pool at the back of the hotel. We meet with the new people, but I get the distinct impression that, as I had thought, they already have a deal with someone else. I don't know who it is, but it becomes apparent that some of them have already given over their money, so it is unlikely they will switch to me.

The next day, when I come down from my hotel room for breakfast, engrossed in finding a way to get the twenty-seven people to come with me, I run into a tall, good-looking Iraqi guy I met briefly in Iran, who had miraculously survived ten years in Saddam's prisons. He asks if he can join me.

His name is Abud and when we finish eating he asks me in a pleasant tone, 'What are you doing here, Ali? What business are you in?'

'I smuggle people.'

I want to say, 'I am going to do more good for Iraqis than I ever did in the resistance,' but my old training kicks in. I still have a father and brother in prison back home, who could be killed to punish me for my work against Saddam.

'Do you have time to meet again?' he says after contemplating me. 'With you and whoever you work with?'

'Two others. Malik and Resa.'

I am dubious about continuing to work with Resa after what happened with the money he was meant to send me from Lombok, and the childish way he handled things with Eni. But he is the only person we know who has any experience in smuggling people, boats and the sea, all of which are completely foreign to Malik and me.

'So can we all meet later?' Abud asks.

I don't know what he wants, but so long as I am waiting for the twenty-seven people to call I can be tempted to do anything to relieve the anxiety. So I agree.

Next day we meet for lunch at Sinbad's. Malik, Resa and I arrive to find Abud and his offsider Adnan already there. We order some kebabs and chat congenially about Indonesian and Iraqi food.

It is not until we have finished eating that Abud asks me about my smuggling experience. What can I say? I'm not about to tell him I haven't had any yet.

'I help Iraqis who are trying to get to Australia,' I begin bravely.

'So do I,' he says. 'I bring them from Malaysia to Indonesia.'

We both smile and there is a pause while Abud sips his tea, then he looks at me more intently. 'Yesterday you were talking with twenty-seven people who just arrived from Malaysia.'

'Yes,' I nod.

'These people, I brought them here.'

I suddenly realise what is going on and I begin to feel very bad. I like this guy. I would not want to interfere with his business. 'I am sorry,' I say. 'I really didn't know. I mean, I thought there could be but ... I didn't know it was you. They have not agreed to anything. I won't go near them again.'

I am genuine in my sentiment. My taking Omeid's people is between him and me, but I would not want to get a reputation for doing it to anyone else, except Zaqi perhaps. I am beginning to realise how complicated this business could potentially be. I have only just begun and I'm already standing on toes.

'It's okay, that's not what this is about,' Abud says quite amiably. 'You see, I just want to know if you would like to work together. I agreed to take these people from Malaysia to Australia. I came here to secure a deal with an Indonesian guy who is meant to be taking them from here by boat to Ashmore Reef.'

'Why would you go to Ashmore from Jakarta?' Resa pipes up. 'Christmas Island is much closer.'

Abud looks at Resa. 'I don't know,' he says with a pause, and I realise Abud is like me, he has people and money but he doesn't know what to do next.

'I'm not really sure about this guy,' he continues, 'so if *I* know how to send people from Malaysia to Indonesia, and *you* know how to send them from Indonesia to Australia, why don't we do it together? I have people, you have people. We help each other. We send them all the way in one group, then we split the profits between the four of us.'

We all agree and shake hands. I couldn't be happier. I have had growing concerns embarking on this venture with just Resa and Malik. Abud seems to be a self-assured businessman who knows what he is doing at his end of things. The only stumbling block is that I don't know what I'm doing at my end yet. But I decide this is not the time to confess.

I now have a legitimate partner, who will send me people, twenty-seven of whom are already here to fill our first boat, and if everything goes to plan I might make a little profit and be able to reassure my mother she will be on her way soon.

Abud turns to me. 'There are about fifteen of my people who haven't paid yet.'

'You should get it from them as soon as possible,' I stress. What Abud doesn't know is that these people *asked* to talk to me, so they are at least considering someone other than him.

So Abud and I go to collect their money. They know him from Malaysia so they are happy to see him, and are glad a decision about me is no longer required because he and I are working together.

Several of the fifteen have amounts owing to them in Iran, which they say they will get soon but can't say when. Then a woman takes off her jewellery and hands it to us sobbing. I could never withstand my mother weeping, so I don't do well with this.

But Abud becomes tough. He looks around the group. 'You will have to raise the money or we can't take you.'

I try to do the same but I empathise with their plight too much. 'Wait Abud,' I say, handing the jewellery back. We can't leave them behind like Omeid would and I'm thinking that some money is better than none. 'How much do you all have?'

'One thousand, three hundred dollars for the two of us and three children,' a frightened young man begs, while his wife and little ones look at me with pleading eyes, and I buckle.

'All right, we send you but you have to get the money to us when you get to Australia. We don't take money for the children, so you only owe us seven hundred dollars.' I look at him severely.

He nods. 'Thank you, brother. We promise we send you the money.'

I expect Abud to chastise me, but instead he shrugs. 'Okay,' he says. 'You know what you're doing.'

I wish I did, and that he knew what a moral dilemma every compromise is for me. Each person who doesn't pay is less money to bring my own family here.

All the money is deposited in the safety box at our hotel. Abud goes back to Malaysia to wait for more people, and Resa, Malik and I get to work. Our first thirty are now aware we have the numbers, so the pressure is on. I don't know where to start but Resa does.

'I have a contact for a guy who sells safety jackets and lifebelts. He'll also have maps and a compass.'

'What about a captain?' I ask.

'I can get one. I know people. I have been here a long time,' he says with confidence, making me glad I put up with him.

I discover the closest Australian territories are Christmas Island and Ashmore Reef. While the trip from Jakarta to Christmas Island is very quick, the Sunda Strait is treacherous and the rest of the journey is through the Indian Ocean, which is wild open sea with no land in sight. Whereas with Ashmore Reef, where the sea is flat and it's easy to land, from almost anywhere down the archipelago beyond Surabaya most of the trip is through peaceful waters, amongst islands where you can stop if there is a problem. So despite having to transport people overland to the far reaches of Indonesia, considering the safety implications, we agree we will send our boats to Ashmore Reef.

Resa insists we should depart from Bali, even though I have heard it is crawling with tourists, and therefore unsuitable. But Resa is the one with experience so I go along with it. I need to stay with our two groups in Jakarta, but Malik could be good backup for Resa, so I suggest they go together.

I soon get a call from Resa. There are no appropriate beaches in Bali so they are on a ferry to Lombok. It is four or more hours away. That's the best part of another day gone, and the people here are becoming increasingly restless.

On Lombok there seems to be a problem finding a middleman to help get a boat. Being foreigners evidently we can't just buy one. The only way is to find an Indonesian who, for a price, will buy and register it in his name, then hand over the papers.

I didn't ask but probably Resa found he could no longer use the contacts he thought he had through Omeid, and being relatively spineless in these situations, had retreated. He heard Labuan Bajo is safe to leave from at the moment, so he and Malik are now on their way there.

I still know very little about Indonesia so I go out and buy a map and come back to my room and spread it on the floor. Labuan Bajo is further towards Timor, on the west end of Flores Island. There goes another day or two.

Because he had been in the navy I presumed Resa was well endowed for the job, but now I begin to question if perhaps he hadn't made more of himself than he actually is. I begin to wonder if partly why he wanted Malik and me on board with Omeid was to compensate for his deficits.

While I wait I call Eni and we resume our nightly courtship through Indonesian lessons. Our conversations are still tortuously slow but I persuade her to come in for the day and can't help building up expectations.

We have a long languid lunch and I am beginning to feel secure when she says she has to leave. This is becoming too hard for me. I'm not experienced with these things and I don't know how to handle the uncertainty. Our phone calls are full of tantalising closeness but when I finally get to see her she is like a young filly about to bolt.

I let her go graciously but I decide I will not chase her. Next time I will let her contact me.

It is a relief when Resa calls from Labuan Bajo and I can immerse myself in the business again. He has found a middleman, a boat and a good beach to leave from. The boat will cost $US35000. It seems very expensive to me but I have nothing to compare it with. It is larger than we need but Abud has more people coming through Malaysia, and with a bigger boat we can take them too.

After Resa's call I go to the hotel desk and ask for my safety deposit box. I take it to a quiet corner of the reception area and open it. My stomach churns as I count out the money for the boat. I remember that night with Malik. How easy it would have been to take it and run. I look back into the box. About $US15000 is all that is left to pay for hotels, food, lifejackets, trains, ferries, middleman, captain and bribes. I don't know if it's possible. I hadn't known there were so many things.

I put all the money in a bag and clutching it to me, go out on the street and exchange it for rupiah. I get a better price than at the bank, where I later take it to make a transfer to myself in Labuan Bajo for the boat. To my amazement the teller doesn't blink an eye at the bundles of cash I hand over the counter. Then with the remaining money in my bag I get a taxi to the airport. I buy a ticket to Bali and on to Lombok, where I can get the ferry to Labuan Bajo.

I have told the people back in Jakarta to stay in their hotel rooms, to call my mobile if there are any problems, and to be ready to leave when I get back in a couple of days. I don't trust either Resa or Malik enough to let them go ahead with the deal or handle the money alone, but when I arrive in Labuan Bajo my doubts about Resa dissipate.

It is perfect. A small sleepy fishing village on a picturesque bay filled with islands. Our middleman, Ghalib, is in his fifties. His background is Arabic but his family have been here for generations, so the

Labuan Bajo people and police are happy to deal with him.

Ghalib takes me to an isolated beach outside the town. An old colonial hotel, surrounded by coconut palms, sits on the edge of the sand. A deal has been made with the owners to empty it before our people arrive, so there will be no one to see us loading them into the boats. I collect the $US35000 from the bank and give it to Ghalib, then he shows me our purchase.

We climb on board a large wooden fishing boat, and I check whatever I can think of without admitting I have never been on a boat before. It is solid and well built and I imagine it will stand up well to a storm at sea. Then we sit on the deck amongst tangled fishing nets and work out what needs to be paid to the authorities.

'First there is the navy, because it is their harbour and you only have a permit for fishing,' Ghalib explains. Then, he tells me, there's the police and the harbour authorities. I am shocked so many people are involved, but then I remember Zaqi and his crew standing on the beach while we waited to depart on Omeid's boat. Fortunately for us Labuan Bajo has not yet become a popular place for smugglers, so the price is lower than it could be.

I go back to the main beach as the sun sets between two small islands, turning the still waters of the bay orange and red. The sorrowful call to prayer from a mosque wafts across white, palm-encircled beaches to the arid hillside behind. Looking out at the small fishing boats becalmed in their watery painter's pallet, I wonder if it could possibly be this easy.

After a day and a half's travel I get back to Jakarta and the people are more than happy to see me. After weeks of being cramped into overcrowded rooms, homesick, irritable and afraid, they have begun to bicker and fall out with each other, and are desperate to get going.

I divide them into groups of seven or eight so they will be less noticeable. If they attract attention the police are likely to ask for their ID, and on close inspection find their passports or visas to be false, and arrest them. Then I take them, one group at a time, to the Gambir train station, its lime-green ceramic façade glinting at us in the morning sun. I buy tickets from a scalper on the street, and shepherd the people onto a train to Surabaya, a large port city to the east with wide streets and one of the oldest mosques in Java at its centre.

Resa will meet them there and put them in hotels. Once they have all arrived he will bus them to the port where they will catch a ferry past Madura, Bali, Lombok, Sumbawa, and Komodo of dragon fame, to peaceful Labuan Bajo. Malik will be waiting for them and take them to the hotel overlooking the beach. It is all organised and I have to trust Resa and Malik can carry it off, because I need to stay in Jakarta to receive the last of the people.

When I call Abud in Malaysia to get an update, he says they are not there yet.

'But there is another family waiting in Surabaya,' he adds. 'Get Resa to combine them with our group and collect their money. They only have $US7000 for twelve of them but it will help.'

A few days later Malik calls from Labuan Bajo. 'Resa has collected the family in Surabaya. What about Abud's people from Malaysia?'

'They still haven't arrived.'

'Shall we wait for them?'

'Can you?' I ask hopefully. 'We make nothing on this boat without them.'

'The captain has arrived. Lifejackets, food, everything is on board and ready to go. The police have been paid. Even if the new people arrive in Jakarta tomorrow you still have to get them here.'

When I don't answer he goes on, 'The hotel bill is growing, and tempers are fraying. If we let them go, they will be in Australia in five or six days.'

I sit in silent dread. I wonder how I will tell my mother it might now be many months before I can afford to send for any of them.

'Let the boat go,' I say finally, and hang up. I sit on the bed staring blankly. In terms of my family's plight the whole venture has been pointless.

It has not been as easy as I had thought it would be and now the stress will really begin. We are unlikely to hear anything until the boat arrives at Ashmore Reef. Resa and Malik want to wait in Bali, so I am alone in Jakarta. I stay in my room for the rest of the day, licking my wounds, then at six o'clock the phone rings. I jump upon it expecting bad news, but it is Eni. The sweetness of her voice washes over me and nothing she has done in the past seems to matter.

Despite not having spoken for some weeks, we talk in our usual friendly manner, with her correcting my every second word. I grin at how she dares to go where no one else would tread, and how much I enjoy it. If it was my mother we would be at blows by now. I have my usual problems understanding what she is saying but my Indonesian is getting better, and before long I realise she has rung to tell me she is coming to Jakarta tomorrow.

I am desperate to see her but it will be difficult without telling her what is going on, and it is unlikely to improve our already unstable courtship if I share it with her. Not that Indonesians think badly of smuggling. They have no personal experience with it because they don't need to escape their own country. When they hear terrible stories they just think it is the result of police corruption, which they know exists. But Eni would know it is a dangerous and unpredictable business and I instinctively sense I will never be able to tell her about the work I do.

I invite her to lunch, after which I decide I will take her to the seashore at Dunia Fantasi. I usually go there to be alone, but I suddenly feel I want to share it with her.

Over lunch she takes my hand in her usual way, wiping away my anxiety about the boat with a surge of desire. We linger over cups of tea and she seems bright and happy as I tell her in my broken Indonesian how much I enjoy seeing her. But as I pay the bill she says she has to go, killing my fantasy of wandering hand in hand along the lovers' boardwalk by the sea.

Perhaps the extra pressure I am under makes her erratic behaviour harder to deal with, but I am raw to the new emotions she generates in me and I don't have the resilience for her changeability. 'I can't cope with this,' I say with all sincerity. 'I have to finish it.'

She doesn't argue, just backs away, but then at the door she turns and I see tears in her eyes. I am swamped with confusion and regret, but I know for self-preservation it is how it has to be.

And so the stress of waiting to hear news of the boat returns. As the days go by I eat less, and drink more coffee. I pace the streets and three days pass with nothing. I should hear something tomorrow or the next day. But no news. Eight days go by and still there is silence. I am now convinced some disaster has occurred, and the feeling of responsibility for the lives of all those people is appalling. This is mixed with getting over Eni. She had filled a void, which is now empty again and I am angry.

On the ninth day I go to the Atrium and sit in my old coffee haunt. I stare vacantly down to the entrance where Malik and I used to watch the girls come in to shop. I become aware of a pretty, shiny-haired girl looking back at me, and when she catches my gaze she gestures that she would like to join me. I nod and in no time she is sitting at my table. I buy her coffee and I chat in my limited Indonesian, shamelessly using phrases Eni has taught me. Then, in an attempt to distract myself from escalating anxiety and to quell the loss of Eni, I invite the shiny-haired girl to spend the day with me.

By the afternoon she is happy to come to my room and we have several exquisite hours of sex. I am lying on my back limp and satiated, her smooth languid body draped over mine, when the phone rings. I reach for it and see an Indonesian number I don't know. It can't be someone from the boat, they have to be long gone from these waters by now.

'Hello,' a man says, 'it is Thalma.'

Thalma was on the boat. He is an Iraqi I knew when I was living in Iran.

'Thalma!' I exclaim in a panic. 'Why are you still in Indonesia?'

'We have big problem.'

My heart sinks.

'The seas were metres high with strong winds. Most of the people have never been on a boat before so they were terrified. Then a man you had let on the boat for free took too much food for his children, and the squabbles that had begun on land erupted.'

I lie frozen as his words tumble out.

'They formed two groups and started yelling and bashing each other. No one could speak Indonesian and the crew couldn't speak Arabic, so the young captain had no way of knowing what was going on and became frightened. We were passing Raijua Island and one group told him to stop, so he did.'

'Oh, no,' I whisper. I remember from my map Raijua is a tiny, remote island between Sumba and West Timor. I had heard the beaches are surrounded by rocks and heavy surf. I just want to hang up but instead I ask tentatively, 'Is everyone all right?'

'Well, yes … but the boat isn't.'

I can feel my blood running cold. I await his next words with dread.

'We landed on a beach with rocks. We all got off the boat but the island is tiny with small villages, so there was nowhere for all of us to hide, and the police soon picked us up.'

'Thalma, what about the boat?' I say, hardly breathing.

'The captain and crew left it on the beach. It was soon squalling and the wind began swinging the boat left and right and left, crashing it on the rocks until it smashed. And then it sank.'

Thirty-five thousand American dollars gone to the bottom of the sea. I want to be sick.

I get up, forgetting the shiny-haired girl as she slips off my sweaty body and onto the tangled sheets.

'What is it?' she says tenderly.

'My father is dead,' I reply, instinctively looking for something as catastrophic as this. She believes me and leaves with a gentle kiss.

I stand naked in the middle of the room, staring out at the thick pall of smog hanging over Jakarta's multi-level roofs. I feel myself descending into a crater of despair.

I call Resa and tell him what has happened.

'It is not our fault,' he responds immediately and I can tell he is going to be no help.

'How much money is left from the people who paid you in Surabaya?' I ask.

'Nothing. It's all spent.'

I am shocked, but this is no time for a dispute. When I try to call him later he has switched off his phone. Then he disappears, with no way for me to find him. Resa, after all, is finally showing his colours.

So I am left with Malik, who at least comes back to Jakarta to try and be of help. But of course he has no money. In Malaysia Abud says simply, 'Let them drink from the sea,' an Arabic saying which means 'Let them go to hell, it is not my problem.'

'We send them, they want to fight, what can I do?' he adds. 'I'm not a millionaire, every time they argue with each other they expect us to send them again?'

'Well, we have to fix the problem,' I say shortly and hang up.

As I stand wondering what to do now I am struck by an apprehension that I had not anticipated. With my first boatload of asylum seekers now in the hands of the authorities, my name will be known. When asked who their smuggler was, considering their circumstances, these people are unlikely to be concerned about passing on information about me. At this point I am unsure what this means, but I am aware that what began as a well-meaning and good idea to solve a personal problem has potentially pitched me back into a life on the run.

To save money I take advantage of the deal I struck for a free room and food at the hotel the people were staying at. Malik moves in with me but he is little support. He is happy to go along but not to take responsibility. He manages to put it all out of his head and just eats, sleeps and goes with women. It makes me so angry I start swearing at him.

Every day the people call me and I am so mad at them I can hardly speak. 'I will try to send you again, but stop calling me,' I yell. 'You got yourselves into this situation, so don't give me a headache or I will switch off my phone too.' This scares them.

'Okay,' Thalma says on everyone's behalf, 'we are sorry. We trust you.' This only makes me feel worse because I don't know what I can do.

Then I begin to discover that some of them have money but are denying it. This fuels my rage. It is hard to imagine why, in a situation like this, they won't help each other, but I had not lived in Iraq during the worst of the sanctions. More evil than Saddam, this inhuman penalty imposed on us by the rest of the world to punish him left hundreds of thousands of ordinary Iraqis watching powerless as their children died of disease and starvation. I heard UNICEF estimate half a million children have died already. It is worse than war, where you get shot and that's the end. With sanctions you suffer every day, starving slowly to death.

So perhaps it is not unexpected that they would protect only themselves and their young, hiding their food and money. But what I find worse is that they give up. The boat is completely destroyed so they don't think, We must get another one. Instead they just crumple. But by the time they have escaped Iraq their money is their life, if they lose it they lose everything. Maybe if they knew that tomorrow they would be in Australia they would be generous, but the uncertainty makes survival utterly tenuous.

Before long, the police move our people from Raijua to Savu, a slightly larger island to the east. They are afraid, and now entirely at the mercy of the police, who can tell them nothing because they speak no Arabic.

Several days later they are given to the navy, who take them to Kupang in West Timor, and put in detention. They find about two hundred Afghanis there in custody. The Afghanis had paid their smuggler, who put them on his boat to Kupang, unloaded them there, then ran away with their money. Resa's phone being turned off has made the Iraqis afraid they are facing the same fate.

In panic Thalma calls me again. Kupang is a small, depressed outpost and cannot afford to look after this influx, so the police have asked the United Nations to pay for their shelter, and now the people must apply to the UN for formal processing. They are desperate to escape before this happens.

They have heard that less than two percent ever get resettled through the UN, often not in their country of choice, and most of the rest languish in detention for anything up to fifteen years, while their lives leach away and their children grow up without a country, education or liberty. So now I start getting calls from America, Iraq, Syria, Jordan, Iran and Europe, where they have friends and relatives. 'Please help these people.'

And some from Australia, where family await their arrival. 'What is happening? Can't you do something? Please.'

The pressure is becoming extreme and all the while I am worrying about my own family. But I can't help feeling sorry for the people despite their apparent stupidity. They behaved badly, but they have come from decades of brutality and war, which brings out the best and the worst in people. I identify with those it renders dysfunctional. Even now, when I think of my brother Ahmad it tears at my soul and threatens to make me behave irrationally.

Two weeks have passed with no progress. I go back to the hotel after breakfast, carrying coffee for Malik. He is still in bed. He has been out all night and has little to contribute, but at least he tries to be attentive to my struggle.

'Resa could have stayed around to take his share of this,' I say, sitting on the edge of his bed.

'He wouldn't be much use,' Malik mumbles, half asleep.

'Well, he knows more than us. He worked with Omeid and had experience in the navy.'

'That was bullshit. He was never in the navy, he doesn't know about the sea. The boat shouldn't have left while the monsoons were starting.'

I gape at Malik. 'You mean those people had good reason to get off the boat?'

Malik shrugs. 'High seas might have made things worse. And he got a captain from Jakarta, who wouldn't have known those waters.'

I stare at Malik and shake my head. I shouldn't be surprised, but I am rocked by Resa's lies. Could this disaster have been avoided if it hadn't been for his deceptions?

I need to get out of the hotel room. I go downstairs and catch a taxi without knowing where I want to go. 'Dunia Fantasi,' I blurt with a hankering for escape. But when I see the big dipper there is none of the usual joy. I buy a ticket then give it to a kid. I am out of my depth and don't know what to do. I want to walk away but I can't leave sixty-nine of Saddam's victims in a prison in Kupang.

Overlooking a small stretch of reclaimed seashore near the fun park is a line of kiosks with chairs and tables under the shade of tall palm trees. I buy a fresh coconut and take it down to the nearby rocks, which have been neatly piled along the coast to hold back the sea.

I sit on the edge where foam and debris lap the rough black boulders and stare out at the ocean. Small fishing boats bob on the choppy brown water. I want to be that little boy on my father's shoulders again, and I want to be in my own country where I understand the rules.

My homesickness makes my body ache.

Behind me lovers wander along the boardwalk, and I smart at the thought that I could have shared this with Eni. But then I am reminded of Intisar and our foiled love affair, and a deeper pain sets in. I sip at my fresh coconut juice and squint into the wind as it gusts salty sea-spray into my eyes and I am not sure if I am crying.

THE CARDS WE ARE DEALT

After an hour or so, with hands deep in my pockets, like those restless days when I had my gang on the streets of Diwaniyah, I head west towards the old port of Sunda Kelapa and its amazing collection of brightly painted wooden sailing ships. They tower over me as I walk along the heavy timber slabs that make up the wharf. I stop to gaze upon one spectacular vessel, when my phone rings. It is Abud, calling from Malaysia.

'In a few days I am sending you sixteen Iranians,' he says, completely out of the blue. 'Each one will pay you $US3000. I didn't take any money from them for my end of things, so that you can collect the lot and organise another boat for the stranded people.'

I stand listening to the wind slapping ropes on the masts, and wooden hulls groaning against their moorings. With that amount of money I can easily pull the show back on the road and get everyone out together. I had planned only to take Iraqis, but we had been given sanctuary when we most needed it by the Iranians, and they too have suffered hideously under their regime.

'Thank you, Abud,' I finally say, my spirits already lifting.

'There's also $US9000 left from getting those last people to Jakarta. I'll wire it to you. It was to be divided amongst us all, but take it to fix the problem.'

My head is whirling but there is more.

'And the Iraqis you were waiting for before the boat left are on their way. They couldn't afford passports so I put them on a fishing boat to Sumatra last night. There are only twelve and they don't have much money, but altogether this might get you on your feet.'

Somehow I am not surprised. I had thought Abud was a good man. I was more surprised when he had refused to help.

'Thank you, Abud,' I say in a daze.

In one short but miraculously well-timed phone call my problems appear to be solved. I jump in a taxi to my hotel, but then change my mind and head back to Dunia Fantasi. I buy a ticket for the big dipper with the relish of a child, and climb on board with a bunch of excited children. As we fly around that crazy maze of slow climbs and manic descents I throw back my head, and with the wind in my hair and relief in my heart I scream with the kids at the top of my adult voice.

That night I call my mother and tell her to get Khalid ready to go. Khalid is the obvious first. Of my surviving brothers, Asad is still in jail and Basim needs time to recover from his brutal incarceration, whereas Khalid is young, fit and employable. He will be able to get a job in Australia to prepare for the family's arrival and to support them.

My mother's brother Karim, who I idolised when I had my gang, and who was hit in the head with shrapnel during the Shiite uprising, is also on the run and she wants him to travel with Khalid. Some of the people on the boat who couldn't pay the full amount have money owing them in Iran, so my share can be passed directly to Khalid to buy their tickets and passports. Via a somewhat circuitous route, my original objective is becoming a reality.

Next morning at breakfast, while I am telling Malik the news, the phone rings. It is one of the twelve Iraqis who are being smuggled overland.

'We are on a bus travelling through Sumatra,' a man says in a subdued voice.

'That's good. When will you be in Jakarta? I'll be there to meet you,' I reply brightly.

'That is uncertain.'

Then that dreaded pause. My joy dissipates before I even hear the words.

'The police have caught us.'

After such a high last night I almost want to shout at him, 'How could you let that happen?' But I remember my many failed attempts to get into Iran, and then of course there was Turkey, the defeat we felt, and the fear of what was going to happen, especially for those with children or families left behind. So instead I say, 'Don't worry, we'll work something out. Just keep in contact with me until you arrive in Jakarta.'

I know the police won't deal direct with me. I am a foreigner with minimal language skills and no fixed address. So I need to find someone else to do it, and Francesca is the obvious choice. She is capable, tough, and while she is Chinese, she sounds Indonesian. The main impediment to the idea is that she is Resa's girlfriend. But as we are still partners I will have to deal with him eventually, if he turns up.

I call Francesca, and fortunately there is no sign of Resa. I promise her another lunch and she happily agrees to help. So with me side-coaching she calls the police. She negotiates them down to $US200 each, but it is still too much for the Iraqis.

'The police won't let you go for any less,' I tell their spokesman on another phone. 'So you will have to stay on the bus. Where are they taking you?'

'To Immigration in Jakarta, where they will decide whether to take us to the UN or prison.' The man is clearly terrified.

'Okay, keep calm, and when you get to Jakarta call me.'

I know it is a long drive through Sumatra to where they cross the Sunda Strait to Java, then more bus hours to Jakarta. It occurs to me that on these kinds of journeys everyone is exhausted, including the custodians. In my experience, after several days together a certain camaraderie can develop, and the demarcation between the guards and the guarded blurs. So when someone wants to stop for the toilet or food everyone is fairly relaxed about it and the guards are not like Nazis, but let them wander freely and attend to their needs.

So when they are finally approaching Jakarta and call me, I say, 'I know you are tired and scared but I'm going to ask you to challenge yourselves. Are there women and children?'

'All men, except for one family.'

'Okay, I need you to really have courage.'

'What do we have to do?'

'Can you all run?'

'Yes, it's easy to run.'

'All right, as you come into Jakarta you have to get word around the bus. Someone has to tell the police they need to go to the toilet and another wants to buy a drink. When the bus stops you all get off, then in small groups of twos and threes you make a run for it. Not all in the same direction, scatter separately. One group go left, one go right, to create maximum confusion. For a couple of minutes you will have surprise on your side so go as fast as you can. When you stop running you call me with your locations, then I will drive around and collect you.'

There is silence, then a tentative 'We will do it.'

Unsure of how many more lunches I can take Francesca to without complications arising, I offer to pay her for her green van, and she agrees. I had planned to put Malik at the wheel but Francesca knows her way around Jakarta, so I am relieved when she says she will drive.

We are waiting and ready when we get a call giving us the general location. We speed off through as many backstreets and short cuts as Francesca can find. Before long individual calls start coming and we begin circling the area, with me perched in the back, ready to pull them in.

'We are behind a food vendor by a telephone box on the main street near the mall.'

'What is the street called?'

'We don't know.'

'You have to find out!'

'We can't see a sign!'

'It's okay,' Francesca shouts from the front, 'I got them.'

She swerves into the kerb and brakes as I throw open the door. Three young Arab men jump in and I yank it closed.

'We are hiding behind rubbish on the street in front of the markets.'

Francesca, hunched over the wheel, drives madly through the traffic. She soon locates the markets and two men run towards us. I haul them inside and the door flies shut again.

They are wild-eyed and pumped with adrenaline and fear. I praise them and try to settle them down but I am as nervous as they are until we have got them all.

Once we have ten, there is only the man with the family to go.

'I don't think he will come,' one of the men says. 'He has a wife and two children. I didn't see them run.'

They have his mobile number, so I take the risk and call. 'What are you doing? We are waiting for you.'

'I called my brother in Germany. He said not to run. He said it's better to let them take us to the UN to be processed. Once they are sure we are refugees they will send us to Australia on an airplane.'

I try telling him it is more likely his children will have grown up behind wire before he is put on any airplane and resettled anywhere. But he won't listen so I give up. 'Please yourself,' I say. 'But why do you think so many people risk going on boats if it is so easy with the UN?'

He doesn't answer.

'There would be no need for people smugglers if the UN did what your brother says.'

He remains silent. I feel sorry for him, torn between someone he trusts and someone on the ground, but I can't risk the police spotting us and endangering everyone else, so I wish him luck and tell Francesca to go.

When we reach the hotel there is another problem. They of course have no passports, and I made no deal, so I have to give the receptionist money to let them stay. I am already eating into our budget, but I am on a high. We have beaten the police and have got these people to safety. I feel on top of things.

Next morning there is a devastating blow. Unbeknown to me and forgotten by Francesca, her mobile phone is with a company that registers your details with the government. The police have her number from when she called to negotiate with them, and now they know who she is and where she lives.

No doubt humiliated by our tactics, they start calling her and demand double the money they had previously asked for. We consider ignoring them but we both know this is not going to go away, and soon they will work out who she is in cahoots with, and be on my tail as well. I decide to give the police half, and see if that will keep them quiet. It does for the moment, but they make it clear they will be back for the rest.

Amidst this wrangle, Abud's sixteen Iranians arrive at the airport. They have passports, so there is no problem getting them into the hotel, but they don't all pay the agreed $US3000. We are getting used to this. It is usually the majority that don't have the full fare.

So I now have twenty-six people ready to go, and even after paying the police we still have a reasonable stash in my safety deposit box, but strangely, this is where I have a lapse of faith. Or perhaps it is a flash of commonsense.

To get everyone on the one boat I would have to transport the twenty-six overland to Labuan Bajo and co-ordinate this with getting the Kupang people out of jail to meet them there. This kind of manoeuvre requires a team of professionals. If Resa doesn't show up again it is just Malik and me.

I hear Zaqi needs more people for a boat he has ready to leave Jakarta for Christmas Island. Unlike me, he is an old hand at this dangerous but short route. I begin thinking the unthinkable. If I could negotiate a deal for the twenty-six that would leave enough money to get the others out of Kupang on a separate boat, it would probably give everyone their best chance. Abud and Malik agree, so despite the distaste it causes me, I call Zaqi.

'How many people have you got?' he asks matter-of-factly.

'Twenty-six. I will give you $US10 000.'

'No, too cheap.'

'It's all there is. Hotels and everything else is paid. It's just for the day at sea. I have people stranded in Kupang that I have to get out.' Then I swallow my pride and add, 'I need your help.'

There is a long pause. Then, 'Okay, I help you. You bring the money tomorrow to the Beja Hotel at three pm.'

So Malik and I go to meet him and make an agreement. He will let me know the location of the boat in the next few days. I give him the money and leave feeling the weight of responsibility lifting. But Zaqi never calls, then after two days he switches off his phone.

Maybe this is payback for getting our money back from Omeid, I don't know, but I do know I have just lost $US10 000 and I am seething. I want to hunt Zaqi down, but so long as my family is unprotected in Iran I have to be careful. In these circles reprisals against them could easily be carried out, even on another continent.

As I sit in the hotel room like a kid who has lost his ball I have to face that it was an ill-conceived idea, and try to put Zaqi behind me as an unfortunate setback. I can hardly lie around and brood while twenty-six people, whose money I have just lost, are in their rooms in a nearby hotel depending on me. Not to speak of the sixty-nine waiting in Kupang.

As I am trying to find a way to get back on the horse, Thalma, who has been keeping me up to date with the people in Kupang, calls. 'Plenty of boats are going from here to Australia. It's only a couple of days to Ashmore Reef, where the sea is flat and it's easy to land. And there are hardly any police.'

I tend not to believe him. The police are always lurking somewhere with their hands out, but the people from the first boat are already there and ready to go, that is, if I can get them out of detention. And I would not have to move them to Labuan Bajo if we could leave from Kupang.

'We are not in a jail,' Thalma adds, 'they put us in the Police Training School and we can come and go as we please.'

This is music to my ears. I go to the hotel where both the Jakarta groups are staying. I tell them to pack up and prepare to get going. I instruct Malik to meet Khalid and my Uncle Karim when they arrive, and send them on by plane to Kupang when it's time.

Within a few hours we are all on the train speeding through the hot starless night to Surabaya. When we arrive I bus them to a hotel and then I get a room in another place around the corner. Next morning I go to the port to find out when the ferry leaves for Kupang.

I stare out from the terminal to a long wharf where an enormous pale yellow and white ship bound for the island of Madura is being loaded by lines of barefooted men. They carry huge piles of heavy goods on their heads, up the steep ramp and into the hull like ants. At the bottom of the ramp police, coastguards and security are watching their every move. Thalma may be right about Kupang but it is not looking good in Surabaya.

I find the ticket office and check out the price and timetable. There is a ferry to Kupang leaving tomorrow. With no other Arabs around I already stand out, so I know I will draw attention with a group of twenty-six. The closer we get to remote islands, the more the authorities are going to be watching. So I deliberately linger a little too long and soon get approached by two port policemen. I take the risk and tell them I have a group of Middle Eastern tourists who want to go to Kupang.

After a quick discussion between them, they turn back to me with a price which is more than twice what I was quoted at the ticket office. The extra is clearly for them and their protection. Whatever it takes. If I pay half now they agree to take care of things and I can give them the rest tomorrow.

I head back to the hotel happy I can give the people the good news that we will be leaving in the morning. I go straight upstairs and knock on the first of their doors, but no one answers. I move from one to the next getting faster as I go, but no one is there. I am both annoyed and worried they might have gone out against my instructions, but when I get back to the lobby the receptionist is waiting for me.

'The people are gone,' she says, obviously distressed at having to deliver such bad news. 'While you were away the police arrested all twenty-six of them.'

'Is there no end to this?' I say to myself, and she politely shakes her head.

My body sags and I am swamped with inertia. I go back out onto the street, where cars and motorscooters stream by, filling my nostrils with exhaust fumes. I look blindly into the busy road, my mind wandering aimlessly through a life unfulfilled until it finally lodges without logic on that day when I was ten, waiting at the palace gates for Umi to return from confronting Saddam Hussein, face to face, to save my father. And I am ashamed.

I square my shoulders and draw my lifeless body back into shape. I will never know who betrayed us but there is no point dwelling on it, or trying to understand what kind of person would want to further punish people who are fleeing persecution, especially when everyone along the line is making money out of them.

I'm pretty sure I paid the police at the port enough that they wouldn't have informed on me. So I take a chance, go back, and tell them what has happened. They won't give my money back but they do tell me the people are being taken to Kupang, and then advise me to make myself scarce.

Now everyone for my next boat is in custody. But at least, I think, trying to stay positive, they are all going to be on the one island, without me having to ship them there. So I head for the airport and buy a ticket to Kupang. I have no idea what I am going to do when I get there. I have no clue.

Kupang is the small, provincial, predominantly Christian capital of West Timor, which has its own share of turmoil. There were recently anti-Muslim riots, and it was also an important location for the Indonesian militia during the conflict in East Timor. And from what I can see, despite Thalma's assurances, all the forces still have an ongoing presence here.

With the help of a taxi driver I find a comfortable enough hotel in the main part of town.

'Where are you from?' he asks and I am pleased to engage. At the moment he is the only person I know who is not in custody in this remote outpost. His name is Wayan.

'I'm Iraqi. I'm just here for a holiday.'

Despite his apparently premature receding hairline he is a young, friendly guy, with that distant look of hope that one day something will happen to change his life for him. So when we get to the hotel I ask if he can wait for me and show me around.

My intention is to try and get Wayan relaxed enough to inadvertently give me information about the sixty-nine people from our boat wreck.

'I stay,' he says, happy to get the business. Kupang is desperately poor and in need of tourists so the locals can't do enough to please. He lights up a cigarette while I check into the hotel, shower and change.

When I return Wayan drives me down the potholed main street, with its rather downmarket collection of retail businesses, restaurants, government buildings, hotels, and workshops offering bottles of petrol and motorbike repairs. The road leads to the foreshore where the city looks out over the flat calm waters of Kupang Bay, which is circled by distant forested hills.

We head out of town to the port where the ferries arrive from Surabaya, then back past a sandy beach with fishing boats of all sizes swaying on their moorings. We stop at a large restaurant under an open pavilion, which sits on a point looking out over the bay. It is clearly a tourist destination so I ask Wayan if he can take me to where the Kupang people eat.

If he gets a cut for bringing tourists here he doesn't show it. He quite happily drives me further along the foreshore to a small family restaurant on a dusty road opposite the Kristal Hotel. We sit under a low tin roof on a dirt floor with the owners and their kids. Uncooked food is displayed in a glass cabinet and barbequed over glowing embers in an oil drum cut in two. I try to chat in my budding Bahasa as we drink avocado juice and watch our marinated chicken being basted with a sweet sauce over the fire.

When it is cooked we eat inside at a small table amongst a few local people. The young wife brings the chicken with steaming hot rice, fresh vegetables, salad, barbequed tofu, and finger bowls.

'Is there an Arabic disco in Kupang?' I ask Wayan as we eat.

'No, not in Kupang.' He laughs.

'Why not? There are plenty of Arabic people coming here for holidays.'

'No, there is not. We only see them when they are stuck here in the police.'

'What do you mean, stuck in the police?'

'These Arabic people come here to go to Australia.'

'Which people?'

'Iraqi people. Sixty or seventy of them. Their boat sank.'

It didn't sink, they left it to wreck, I stop myself from saying by concentrating on my food. 'Can you show me these people?' I ask, knowing I am getting into dangerous territory, but Wayan goes on blithely without suspicion.

'Yes, I can show you.'

We drive the short distance back into town and come to a street where a solid concrete building with high windows and large double front doors sits on a quiet corner. Wayan drives slowly towards it.

'It used to be a school or something but now they use it to keep the Iraqis.'

There is a sadness to his voice that prepares me for what I see. It is close to sunset and they sit outside like people who have lost their children. Even the faces I remember from Abu Ghraib had more hope in them than these. Despair has taken over and they have abandoned any prospect of a future. It is terrible to see.

'Wayan, can you stop the car?'

I get out and stand for a moment watching them, but if they see me they don't register. They have given up any prospect that I would come for them. I can't help seeing my own family when we were adrift in the refugee camp in Duhok.

I walk cautiously through the gate, remembering how alive they were back in Jakarta when they agreed to come with me instead of Omeid. A little girl playing aimlessly in the dust stands up and comes over. Wide-eyed, she gazes up at me and I forget Wayan is watching and pick her up tenderly. She touches my face and whispers, 'I knew you would come.'

I restrain myself from telling her, 'I don't know what I can do.' And then I look at those desperate people and I want to yell at them, 'Why did you argue? Why did you get off the boat and let it smash to pieces on the rocks? Why didn't you help each other like I said?' But instead I walk towards the parents with a lump in my throat and hand them their little girl and they look at me as if

I have just come down from the sky.

They hug me and others begin running my way; some are weeping, some laughing. For a moment I am exhilarated by their glee, but then I come back to my senses and tell them urgently, 'Stop, or you are going to get me caught like you. Please, go back to where you were, keep quiet and act normally.'

I look around at their hope dissolving again and quickly add, 'I'm not leaving. I'll do something, just be patient. I will contact you by Thalma's phone.'

Thalma has just appeared, beaming, but I wave him away and hurry back to Wayan's taxi, hoping I have not already been seen, and that Wayan will not report my behaviour to some official.

Back in the car Wayan looks at me questioningly. 'So you know these people?'

'I know them from back home, and some of their families called me to come and see them because I have business in Indonesia. I work in timber. Import and export.'

'The guy who tried to send them to Australia was really stupid.'

I want to leap to my own defence and tell him that for my part I'd done a pretty good job. 'How?' I ask, wearing it instead.

'It wasn't hard to see it was the wrong weather. He used the wrong captain, the wrong crew. He didn't know who to deal with or what he was doing.'

I curse Resa under my breath. If he had really been in the navy he would have at least known some of these things. But it is not entirely his fault, we were all novices.

'Do you know the right people? Someone who can help this lot?'

'Yeah, I know a guy. Hadjib Mohammad.'

'What does he do exactly?'

'He's a fisherman.'

'Can I meet him?'

'Yeah, no problem.'

That I would find the right man through a taxi driver within a few hours of being here is all too incredible. But of course it is a small community.

We meet in the lobby of an inconspicuous hotel in the centre of town. Hadjib Mohammad is in his fifties and seems to know what he is doing. There are no games, he is straight up. But of course I am desperate, and you can never tell in these brief meetings, when you don't speak the language well, what is really going on. I am Arabic, so no matter how civil they are to me I will always be an outsider to the Indonesians.

When I ask how much he would charge to take the whole group of ninety-five to Australia, he says $US20 000.

It makes me ill to think of how much we paid for the first boat. Hadjib's offer is $US15 000 less.

'Is that for them all?' I ask cautiously. 'There are sixty-nine and another group of twenty-six on their way from Surabaya with the police.'

'All of them.'

'That's good.' I pause and take a breath. 'But I don't have $US20 000.' After losing $US10 000 to Zaqi, then the hotels, planes, trains and buses, I only have $US15 000 left for a boat. 'I will owe you $US5000, if you trust me?' I tell him.

'I will trust you,' he says, looking me straight in the eye.

'But I don't pay one dollar until they arrive in Australia.'

'Okay, when they arrive in Australia and you hear the news, then you pay me.'

'What happens about the police, and transport to the beach?'

'I'll do all that and then charge you for it. Police, bus and every-thing, about $US2000.'

'Okay,' I say, thinking that it is cheaper than I anticipated. Maybe Thalma was right about Kupang. 'When do you send them?'

'The day after tomorrow, or the next day. From here, one or two days to Ashmore Reef.'

We shake hands and I walk out feeling lighter. Both groups could be in Australia in the next few days. I want to sing. The unfixable has been fixed.

Wayan drives me back to the hotel and I pay him twice what is on the meter. As soon as I get to my room I call Thalma and tell him they will be leaving in the next couple of days. He repeats it loudly and there is an outburst of joy. I get goosebumps at the sound of their excitement and relief.

One day slips by, and then another and another. For me these three days are like three years, as my fears that something will go wrong grow and flourish. Thalma has told me that a lot of the police already know about the deal, but I don't know if Hadjib has paid enough. I am not entirely sure Hadjib knows either, but I have no experience by which to judge him. Maybe the police will just take the money and put me in jail; no one knows I'm here so they could do whatever they want with me. I am just a refugee.

On the morning of the fourth day Hadjib finally calls. 'Everything is organised. Tomorrow they will go to Australia.'

'What about the Surabaya people?'

'They have arrived. Some are with the navy, the rest are with the police. I will organise it.'

I breathe a sigh of relief.

I call Thalma and tell him to get his group ready. Then on the spur of the moment I ask Thalma if he would be interested in staying and working with me. Now that I have found Hadjib, maybe next time things will be easier, and the way it is looking we will need someone who speaks Arabic to replace Resa.

'You seem to know your way around here, and you could work with Hadjib while I am in Jakarta,' I say. 'If you stay I will take your wife and kids to Australia for free, if that is what you want.' I remember when Omeid made me the same offer, how you will do anything to save your own flesh and blood.

I am not entirely sure I trust Thalma, he is from a decidedly bad background. I've heard he robbed the shop he worked at in Iran and ran away to Pakistan. But because he needs me and I need him, he will probably be okay. He says he will think about it. Then I call Malik and tell him to send Khalid and my Uncle Karim.

When they get off the plane I realise Khalid is no longer a boy but a man, who has been shouldering the burden of supporting the family. As I put my arms around him my uncle watches smiling. We only have one day together, then they have to cross an ocean with strangers to an unknown land, and as with each time we separate, we might never see each other again.

Wayan takes us back to the family restaurant and leaves us to talk away the night, reminiscing and laughing until it is almost dawn. The owners pack up and go to bed, leaving us under the lean-to out the front in rickety chairs, beside the smouldering barbeque.

At seven o'clock the next evening three buses collect the people. I get Wayan to take Khalid, my uncle and me in his taxi. We drive out of town a short distance behind the buses, past the ferry terminal and along a winding road lined with palms and thatched huts nestled amongst the leafy folds of banana trees. It is dark by the time we turn onto a rough dirt track, banked on either side with high grass and scrubby trees. The tail lights of the buses bob in front of us but otherwise we could be lost in the wilderness.

Eventually the foliage opens out and we pull up in a sandy clearing. I can see in our headlights the people hurrying off the buses. But as I watch them, I don't see any of the ten we rescued off the bus from Sumatra.

I leap out of the taxi and run to the beach, where I grab Hadjib and yell, 'Where are the other people?'

'Some are still in jail,' he replies sheepishly. 'The navy has them. I couldn't get them out.'

'You agreed to get them all! That was your job.' I am holding him by the shoulders and am inches from his face. 'Why didn't you tell me?'

I want to hit him because there is no one else to blame, but I turn away. Flashlights slash the beach as dark shapes clamber onto small boats, their motors idling in the shallows. Hadjib stands tentatively by. No doubt he has done his best, but this is a royal fuck-up.

'Do you want me to stop the boat?' he asks hesitantly, looking out into the dark where the large vessel lies waiting. 'I don't know if we can get the other people unless you have plenty more money, which you told me you don't have.'

What can I say? Hadjib's contacts probably didn't extend beyond the police. He was not to know one group would be kept by the navy.

'It will cost a lot more to get another boat,' I retort. I am digging a hole so deep I will never be able to get out, and every dollar spent leaves the rest of my family more resolutely behind. But to delay these people again would be more than they could take. 'Let it go,' I say, trying to simmer down.

Khalid appears and I put my arm around his shoulder. 'Are you ready?' I long to keep him with me, but someone has to go first, plus he will be the one to take over the family if anything happens to me. I look around for my uncle.

'Where are your passports?' I ask. 'I know how bad this feels when you have never had one before, but you can't keep them. The Australians won't believe you are refugees if you have one. If you are being persecuted or chased by your government they would not have given you a passport, and if you tell the Australians it is false, they'll say you are a criminal. It is better to have nothing.'

I can see Khalid's fear growing. I don't want to frighten him more, but I need to prepare him with what little I know.

'If the people on the boat say you are the smuggler's brother, make sure you tell the Australians you never took money from any of them, that you only spent one day with me, and that you are an asylum seeker just like everyone else on the boat.'

He nods as the reality of what might await him hits.

'It will be okay,' I say with a final hug. 'I will get Umi and the others to you as fast as I can.'

It is almost dawn by the time I get back to the hotel. I don't know how many police would now know I am involved in this venture but I do know it would be prudent for me to stay on the move. So I check out and get Wayan to take me to the Kristal Hotel. They have more of a hotchpotch of internationals, and I will be less conspicuous. I get a room with a view over the bay and sit at the window smoking cigarettes, expecting any minute to see the coastguard shepherding my boat back through the early-morning waters.

After a day and night on coffee and cigarettes I am strung out and shaking like an addict, when I get a call from a guy in Australia whose family is on the boat.

'I just saw my wife and kids on TV,' he shouts down the phone. 'They've arrived! They are on Ashmore Reef.'

'Thank you for letting me know,' I say with a surge of relief. 'I am very glad. So now, what about the money you owe me for sending them?'

He had pleaded with me, and relying on his promise I let his wife and two kids on the boat for no charge. One was just a baby and I even paid for its nappies, yet now I hear him hesitate.

'I have no money.'

I know what is going on. He thinks I am rich because I am a people smuggler: the people line up, I take their money, put them on a boat, and make a big profit. There is no way he will believe that I am so in debt that I will have to get another boat up before I can pay back the people left in Kupang with the navy. There is no point going there.

A few days later Afrah calls. She has a message from Khalid. He is in detention somewhere in the desert, in a place called Woomera, but hopefully not for too long. I am happy. I have achieved my first objective. Only five more of my family to go.

I pay Hadjib Mohammad, shake hands and assure him I will send the rest as soon as I get more people for the next boat. I say goodbye to Thalma, who has taken up my offer to stay and work with us. Then I call the people left in jail and promise to do what I can, but I hear the disappointment in their voices. The boat they should have been on is already in Australia. It wasn't my fault they were arrested, everyone embarking on this journey knows the odds, but as I get on a plane to Jakarta I am full of angst at not having been able to get them there.

UNSPOKEN BONDS

Once the boat landed in Australia the people called their families to tell them they arrived safely and it is passed around how I had helped them get there even after they left the first boat to wreck on Raijua Island. So by the time I reach Jakarta, I start getting phone calls from Iraqis everywhere.

Before long I am on the phone for hours giving directions. I try to make them feel safe and at the same time warn them of the possible problems, but I can tell my warnings fall on deaf ears. To even enquire about this kind of journey means that nothing could be more terrible than what they are running away from.

Meanwhile I need to get my house in order, if such a thing is possible when you are in business with three other stateless people with hideous pasts. I call a meeting of the four original partners, Abud, Resa, Malik and me. We need to look at why the first boat was a disaster, and Resa has a lot to answer for. Apart from lying about his background in the navy, the $US7000 from Abud's Surabaya people seems to have vanished. And his own disappearance when we had a calamity was for me unforgivable.

I send him a message through Francesca, and surprisingly he turns up, but when I confront him about the missing money he responds with antagonism, and I know he is lying.

'Look, people have been left behind, who we have to pay back,'

I say, tired of arguing.

'No one else does. Why should we?'

'If we do the job we take the money, if we don't we give it back. I made a choice to help my family, but not to become like Omeid or Abu Quassey to do it. I don't want to have a bad conscience, or have someone point their finger at me shouting that I am a thief. I don't want to have to change myself to do this.'

Everyone falls silent and for a moment Resa looks like he might agree, but Abud is not about to let him off lightly and jumps in. 'So what happened to the $US7000?'

Backed into a corner Resa gets nasty and raises his voice. 'Are you calling me a liar?'

When no one responds he takes his stand by leaving.

'So he just walks away,' Abud says angrily.

'We can hardly go to the police,' I quip.

'Just the three of us then,' Malik speaks up.

'Well yes, so let's get back to business,' I say with no regrets.

We start to build up again for boat number three. I tell the others about Thalma and we agree to sail from Kupang again. But first I contact my mother, who has been expecting Basim to come next, to let her know I can't bring him yet. I can tell she is distressed. Without Khalid's income they are doing it tough, and with the failure of the last boat to make a profit I can send them nothing.

Then one morning it hits me. If asylum seekers are going to have to pay someone to get the right documents to enter Indonesia, it may as well be me. They are expensive and difficult to get, but I find out what things cost and how it all works, then after some bungled attempts, I build up some good contacts in the Immigration Department, and develop a reputation for being able to acquire visas.

I begin to be approached to help people whether they are going on my boats or with other smugglers. The small percentage I take becomes an unexpected avenue to keep me afloat, and I will be able to send money back to my family even if we make nothing from a boat.

Before long we have about sixty people, either in Jakarta or on their way. I call Abud in Malaysia to let him know Hadjib has found a suitable boat and that I am heading off to Kupang to get everything organised.

'Why do you have to go to Kupang?' he surprises me by asking. 'Thalma can do it. I've spoken to him.'

My affection or trust has not grown for Thalma in the short time I have known him. But I do trust Abud, and if he believes Thalma can organise the whole Kupang end of things it will save me running myself into the ground. 'Okay, if you think he can do it.'

'He's been in Kupang long enough to know his way around. He's already talked to the police.'

'Are you sure about this?' I say, trying to hide my uncertainty.

'Yes, a hundred percent,' Abud insists.

So I leave it all to Thalma and fly in when he is ready for the people. Thalma meets me at the airport.

'There is nothing to worry about,' he smiles, 'everything is organised. Tomorrow when the people arrive we take them to a safe house, then when it is dark, to the beach where the boat is already waiting.'

So next morning we go to meet the ferry. The terminal is already bustling with people so Thalma and I stand outside, watching a slim grey navy boat moving slowly along the horizon. Then a coastguard vessel cruises towards the wharf and I glance at Thalma.

'Stop worrying,' he says as we hurry back inside.

It is not long before the crowd begins to stir and we see the ferry lumbering towards us across the still waters of the bay. It is a heavy, square-shaped vehicle, big enough to carry hundreds with their goats, pigs and produce. It heaves itself against the wharf and doors begin to open. Iron staircases are wheeled into place and the passengers emerge. Despite the human mass that floods along the pier, our group are not hard to spot. They are the only Arabs.

They are frightened and hurry into the terminal looking for a familiar face. I hang back for a moment, this can be a dangerous time. A couple clutching two small children see me, and with relief begin pushing their way through the crowd in my direction. Suddenly a policeman appears and steps into their path.

They look back to the others for help but the whole group has been surrounded by police. They turn to me again with fear in their eyes as I back away.

'Wait, what's going on?' the woman calls, hands reaching out, but I will be useless to them if the police catch me too.

I look quickly away and let the moving mass of people carry me to the exit, where they mill amongst buses, taxis and exhaust fumes. A motorbike pulls in front of me.

'Hotel Astiti,' I yell, and jump on.

We ride at a dangerous pace back to town. His recklessness is exactly what I need. With the cool air blasting in my face I can try to get my anger at Thalma under control and work out what to do. As we pass the sleepy beach where the fishing boats are moored I get my driver to stop. He skids to a halt near the lapping water's edge.

I take a deep breath and call Thalma. This is not the time for accusations, I just want to know what can be done, but once I hear his voice I fly at him. 'You told Abud you had dealt with the police. Last time we had to leave ten in jail, this time they were waiting for us.'

'I'll go and talk to them now,' he says, and hangs up before I can respond.

Back at the hotel I pace the floor. Sixty people are a lot to get out of jail in a remote town where I am at the mercy of Thalma and his dubious contacts. After an hour he finally calls back.

'They will release forty-five.'

'What about the other fifteen?'

'I don't know why, but they won't let them go. I have told them I won't give them any money until the boat goes, and they have agreed.'

I don't bother arguing. There is some game going on here I don't understand.

It is not until dawn that I fall asleep. At midday the phone rings and I grab it expecting more bad news.

'We'll be leaving for the beach at seven o'clock,' Thalma says.

'No more news on the fifteen in jail?'

'None.'

'Okay,' I say, gritting my teeth but knowing there is nothing I can do.

I don't want to get caught on Thalma's bus if he has made another cock-up, so I track down Wayan and his taxi. It is a couple of hours' drive to the beach. When we arrive the moon is up and I can see the silhouette of the boat anchored out in the deep waters of the small sandy cove. Apart from the occasional fishing craft moored in the distance we have the place to ourselves.

Two small wooden boats start their engines, and standing knee-deep in the water I help the women and children on first. As they head off into the dark I pray there will be no more complications.

A seven-year-old boy stands shivering beside his mother. I squat in front of him while we wait for the next boat. 'It's okay to be scared,' I say, thinking of little Hashim, 'but you are going to a new life where anything is possible. You can learn to swim and play computer games.' In the moment this is all I can remember from Afrah's letters, but it is enough to get a smile.

'I had to leave my dog in Baghdad,' he sniffles. 'There is no one to look after him.'

'Someone will care for him,' I say, knowing Iraqis are having enough trouble caring for themselves, but hoping someone like my father might come along. He had a handsome brown dog who went to work with him. It was near the main petrol depot, so when the Americans began bombing Diwaniyah after they invaded Kuwait in 1991, everyone ran from the shop in such panic that the dog was left inside.

For two days no one went out, they were so scared. Then my father said, 'Fuck it, I go for my dog.' The fuel dump was already ablaze and the Americans were trying to hit the tankers. About a kilometre away he started calling, 'Chalabi! Chalabi!' through the roar of fires and acrid smoke. He had named him after a famously powerful Iraqi family. To cut someone down to size you would say, 'What do you think you are? A Chalabi?' My father liked to endow his dog with the strength of a president.

Even at that distance the dog heard him and began to howl. With the bombers overhead, my father used the barking to guide him as he ran. It was at fever pitch by the time he reached the shop. My father kicked down the door and grabbed his dog just as a petrol tanker near them exploded. When he reappeared from the carnage with Chalabi by his side we had already assumed they both were dead.

I am pulled out of my reverie by raised voices. I pat the boy's shoulder and stand up to see what is going on. The police have arrived and three of them are arguing with Thalma, who, to his credit, is holding his ground. 'You'll get the money when the ship has gone,' he yells.

I sigh, wondering if Thalma is unable to lock a deal down, or if every transaction in Kupang is open to being broken.

'How do we know you won't disappear once they are all on board?' a policeman responds stubbornly.

'Because we had an agreement,' Thalma persists.

'But we don't know you!'

This of course is the trouble with us not being Indonesian. Neither side can trust the other.

They have already started to push Thalma around as I run up the sand towards them. One of the police sees me approaching, ready for a fight. He pulls out his gun and shoots it in the air. But I am too angry to stop. I grab him by the shirt.

'You think you scare us with your gun?' I yell into his face. 'We lived under Saddam Hussein, you fool!'

I glare at him, and as he lowers his weapon I wonder if I have become my father. But he of course feared nothing and I still fear plenty, just not guns and violence.

'We don't give you a cent until the people go,' I glower at him. He gives in, and I remember from watching Baba how genuine fearlessness renders others powerless.

Thalma and I hurry back to the water where there is a scramble to get on the small boats. While I try to gain calm, I keep glancing over my shoulder, but the police are now sitting on the sand, resigned to waiting until we are loaded. When everyone is on board the main vessel and we hear the rumble of the engine grow faint as it heads out to sea, we pay them.

I should be happy they are on their way but I am smarting over the fifteen left behind. Then, when Wayan drives me back to Kupang and our phones come back on, we discover that for some reason I do not understand the police released them while we were at the beach.

An Indonesian guy who works with us took them back to the safe house, where they desperately tried to call us, but we were out of range. There were tragic scenes of the women shrieking, children crying, and the men trying to make our guy tell them which beach the boat was leaving from. But of course he didn't know. We couldn't risk telling anyone. Thalma and I were the only ones who knew and we were unreachable.

Next morning I go to the safe house. 'I thought the police were fixed,' I tell them with a certain amount of bitterness. But the people have already created their own scenario. They think I only sent the ones who paid me, and left those who paid Abud.

'No,' I say. 'Abud and I share the business. It's just the guy who organised everything here messed up. I am sorry.'

I catch a taxi to Thalma's hotel. 'We need to give the fifteen who were left behind their money back,' I say abruptly.

'I've spoken to Abud and he says he is going to keep the money and send them to Australia himself on another boat.'

'Why would Abud do that?' I retort, confused. Even if Thalma has begun playing behind my back, I can't imagine why Abud would go along with it. 'All right,' I say, my irritation growing, 'but you pay for their food and a place for them to stay.'

We both know it could be months before he can get enough people for another boat.

He glares at me. 'Okay, fine!' he says and slams the door.

It hasn't taken long to fall out with Thalma. I wonder how long he will last with Abud if what he says is true. He is no loss to me after this debacle, but the possibility of Abud's betrayal hits me badly.

I wait until I hear the boat has arrived safely, then I fly back to Jakarta and call Malik to organise a meeting with the three remaining partners. Malik, Abud and me. I catch a taxi from the airport and sit gazing at the clusters of motorbikes banking up around us as we stop at a red light.

Next to my window a scooter idles. The driver is sandwiched between his wife, perched behind him cradling a baby, and his little boy between his legs. As we take off he is still rolling a cigarette with the hand that holds the steering and talking on his mobile phone with the other. A few wrong inches could wipe out the whole family. I wonder how he could be so cavalier with such precious cargo.

When I get to the apartment Malik and I have been sharing, I decide to say nothing about what happened with Thalma. I will wait and see how Abud behaves. I just want to discuss how we need to do things differently on the next boat. When I arrive I find Abud and Adnan, a smartass we had previously met with Abud, already waiting for me. For some reason the atmosphere is hostile.

I put down my bag and look at Abud. 'What is Adnan doing here?' I ask as civilly as I can.

'I want my money,' Adnan replies for himself.

'You and I don't have any business. What money are you talking about?' I am genuinely confused.

'You know what money, you owe me a share.'

'Nothing I do has anything to do with you.' I look at Abud, bewildered. 'Do you hear what he's saying?'

When Abud doesn't respond I begin to realise it is true. He is moving on, and Thalma and Adnan are now working with him.

Then Adnan snaps like a dog. 'You must still have some of the money you shared with Zaqi.'

Suddenly, and to my horror, I see the bigger picture. They think I had a deal with Zaqi when he stole our $US10000. 'For God's sake, Malik,' I say when he doesn't come to my defence, 'you were with me when I gave Zaqi the money.'

But Malik remains silent. They must think I met Zaqi later and got a cut before he disappeared. I turn to Adnan. 'I have no business with you. So get out of my apartment.'

He stands defiant so I try to push him towards the door. But Adnan wants a fight and I find myself ready for one. I am appalled by the accusations and in no mood for his games. I have had to leave fifteen people in Kupang with an incompetent who thinks he can smuggle them to Australia, most of my family are no closer to getting out of Iran, and now a complete stranger has turned my only friends against me.

When Adnan pushes me back and neither Abud nor Malik intervene my temper flares and I instinctively reach for an empty Coke bottle that sits on the coffee table. Fortunately I don't knock the bottom off it and threaten him with the jagged end, but he gets the idea.

'Okay, okay,' he says, backing away. 'Okay, we solve this by talking.'

'No, you motherfucker, I have nothing to say to you.' My blood is up and I am no longer interested in conversation. Adnan is just a fool, and Abud a disappointment.

My friendship with Malik and Abud had given me a safe port in a bleak and lonely landscape. But as I stand poised with my Coke bottle in the air, I realise that while I would like to do some damage to Adnan, I should instead use the energy to make myself walk away from them all. I toss the bottle from my right hand to my left to lighten up the situation, set it down on the table as if it had never been intended as a weapon, and look at Abud. 'Our partnership is finished.'

I glance at Malik as I go. 'With you too, my friend. It's over.'

Loneliness hits me as soon as I walk out onto the street and look up at the window of the apartment. In the grey light of evening it emits a warm glow and I am stricken with a deep longing for my dead brother. I miss the gently unspoken bond we shared that meant trust and caring were implicit. Feeling utterly bereft I head off to find yet another bland hotel room. The apartment had at least resembled a home of sorts.

I go back to the Matraman and ask to be put on the top floor, as far away from humans as I can get. There is an uncomfortable armchair in the corner where I curl up like a wounded bear. In the future, no more partners. I have learnt enough about the business now to go it alone. I will employ people, they will work for me, and any profit goes straight into getting the rest of my family to Australia. Then I get out of this place.

After three miserable days I decide to go to Malaysia to find a replacement for Abud. As I pack my few belongings into my Adidas bag the phone rings. It is Francesca.

'The police want the rest of their money,' she snaps. 'While you were in Kupang they have been harassing me.'

It has been hanging over me that the balance of the money for the Sumatra bus is still to be paid, but I somehow hoped with time they would forget, or other more pressing things would take over. But Francesca has remained loyal and I cannot risk her being left in a threatening situation. There is nothing for it but to pay them.

'Don't worry,' I say flatly, 'I'll bring it to you.'

On my way to the airport I stop off at her place with most of what little I made from the boat. 'Thank you for all your help. We'll have lunch again some time,' I say, knowing that with Francesca, too, I am closing the door.

I land in Kuala Lumpur airport on a new Turkish passport. Now that I know how things work it is not hard to find people involved in the smuggling network, and before long I hear about Rahim. He was born in Iran but his ethnic background is Arabic and he has a good reputation. Like Abud, he meets the people at the airport and takes care of transport, hotels, tickets, visas, and whatever they need to get to Indonesia.

Rahim tracks me down before I can find him.

'I have twenty-two Iraqis coming who want to go to Australia, and I'm having difficulties getting visas to Indonesia at the moment. Can you help with that?' he says after we have made small talk over tea.

I know that Immigration are sensitive to political pressure and sometimes not prepared to deal with us. As the Australian authorities have been in Jakarta recently I have no idea if any of my contacts will oblige. 'No problem,' I nod as confidently as I can muster.

As luck would have it, one of my associates back in Indonesian Immigration is happy to assist for a few extra dollars, and by the end of the week the visas are ready to be collected from their embassy in Kuala Lumpur. My credentials established, it is agreed I will return to Indonesia and organise to get Rahim's twenty-two people to Australia.

When they arrive I take them to a rented villa in Bogor, while we wait for more people. Amongst them is a suave Iranian who Saddam wanted to execute for demonstrating against the government. He is interesting, charming and fun to be around. I get to know him when I visit the villa, and sometimes he comes back to Jakarta and we eat together. One night he persuades me to go to a club, and I surprise myself by dancing and having a good time like other young men in their twenties.

One day he says, 'I met two young Iraqi men who know you.'

'Oh,' I reply abruptly, expecting it to be Abud, Resa or Malik, so not really wanting to have this conversation.

'Haider and Shahin. They were left behind from one of your last boats. They'd like to see you.'

I still haven't paid them back, so no doubt that is what it is about.

We meet in the Atrium where Malik and I used to hang out. 'If you still want to go to Australia,' I offer, getting straight to the point, 'I will put you on my next boat. If you don't want to go, I'll give your money back.'

'We didn't give you money. We gave it to Abud.'

I look into their friendly open faces with some confusion. 'We were partners, so I will help you the best I can.'

There is a pause.

'We are not asking for money, we would like to work with you, Ali.'

So Haider and Shahin become my first employees. They are Iraqi but born in Iran, so they speak fluent Farsi as well as Arabic, and while in Indonesia have learnt Bahasa. They start picking up people from the airport, bringing them to a hotel or the villa, buying train, plane and ferry tickets, and taking the people where they need to go. I just have to spend the time on the phone, organising everything. At night we often eat together. We laugh and talk a lot and enjoy each other's company, but I never let it interfere with our work. So, apart from the ever-present worry about my family, I begin to have a somewhat normal life. Then one day the phone rings and it is Eni.

I feel a rush of pleasure at the sound of her voice. It is weeks since we last spoke and because my Indonesian is so much better we are able to have a real conversation. For the first time she can explain why she always has to leave early. She lives with her family in Bandung, about four hours out of Jakarta, and she also has a job. Then there is her father, who doesn't want his daughter coming to meet a man if she has to stay overnight because of the distance.

I feel guilty for having dispatched her so summarily, but relating across cultures is difficult enough without trying to do it with almost no language. She still corrects my sentences but I like the familiarity of it, and with the intimacy of understanding comes a longing to see her again. So despite some trepidation I plunge in and ask if she will meet me.

She agrees and a few days later she comes to Jakarta. I am so pleased to see her I almost pick her up when I hug her, and she beams. I take her to dinner at Café Batavia, in a Dutch colonial building in the old part of Jakarta. I had often stopped and looked up at the high shuttered windows on my walks to Sunda Kelapa, where the mighty schooners are moored. I had thought about entering, but it has a certain romance that demands a companion.

It looks out over the original town square. Families, teenagers, kids and lovers gather there to play music, picnic, and even get tattoos. Tonight it is alive with the sound of kendang drums and singing. Jugglers toss firesticks in the air and pretty girls in vibrant colours sway to the rhythm while young men swagger or lean against two ancient ship cannons and observe.

Inside the cool interior of the Batavia there are high ceilings and a large chandelier. Signed photos of famous people line the panelled walls and waiters stand poised behind a bar made of cowhide. Upstairs the restaurant has dark-timbered beams, ancient hardwood floors, and potted palms.

We are ushered to a white-clothed table next to a window and the waiter slides open the heavy wooden shutters. Ceiling fans whoosh slowly overhead like giant sea birds circling, and I feel transported to the European splendour I read about in the Arabic translations my friend smuggled to me while I was hiding in Diwaniyah.

We linger over our food, and with my improved Bahasa I find myself venturing into personal areas I have never talked about before. Eni's affection for me is clear, and at one point she takes my hand. 'Why don't we get married?' she says, her eyes softening.

Despite the bizarre circumstances of my situation, I smile. The thing I have wanted most passionately in my life, apart from my family's safety, is a wife and children. One would have thought raising younger siblings would have doused my paternal flame but strangely it has done the opposite. On the filthy concrete floor of Abu Ghraib, sandwiched between the bony bodies of my comrades, Intisar and the desire for a child with her became my antidote to pain as the long nights inched away. I have lost Intisar. I don't want to lose Eni too. It might be an inopportune time but I want a family of my own.

'I would love to,' I beam and clasp her hand.

For the rest of the evening we talk intently about the possibility of a life together, and we leave the restaurant on a high. But as we walk away from Batavia's imaginary European world and back into the hot muggy night, I realise how deeply I have been lost in a fantasy. If I want to marry officially, I have to go to the Iraqi embassy and I can't do that. If I tell Eni I have no real passport or ID and that my business is one of the most dangerous in Indonesia it would scare her, and knowing how flighty she is anyway, I might lose her for good.

Eni begins coming to Jakarta more regularly and sometimes I go to Bandung with her, but every time she mentions getting married I have to keep saying, 'Soon, soon.' I have already been through this once with Intisar, and now again with Eni. It seems that what is normal to most human beings is, for one reason or another, always out of my reach.

Before long Rahim has sent us thirty-eight more people. Despite my unfortunate dealings with Thalma, I decide to depart from Kupang again. It is a short, relatively easy trip to Ashmore Reef, and while the police are difficult I know what I'm dealing with. I plan to organise everything in Kupang myself, leaving Haider in Jakarta, and Shahin in Bali.

I give them both clear instructions. Haider is to send the people by train to Surabaya, then by bus to Denpasar. Shahin will meet them and put them on a plane to Kupang, where I will be waiting. Because these people are frightened and confused, it is easy for them to make a mistake, so someone has to be with them all the time. Now that it is entirely my own business, I am beginning to take pride in how it's run.

'Can my girlfriend come with me to Bali?' Shahin asks at our final meeting.

'No,' I say firmly. I am shocked that he is not taking things more seriously. 'We play after, but now we do the work.'

'Okay,' he says, and I am relieved we don't have to fight about it.

I head off to Kupang happy that everything is securely in place. It is late May 2000, six months since I left Iran. This is the fourth boat and I am determined to get it right this time.

Hadjib is working with Thalma so I find another middleman called Mushbah. He is young, maybe early twenties, and while I am unsure about him, it is a small town and the supply is limited.

He finds a boat and a captain, who is even younger than him. This strangely doesn't make me as nervous as Mushbah himself, because while the captain is little more than a boy, he is fearless, and from generations of fishermen who know the sea. They grow up on it and can find their way to Ashmore Reef, which they call Pulau Pasir, with their eyes shut.

They navigate by the stars and the sun, they know the weather, and if they are young with no commitments they are happy to spend two years in an Australian jail when they get there. The money they make for a few days at sea will buy them a fishing boat of their own and set them up for life.

'Sometimes,' Mushbah says, enjoying teaching me the ropes, 'the older captains get someone to pick them up when they get near Australian waters, so they don't get arrested, leaving the crew to take the boat in.' He laughs cynically. 'And then when the Australians try and stop us by destroying our boats, they think it sends a message if they burn it to the waterline in front of our eyes. But the passengers don't care. Nor does the captain. They don't own it. It just means that the smugglers charge the people more because they have to buy a new boat each time. And as they don't expect to see the boat again, they don't care what condition it's in.'

He pauses for a moment, then looks at me with his boyish grin. 'So that's why you need me, or, because you're a foreigner, the fishermen will sell you any old piece of leaky shit they want to get rid of.'

I rent a house in Kupang and over the next two days the people arrive in small groups without a hitch, but I hear a few complaints from them about Shahin in Bali, and he did bring his girlfriend with him. It would seem he can't stop thinking about women. I call him several times but his phone is switched off.

Late the following night we skirt the city in a rented bus and head out along a winding road to another lonely beach. Mushbah and I load the people onto two small launches to shuttle them to the main vessel. While there are only thirty-eight people, it is the first boat I have done without partners, so I am alone with the responsibility. As it sails away I feel both acute anxiety and a great sense of accomplishment.

By the time I tie up loose ends with the house and Mushbah it is afternoon. I go back to my room and crash until the early hours of the next morning. The hotel is cheap and nondescript except that it sits right on the beach and has a large open restaurant that looks across the bay. I know I won't sleep again until the boat reaches Australia, and I can't walk the streets like I usually do in Jakarta, because Kupang is so small that before long I would be in a wrangle with the police. So I sit amongst the empty tables and gaze out at the tiny lights on the fishing boats creating silver circles on the sea.

As the grey dawn becomes golden and colour seeps into the mountains behind the now glittering bay, the hotel staff begin their chores. Being the hospitable, welcoming people the Indonesians are, they are happy to serve me coffee for as long as I want, making me so wired I can hardly hold the menu when they suggest breakfast.

It is late afternoon before my phone finally rings. The lunch clientele have been and gone, and now the evening crowd is arriving. I am still sitting at my table, slowly threading my paper serviette into spaghetti.

'Ali, it is Nina,' she says and begins to cry.

Nina is a woman I let on the boat for nothing. Her husband and son had been killed by Saddam, leaving her penniless with a small boy. I hold my breath.

'Nina, what has gone wrong? What happened?'

'We made it,' she sobs. 'We are in Australia.'

In the morning I fly back to Jakarta with a stopover in Bali to see Shahin. I go straight to his hotel unannounced and find him in bed with his girlfriend.

'Come, let's go and have some coffee,' I say with no further comment.

We go downstairs to a small café. Nearby a tiny stream babbles amongst lush tropical plants, filling my nostrils with a sweet, fecund aroma.

I ask him how much money he has left from the $US5000 for expenses I'd given him, expecting there would be plenty remaining.

'Nothing. The people needed things.'

'Can you make me a list of what you spent it on?'

He waves his hands to indicate the money has gone this way and that.

'There must be something left,' I say, as controlled as I can.

He shakes his head.

There is a pause, then I hand him a $US2000 roll of notes I have in my pocket. 'This is your pay. You have done a good job, but I don't think you are right for this business.'

He protests angrily but I cut him short. 'Shahin, you didn't listen when I told you not to bring your girlfriend. Secondly, I heard the people were waiting to leave in the morning and you were still asleep. So don't get angry with me. It should be the other way around.'

He doesn't deny it. His face falls and he looks suddenly sad. 'Please, last chance.'

'No, I can't take the risk. These people pay me money to do a job for them. They hand their lives over to me.'

I go back to the airport and take a side trip to Lombok, where I track down the remaining Sumatra bus people left behind from the second boat and pay them back. By the time I get on a plane to head home my money bag is all but empty, but I am at last free of debt and with the next boat I will be able to bring more of my family.

TWO FAMILIES

When I arrive in Jakarta, Haider is waiting at the airport to meet me. Shahin has already called him and admirably only blamed himself for losing his job. But it makes us both feel bad. Shahin had become my friend as well as Haider's.

So Haider and I start building up a fifth boat, with just the two of us, but we need to move quickly. One of the people on the last boat called to tell me he heard that both Interpol and the Australian Federal Police are looking for me, so the pressure to get my family out before some kind of calamity occurs is building. My mother's phone calls are becoming increasingly distressful and my concern for their wellbeing is growing.

That night I toss and turn in my sleep. I am running towards the cellar where we lived in Iran. The police are dragging my mother and my sisters away and they are screaming. Little Hashim stands in silent terror. Ahmad is by my side as I run to help them, but I suddenly see his face is bleeding and all his fingers are severed. I cry out and as I do the phone rings, jolting me into the lonely reality of my hotel room.

'Who is it?' I ask hoarsely, wiping sweat from my forehead.

'This is Asim, in Jordan. I forgot the time is different.'

'It's okay,' I say, checking my watch. It is two am, but I am glad to be woken from my dream.

'I have thirty-five Iraqis escaping through Jordan who want to get to Australia.'

I have a deal with Asim where the people buy a two-way ticket, which is the only way into Malaysia, then when they get to Indonesia I send the return tickets back for refunding as his payment for setting everything up for them.

'Okay,' I say and hang up, relieved we are on the move already.

My relationship with Rahim is beginning to fray, he keeps pushing up his price, so once Asim's people are on their way I go to Malaysia and meet them myself. I put them in a hotel and then go through their individual situations. If, for whatever reason, I can't get them a visa, they need a new passport from a country like Turkey, where a visa isn't required to enter Indonesia.

'How much?' they keep asking me.

'You get what you pay for. If you want a good job, maybe over a thousand US. If you just want to change the photo on a second-hand one, then it may only be a hundred. But you're more likely to get caught. Either way, you have to believe the passport, that the new name and age are yours. Or no matter what you pay, you won't get through.'

What I decide to spare them is that often there are not enough passports. We collect them when the boats depart. People are usually happy to give them to help someone else, but many have already been used several times and after one or two uses you can't reinsert the photos and information without it being detected, so we burn them. Sometimes there could be three hundred people in Malaysia waiting, and we're lucky to get twenty passports we can re-use. The ones who can't afford any documents at all are smuggled out of Malaysia by boat and through Sumatra.

Once Asim's thirty-five are in Indonesia I buy them tickets for the train, ferry and plane to Kupang. Then, leaving Haider to organise their departure, I go ahead and meet Mushbah, who has found a captain and a boat. I tell him to make it more comfortable, old carpet to cover the boards, a large water tank, and to fix up the cooking area.

After each boat I get better at the job.

Soon Haider's group begins to arrive. I hire a van and take them to a house I have rented. While I go back and forth to the airport Mushbah organises the food for the journey: plenty of bananas, canned fish, rice, bread and water. The people are likely to get seasick so we keep it simple.

On the fourth day I send Mushbah to the airport to collect the last people, but when they reach the house it is clear two families, four adults and five children, are missing. Nobody, including Mushbah, knows what has happened to them.

I am kicking myself for not having gone to the airport myself when the phone rings, and I answer to a frightened voice.

'Ali, the police have us in a hotel and say we are not going anywhere.'

'Tell them you are on a holiday while I work out what to do. Try not to worry.'

But they have suffered at the hands of Saddam's secret police and they are terrified.

'I will think of something,' I say with no idea what, and hang up.

So now we have a real headache. Normally the middleman would do the negotiating, but I discover Mushbah is useless. He talks big but does nothing. Three days go by with no results. Kupang is becoming untenable as a place of departure.

On the third night in a seedier part of town, I am sitting with an Indonesian guy from the navy Mushbah introduced me to. I am drinking tea while he drinks beer. I am burning with frustration. I cannot keep the people waiting much longer. The sea is calm because the moon is full, but it will wane over the next few days and the waters will become more dangerous.

I look at the burly navy guy drinking his beer and I take a risk. 'Are you afraid?' I ask out of the blue.

He smirks, sensing a challenge. 'I'm not afraid of anything.'

'Good,' I say. 'There are these people, two families, being held by the police for no reason in a hotel. How about you and me, we go and get them?'

His face lights up. 'Sure.' He gets up from his seat, poised and ready. 'You want to use my van?'

I smile and nod, and grinning from ear to ear, he leaves to get it. Then I call Mushbah. 'I need you to take the people to the boat as fast as possible.'

'Okay,' Mushbah says hesitantly.

'Can you do that?' I ask, having hoped for a more decisive reaction.

'Yes, I can do it.'

'Good. I am bringing the two families the police are holding. Wait for us until one am. If we don't come by then, let the boat sail.'

'Okay.'

'Are you clear?'

'I'm clear.'

Next I call one of the captives in the hotel. 'Get your stuff ready,' I say, my blood pumping now that I am finally taking action, 'and when I call you again, you all go down to reception. Don't talk to them, just give them the right money, and then get out of the hotel. There will be police in the foyer so you will have to run.'

'The police told us they have found out about the house where the others were hiding. They are going to cause trouble for you.'

'All right,' I reply, my shoulders sagging, 'so just do what I say.'

'Okay, we do it,' he agrees nervously.

I call Mushbah to tell him to hurry. 'The police know about the house, they will be on the way any minute,' I say urgently.

'Okay, we're moving,' he replies to my relief and hangs up.

My navy man returns with his van. Like most cars in Kupang it isn't in great shape but it has a sliding side door. 'Let's go,' I say in a military tone of voice.

So we head off, planning our strategy while we drive, and as we approach I call the people.

'Go now,' I demand. 'Get out of the hotel.'

Within a few minutes we swerve into the small driveway in front of the main entrance, but there is no sign of the people.

'Go,' I say, 'go around again.'

The navy man, used to working under command, is remarkably compliant. But the moment we pull back onto the street I suddenly see the children, followed by their parents, flying out the door.

'Back up!' I yell. 'Back up!'

He jams on the brakes, throws it into reverse and revs backwards. Before he even stops I leap out.

The police are following the people out, but when I jump they are scared we might have weapons and pull back inside. I grab the children two at a time and almost throw them into the van. The navy man, leaning over from the driver's seat, catches their hands and pulls the five of them in, then the four parents pile in behind as I push in flailing arms and legs and yell to the navy man to go. He flattens his foot to the floor and takes off. I leap on and hang there until I can climb in and close the door behind me with a bang.

We speed down the main street, with the engine roaring, past the police station, and I imagine how they will laugh if we lose control and crash opposite their entrance. But the navy man is a good getaway driver and we head out of town without incident. We caught the police by surprise, which has given us a good head start, and with a bit of luck the rest of the force will be searching for our safe house, which by now will be empty.

It is over an hour's drive to the beach. Apart from the occasional whimper from the youngest child, everyone is silent. Except the navy man, who chuckles to himself. He knows by now he is aiding and abetting a smuggling operation but it seems to have lit up a life of relative boredom, so all going well he won't betray us until it's over.

As for me I am ecstatic. Probably because of my time under Saddam, outwitting the police is always thrilling, and we should get to the boat by midnight, which is well before the deadline.

I cling onto my seat, my eyes fixed on the rear-vision mirror, the engine clattering and blowing smoke as we hurtle down narrow gravel roads at 120kph. Under the seat I have a two-foot machete, which I am prepared to use if the police appear with their lights flashing and guns in the air. I'm not sure what I will do with it but I have had enough of their tactics, and they are not going to take these people again.

It is nearly twelve when we bounce along the last of the potholed road to the beach. We pile out and stand for a moment absorbing the soundless night, without the growl of the engine. Then I realise there are no other vehicles and I wonder in a panic if we are at the wrong beach. I turn on my flashlight and soon recognise the gnarled trees that encircle us, and the small wooden fishing boat that lies beneath them, half built.

We run over the sandy rise to the beach. In the moonlight we see a speedboat is still on the shore but nothing else. Then one of the women lets out a wail, which echoes through the silence. I turn to see her pointing, and in the distance we all see a small light and the silhouette of the big boat heading out to sea. I check my watch again. It is only a few minutes past midnight. That idiot Mushbah must have lost his nerve and let the boat go too soon.

I was taking these two families almost for free, so there is no financial imperative, but I have been left on a beach myself and I am overwhelmed by the same primal frenzy that could have led to my committing homicide on Omeid that night. I grab two of the children's hands and I run through the dark, down to the water where the speedboat sits empty.

The owner stands by, doing nothing. I hurl abuse in Bahasa but he just shrugs and looks the other way. I lift the children in, then turn back and yell at the others to come quickly. The navy man comes too and he and I load everyone in, heaving and cursing at anything that slows us down. As we push the boat offshore and clamber in I catch my foot on a rock and rip my ankle open.

I claw my way back on, bleeding profusely as I grab the helm. The navy man yanks the motor with his beefy arms and it roars into action.

I open the throttle and we surge out into the black water. Pulling off my shirt and wrapping it around my ankle with one hand, I steer towards the disappearing light with the other. The frightened children cling to their parents as we speed into the dark but no one objects to my actions.

The motor is a decent size and we make good time, catching up with the big boat before it reaches the ocean. The captain cuts the engine as we pull up alongside and a rope ladder is lowered. Together with the navy man I help each one to board, and as they leave they thank us with tears and hugs before they disappear up over the side for yet another traumatic journey. Even the navy man has tears in his eyes by the time they have all gone.

We watch until they are out of sight, then we make our way back to the shore. The navy man helps me into the van and we head back into town. I nurse my ankle, while he sings to himself as he drives. He is clearly invigorated by the heist and gratified by the good deed. When we reach my hotel I thank him and push some money into his hand. Bonded by our experience we laugh and hug, then I hobble to my room.

I soak and wrap my ankle while the adrenaline drains away, and then collapse into a dead sleep on my bed and don't wake properly until the phone rings about twenty hours later.

It is Haider. He is back in Jakarta and has just checked the internet. There is a report that the boat has arrived on Ashmore Reef.

'So you didn't lose any?' he asks.

'Not a one.'

'There was no trouble?'

'No more than usual,' I laugh. 'Tell Eni I'm on my way.' No matter what has happened while we are apart, I am always excited to see her. 'I want to marry her,' I surprise myself by saying to Haider, 'but I can't see how I can do it.'

'There are other ways,' he replies.

I can always count on Haider to come up with something.

'They have a kind of contractual marriage here, which many people do. There is a full wedding ceremony but it doesn't require the usual legal verifications. Ask her about it.'

Next day I go out to Bandung and when I mention Haider's suggestion Eni is delighted. It doesn't seem to bother her which way we do it, so long as we get married.

At last I have made a profit, so Eni keeps busy with wedding plans while I proceed with preparations for bringing Basim to Indonesia. Once he's here I will bring my mother and the younger children together. With no adult male accompanying them they are less likely to be noticed.

I ask a guy in Iran who owes me for taking his uncle and nephew on the last boat to give the money to Basim for his ticket and passport. Then I organise his visa for Indonesia and he catches a flight out of Tehran. But when he arrives in Malaysia he is sent back. Sometimes they just randomly do this, so I try not to blame him.

But he returns via Turkey, where he spends all the money I'd sent him for expenses. I am furious but I cannot stay angry for long. Some of us survive Saddam's jails better than others but none of us escape without scars. So I spend another $US2000 on new paperwork and tickets to get him back again.

Determined that things go smoothly this time I get a friend to meet him at the airport and take him home to his place in Kuala Lumpur. But after a couple of days I get a call.

'Your brother wants to go and live with some crazy Russian he met on the plane.'

I sigh with frustration. 'Put him on.'

Basim gets on the phone and shouts at me like a child. He is having his first taste of freedom, and after the severity of what he went through in Iraq it is impossible to explain to him the seriousness of his current situation.

'Basim, stay with my friend. If you don't I will come to Malaysia now and get you myself.'

I hang up wondering if all my siblings are going to be as off the rails by the time I get to them.

I decide to go ahead with the wedding before my family get here. I don't want my mother to see how I have been living – my clothes in a bag, every day sleeping somewhere different. I want to be settled with a house and a wife. Also, I don't want to risk her putting a spanner in the works, the way she did with Intisar.

We have an Indonesian ceremony in Eni's parents' house. The night before, a traditional artist comes with decorations and costumes. He hangs a red and gold backdrop behind a ceremonial platform and smothers it with sweet-smelling flowers, including sprays of jasmine. We are up all night helping.

Next day we are exhausted but have to stand for hours greeting the long line of wedding guests. Eni has about fifty family and friends, and I have invited Haider and a few other people I know. But Basim is still in Malaysia so I have no one from my family, which saddens me.

Everyone gathers around the decorated podium for the short ceremony with the sheik, we exchange rings and then the party begins. It goes all day. There is a banquet and Indonesian music with singing and dancing. At various stages Eni and I change into different traditional costumes, with ornate headdresses for her, and jackets, hats and ceremonial swords for me.

As bride and groom, we sit on a special couch and watch the proceedings. I particularly like the music and the traditional dancing. I am so absorbed that I am in a trancelike state when the three girlfriends who were with Eni the night we met at the club appear in costumes that match the backdrop.

Then, in a gesture of love for her, they pick up the rhythms of the singing and begin to dance. With delicate hypnotic gestures their hands glide in unison, their bodies swirl and twirl in perfect step, red and gold scarves coiling to their movements.

It is exquisite, fragile, beautiful, and when I glance at Eni I see her eyes glistening. I put my arm around her and drawing her close to me I can feel my own tears rising. There has been so little beauty in my life for so long that I have forgotten how our souls yearn to be touched by it.

Next day we go to Bogor, where we rent a villa in a charming part of the city for a week. For the first time we have our own house in which to indulge each other. We buy food and cook together or we go out to restaurants to eat. We are happy, we laugh, and having waited until our wedding day to consummate our marriage, we have so much sex we are sure we have made a baby.

After a week of bliss it is back to hotel rooms in Jakarta. I now need to focus on my family. With money, contacts and experience everything has become easier. But I find myself split in two. Eni wants my full attention, and what's more she did get pregnant. We discover from the ultrasound it is a boy. I am both exhilarated and terrified. The reality of even more responsibility is upon me too soon.

Then one night I wake to Eni crying. There is blood on her hands and in the bed and she is clasping her stomach and sobbing as if her heart will break. She is losing our baby boy. It is only two months but he is now somewhere down there on the sheets and I don't know what to do. In Iraq we would be living with my family, and my mother and sisters would take charge. In my culture men don't even talk about miscarriages.

At a loss, I tell her we will have another baby but it is the wrong thing to say, it just makes things worse. As dawn breaks and the first bird sounds begin I call her mother. She calms Eni down and says she needs to go to the hospital. I panic. I don't know what this might mean, and I have never ventured inside a women's hospital. I am relieved when Eni says she wants to be with her mother, so I take her back to Bandung. I'm frightened I have made a terrible mistake but I don't know what it is. I'm afraid this is the end. This is much harder than smuggling.

Eni recovers and we rent a house near her family, but I am aware there are differences. She is more serious, possessive, and less flighty than before. She finds it hard that I am away such a lot and she wants to go back home. So we move in with her parents. It's not hard for me because they are extremely nice people. Besides, they are very happy to have her home, which makes things much easier for me. I don't have to worry about her when I am away and when we are together she is happy. So we can enjoy each other once more, and it is not long before she announces she is pregnant again.

The thought of Umi and my siblings being soon on their way makes the idea of a baby more manageable, and I become increasingly excited about both. I am so keyed up by the time their flights are booked that I decide to join Basim in Malaysia and meet them there. I have to wait for the seas to come down before I can send another boat, so we can spend some time together in Kuala Lumpur.

Eni wants to come too but I am worried about another miscarriage, so I suggest she comes later, when the pregnancy is more secure.

Finally the day comes. I am at the Kuala Lumpur airport an hour early, waiting outside. I am used to this process and should be calm, but because it is my own family everything is different. And I know how many things can go wrong.

Eventually the people from their flight start to emerge. I have played this moment over in my head so many times it is hard to believe it is happening. Each time an Arabic woman with children comes into view my pulse increases, but it is not them. I wait and I wait. I am trying not to pace or I will attract attention, so I drag on cigarette after cigarette until there is only a trickle of people and still there is no sign of them.

Then my phone rings. It is a local number I don't know but I snappily answer in case it is business.

'Hello?' a woman's voice replies.

'Who is this?' I ask sharply, dragging on my cigarette and watching a group of stragglers come through the airport doors.

'Inas.'

'Who is Inas?' My anxiety level is so high I can't remember any Inases.

'Your sister,' she giggles.

I laugh wildly. 'It has been so long since I heard your voice I didn't recognise it.'

But then she tells me they have been stopped by Immigration. I rush back to the car where a friend who drove me is waiting.

'Immigration have got them!' I am as close to hysteria as I have ever been. 'Quickly, go and see what's going on. It's too dangerous for all of us if I go in.'

As he hurries off I jam a roll of notes into his hand. He disappears into the terminal and I light a cigarette before I realise I already have one going.

I have a full-blown headache when the glass doors finally open and my friend emerges. His face looks sour. I stop breathing and look away. Clearly things have gone badly. Then suddenly I hear my name being called, and there, running from behind my friend and across the car park is Hashim, yelping like a puppy. He throws himself at me and I clutch him so tight I knock the breath out of him. He is tall now, already ten, but all I see is that little boy I left a year and a half ago in Iran.

Then I look up and see them, Ahlam and Inas. They no longer look like girls, but women. Everyone has changed except my mother, who still wears her black hijab. I look around, wanting to share my joy, and maybe I am overwrought but for an exhilarating moment I think I see Ahmad, standing under a tree to the side of the car park, lit up with his sweet boyish smile, watching us. I glance away to embrace my mother and when I look back over her shoulder he is gone. Instantly it revives the memories that plunder my waking hours as much as my dreams.

I try to lock it away as I hug them all again, but inside I ache for Ahmad to be sharing this with us. I keep hold of my mother, who is crying so hard I am soon distracted and as she kisses me my friend explains, 'I didn't have to pay.' He smiles, pushing the notes back into my pocket through the tangle of my mother's arms. 'They have two months in Malaysia.'

I unwrap myself from Umi and bundle them all into the car and we head off. I glance back at the tree where Ahmad had stood. Then I turn to my mother and she takes my hand.

We drive to a nice hotel I have booked, where Basim is waiting to greet them. They have never stayed in such a place. Huge windows overlooking the city, air-conditioning so quiet it can't be heard, soft carpets and giant, fresh-linened beds. This is a splendid new world and they are free. I sit on the deep comfortable couch and watch their faces. They are so happy I just smile and smile until my face hurts.

When the younger ones were born Iraq was already destroyed. They have never seen towering glass skyscrapers, plazas or malls. So they ride the escalators and wander wide-eyed through the brightly lit stores, whose exotic clothes, shoes and toys they couldn't have imagined. There are hair salons, manicurists, gift shops and sports stores. There are fun parlours with game machines. They spend hours lost in one after another.

One day I am having a meeting in a big mall in the centre of Kuala Lumpur when I suddenly hear Inas yelling my name. I look up and see her with Hashim; they are playing pinball machines like ordinary children. I have never heard them laugh so much or seen them so happy. Especially Hashim. This is what I have dreamt of. This is my reward.

After two weeks I rent them an apartment so my mother can cook and treat it like their home. There is a swimming pool, a gym, and a small mall on the first floor. I show them where the markets are and my mother cooks our favourite dishes. It has been so long I have forgotten how much I craved them.

Every day we eat lunch together. It is not just the food that we like, but the way we eat with each other, and the closeness it creates between us. Our arms brushing as we lean in to gather the rice and vegetables off the same big plate, our hands entwined, our fingers touching and tussling to help each other break up the food or share the tastiest pieces.

At the end of a month Eni arrives and we take a small apartment on our own so I can introduce her slowly. Inas and Ahlam come to stay one night, but while Eni taught me Indonesian so excellently she has no interest in learning Arabic. So all they can really do is smile at each other. From time to time they ask me to translate, but it is difficult to interpret when it's not customary for them to talk with me about women's issues and Eni's pregnancy. As for my mother, in this environment and with Australia within her sights, I think she would finally have been happy for me to be married to anyone.

The only difficulty that arises is when a woman, Mrs Talal, who is on her way to Indonesia to travel on one of my boats, arrives in Malaysia. Her husband called from Australia: 'Please, my wife is scared. Please help her.' So I move her into the apartment with my family. It imposes on the intimacy of our reunion, and my mother has to wear her headscarf when I visit because Mrs Talal is there, which introduces a formality none of us want.

But otherwise it is two glorious months, by the end of which I have organised visas for the whole family. I have to stay to meet a group of Iraqis arriving in the next few days, so I send Umi and the children on ahead to Jakarta, where Haider will collect them. The sea is beginning to come down, so it is coming time to get the boat that will take them to Australia.

I have parted ways with Rahim. He started to become greedy. By the time people were getting to me in Indonesia they had nothing for their fare to Australia.

'You don't have to rob them, what for?' I yell, and burn another bridge.

So now I need someone else to handle Malaysia. I track down Abbas, an Iraqi I know from Iran who has a good reputation for successfully moving people from Malaysia to Indonesia.

He starts sending me people, who I put in hotels to wait, and the same old pressure mounts. Once we have thirty people I can search for a boat for sixty, but I can't actually pay for it until I get the sixty, and the longer it takes, the bigger the hotel bills. My head swims. The police, the navy and coastguard all want money, and if I make a deal with one for more than the others, they all want extra. So it's a juggle, and in the end if anything goes wrong I owe everyone.

When I find the stress unbearable I visit my family in their hotel, and we eat together and I am able to calm down. We snuggle close to each other on the floor, hands weaving and colliding, relaxing into our familiar rituals that re-establish order in our worlds.

Meanwhile Eni's pregnancy is beginning to show. We know it is a girl and we have called her Nagis, which is Arabic for Jasmine. I am torn between organising the boat to get my family out and being with my new family which is growing in Eni's womb. Whenever I can, I drive madly to Bandung to lie by her side and rest my head on her swelling belly, listening for sounds of our baby, and murmuring softly to prepare her for this world. I am determined not to let her suffer like my parents and my siblings have. She is the panacea that will make all our torment worth it.

STARING AT THE HORIZON

As Kupang has become unworkable I need to find a new location for departure. Despite my rift with Mushbah I know no one else who can help so I have to bite my tongue and call him. He suggests Bali, assuring me there are remote beaches that will work, but when I go there, there are too many police and tourists, as I always suspected.

So I fly to neighbouring Lombok. It has secluded beaches and far fewer tourists, but the authorities want big money. Some refugees who are caught exaggerate the sums of money they paid to smugglers, in order to get sympathy. Others tell the truth but forget to mention how much of it went on bribes, transport and accommodation. So the police imagine it is all still in our pockets and they want their share.

I am running out of viable alternatives when Mushbah calls and suggests Bau-Bau in Sulawesi, so I agree to take a look. On the map it looks a long way to go, and travel amongst any of the Indonesian islands is always an ordeal, but we are running out of choices.

So three of us, Mushbah, a driver and me, fly from Surabaya to Sulawasi, then there are two days of hell. We drive from the airport to the first ferry. We put the car on the ferry, and when we get to land we drive to another ferry which is like a fast cat, so we leave the car. It takes us to another island, where we rent another car and drive to Bau-Bau. It is impossible to sleep in the upright seats on the ferry so we sleep in the car. I curse under my breath as I contort myself into excruciating positions to try and rest.

When we arrive we go to an old hotel near the beach and all I want to do is sleep. But in what seems like only minutes, there is a loud banging on the door.

Inevitably my heart pounds as I leap from my bed. For the rest of our lives every Iraqi who has lived under Saddam will experience these moments as a brief encounter with possible death. I take a deep breath and try to relax. I don't want to present myself with fear in my eyes.

It is of course the police. 'We have had smugglers here before,' one of them says, 'but now we have received a letter from Jakarta to say watch out for foreigners coming with these operations. So I am very sorry to tell you, we can't help you.'

Even in my half-delirious state I know the game is up.

Next morning we wake and without talking we check out and get back on the ferry. By the time we reach Jakarta we have wasted five days and considerable expense, and we still haven't found a place for the boat to go from.

By now Haider has nearly a hundred people waiting to go and they are getting impatient. I can't tell them we don't have a boat or a place of departure, or they will go to another smuggler.

'Soon,' I assure them, but they can read my face and some begin to go elsewhere.

I am mad at Mushbah but Bau-Bau was not exactly his fault, so when he calls me a few days later to suggest Maumere, I am ready to say yes to anything. I pull my map onto the grimy hotel carpet. Maumere is down the archipelago on Flores Island, north-west of Kupang, and over twice the distance to Ashmore Reef but mostly through calm waters.

'Okay,' I say wearily, 'let's go look.'

'And by the way, I have found you a boat,' he adds.

'Is it big enough for a hundred people?'

'No problem.'

'Is it a good boat? My family will be going on it.'

'It's good.'

I am troubled at having to let Mushbah buy the boat before I have seen it, but our situation is becoming so desperate that I have no choice.

I take a group of people with me to Surabaya and put them in a hotel, then fly to Maumere with Mushbah. He has heard it is a good quiet place, but he has no contacts there, so I am sure it is going to be another dead end.

Our taxi driver from the airport, who introduces himself as Francis, must have guessed our purpose, because he tells us he owns this taxi and his own business, and asks if he can be any help to us.

'We need a hotel for a large group of people,' I say, beginning to pay attention.

No doubt this confirms his suspicions, because he says, 'The people in this town don't like smugglers. We trusted one because he was married to an Indonesian girl, but he disappeared without paying anyone.' His voice is tinged with bitterness.

'But I will try and help you,' he adds after a pause.

I look more closely at him. No doubt he is keen to milk the foreigner, but hopefully, if I am vigilant, we can make it work for him as well as me. I start to feel more cheerful.

So Francis begins to work for me, and Mushbah goes back to Kupang to find a captain and collect the boat. While he is gone Francis helps me to organise a hotel, a secluded beach, and a deal with the police. I insist he only pays them half up front, and the rest once the boat has left. They agree, but from now on they are watching my every move in case I run away like the smuggler who disappeared.

Haider has already taken the rest of the people, including Basim, to Surabaya, but to fly one hundred people from there to Maumere will cost many thousands more than the ferry. So next I go to meet Haider and we find scalpers to help us buy plane tickets for the sixty people who have paid me in full already. For the forty who have paid half or nothing, we buy ferry tickets. From Surabaya Haider will take them by bus across Bali to a port on the other side of the island, where the ferry leaves for Maumere.

I decide to let Basim go on the ferry with him. The rest of my family will fly in from Jakarta and meet Basim, then all leave together. It has been years of longing for the day when I can dispatch them to safety, but now, after the immense difficulties and stress of pulling this boat together, I am strangely numb to it.

'It's all under control,' Haider says confidently as I leave.

'Keep an eye on my brother. He can be a handful,' I grin.

He laughs and waves me off.

I return to Maumere and the people begin to fly in. I put them in a hotel consisting of huts scattered amongst the palm trees.

At night I toss and turn for no reason. So far everything is running smoothly. Francis is organised to load food and water. Mushbah assures me the captain and the boat will arrive from Kupang before morning. The weather is right, the moon is full, the ferry and everyone, including my family, will be here by tomorrow.

In the morning I meet the people in the hotel as they check out. I tell them to sit by a local beach and picnic like tourists. Then Francis picks me up to drive me to the airport, and to my relief reports that the boat has arrived and is loaded.

The plane arrives with the last group, and then I see my family coming across the tarmac. Hashim runs ahead and I sweep him up, and despite my stress we are all soon laughing.

We drive them to a little beach near the edge of the town, where the other passengers are gathered.

'Wait here for me,' I say hurriedly.

Shortly I'll have another forty Arabs in town, and it's only a matter of time before one authority or another will be onto me.

'I'm going to meet the ferry that Basim is on,' I say, and my mother lights up.

I call Haider but the phone is dead. Connection between islands is unpredictable and the ferry would still be too far out of range to get Basim, but I can't help becoming uneasy. When Francis and I reach the port with a bus there is already a crowd gathering and it is not long before we see the ferry appear on the horizon. I get out and watch it come towards us, almost overcome with relief, when my phone rings. It is Basim. 'We were late.'

Familiar with my worst fears being realised, I remain silent.

'The ferry left without us. We are still in Bali.'

His voice is flat and emotionless. He too is used to disappointment. 'We are back in Denpasar.'

I hang up trying to contain my rage, but then I explode at Francis. 'This is totally fucked up. Ten days before the ferry comes again. We'll have to go without them! Forty people!' I howl with fury, 'Forty people!'

Francis hustles me into the bus before I attract attention. Now Basim will be left behind too. Will this ever end?

Francis turns the bus around and I stare out the window, warding off the powerlessness which threatens to engulf me. I had told Haider to get there early, but I have to stop blaming him. Unlike Malik he takes responsibility, and never fails to come up with good ideas. But sometimes he takes on a venture then becomes overwhelmed with fear. No doubt being deported from his home by Saddam when he was a kid contributes. I should have paid more heed.

I go back to my family, who sit near the beach like good tourists with the others, and break it to them that Basim won't be coming. Their faces drop. My mother in particular, not wanting to be parted from him yet again, is distressed. Before they sense my own agitation I go and get some food so we can sit on the grass and eat together. Our last supper. I have read the Bible. We only have a few hours before they will be gone again.

Sitting nearby is Abbas, who has been sending me people from Malaysia. He has decided to take up my offer of a free passage to Australia, and his friend Jamal is wavering as to whether to go too. Jamal is a few years younger than me and is smart, funny and full of energy. I invite them to join us for some food.

'Why don't you go with your family?' Jamal asks.

'It would destroy their chances,' I reply. 'The Australian police are hunting me, so when they ask who their smuggler is, some passengers would point to me, hoping it would help their case. Then who knows what would happen to my family.' I laugh, but not for long, as the reality of them going to Australia tonight without me begins to hit.

We wait until dark, then Francis brings two large buses and they head off with the people. I follow with my family and Mrs Talal, who has been travelling with them, in Wayan's taxi, to a sandy beach where the boat is waiting. In the light of the full moon we can see it silhouetted against a cloudless sky.

Everyone is nervous and just wants to get going but the tide is out and the small boats can't get through the reef that lies a few hundred metres offshore. For nearly an hour we wait for the water to inch higher and I am worried there is going to be panic, but eventually we hear the engines of the motorboats nosing through the shoal towards us.

Francis keeps the people orderly while Abbas, Jamal and I help them board, then push the boat off and watch as it heads out to the main vessel. Each time one returns, my family step back so they can spend some extra minutes with me. None of us know how long it will be this time, in fact, like when I left Iran, there is no way of knowing if I will ever see them again.

One of the small boats comes back and there is only my family, Abbas and Jamal left. I put my arm around my mother. Like most Iraqis, she has never in her life been in a boat, let alone on the open sea.

'Umi, it is time to go,' I say gently, then turn to Hashim. 'Hashim, come on, climb in, I will come with you to the big boat.'

Once we are all on board Francis is about to push us off when Jamal grabs my shoulder. 'I think I stay, Ali.'

I will be pleased to have his companionship during what is going to be a lonely time. 'That's good, Jamal.'

He hugs Abbas, then drops over the side as the engine revs, and we are on our way.

The huge moon illuminates the mother ship as we draw up along-side it, and I am disappointed in what I see. It is much smaller than I had ordered. Apart from Basim being left behind, I am suddenly glad the people on the ferry didn't make it. The boat would not have been big enough for all of them.

I shake Abbas's hand as he climbs up the steep side of the old wooden vessel, and then I say goodbye to my family. My mother is crying as usual. I hug her with a mixture of joy and despair until the Indonesian crew call from above that they have to go.

One by one I help Umi, Ahlam and Inas up the ladder. Then there is Hashim. I hold him until the hand of one of the crew comes down from the dark and next thing he is being pulled from my arms and dis-appearing over the side. I stare into the shadows until he reappears again and then they are all leaning out above me.

'Ali, Ali,' I hear them calling. 'We will see you in Australia.'

The big boat begins to pull away and in a strange kind of panic I call to my driver, 'Go with them. Please, go with them.'

He opens up his outboard to full throttle and we jump the wake and speed up alongside her big hulky bow. I can hardly see their faces as I stare into the dark, spray whipping my eyes, as we wave our arms and call each other's names. I am crying and I am laughing. I have done what I set out to do. They are on their way, and I am alone again.

'We have to go back,' the driver of the boat yells. 'We're approaching open sea.' He swings the wheel, banks in a circle and heads for the shore. I stare back, watching as the shape of the boat merges into the blackness. It is not until we cut the engine and are about to land that I look around at the beach and see the navy, the police, everyone, waiting for me.

I pay them and they disappear into the night, then I ask Francis and Jamal to wait for me. I walk off along the beach, gripped by a deep wrenching sadness. I thought it would be easier now I have my own child coming, but after what I have had to do to get my family to Australia, it is now unlikely I will ever be able to join them.

We won't get news of the boat for five or six days, so I pull myself together and fly to Bali with Jamal. I leave him in the hotel and track down Haider. 'What happened?' I ask, aware by his appearance that it has been an ordeal for him.

'I heard the police were all over the port,' he says haltingly. 'There was no way they wouldn't notice a group of forty frightened Arabs waiting for the ferry. So I tried to arrive just before it left. Maybe it was the wrong decision.'

'It's okay,' I sigh. 'They wouldn't all have fitted on the boat anyway.'

Next I have to deal with the passengers. Some of them understand, others have been waiting for months to leave and are furious they missed the ferry. As I am now going to have to send another boat to get them and Basim out, I decide to pay Francis and Mushbah later and use their fee to repay the people who don't want to wait.

But when I get back to the hotel Mushbah calls from Kupang. He wants his money.

'You cheated me,' I snap angrily. 'The boat was too small. Just lucky for you everyone didn't turn up. You charged me for a much bigger boat. We hardly have money for food, so you will have to wait.'

Jamal, who is sharing my room, has been listening. 'If you fix me a passport and get me back to Malaysia I can be of help,' he says when I hang up. 'I can take over where Abbas left off and send you people.'

'That would be good, Jamal,' I say gratefully.

That night I can't sleep. I get up for a glass of water and watch Jamal sleeping as I drink. I see us thrown together in this bleak hotel room in a land where we don't belong, with our own lonely thoughts, and I want to rip Saddam's throat out for destroying our country and driving us from our homes.

Haider, Jamal, Basim and I fly back to Jakarta. I organise a passport for Jamal and he heads off to Malaysia. Basim goes back to the rented house where he has already made friends, and Haider and I get a room while we continue to wait for news.

The days drag by. If I sleep I am plagued by nightmares. Ahlam and Inas scream for their mother, her heavy robes ballooning and entrapping her thrashing limbs, while little Hashim flounders silently then slips beneath the surface of an untamed empty sea. I hear their voices calling me, Umi uncharacteristically calm, telling me it is not my fault. I wake dripping. Then on the seventh day the phone rings.

It is an Iraqi living in Australia whose family is on the boat.

'Did my family die?' he asks fearfully.

I freeze.

'What do you mean, die?' I whisper, unsure if the words have come out.

'I heard news about a boat going down. I think it is yours.'

I sink onto the bed in a daze. After several minutes of staring trancelike at the floor I call Mushbah.

'Yes, it is true,' he says and I stop breathing. Then I bash my head with my hand. He lied about the size of the boat, why would I believe him when he says my family is dead?

'No, they arrive!' I scream down the phone. 'They arrive!'

For the next few days Haider comes and goes, bringing me food, which I can't eat, and coffee. Night and day slip by without me knowing which is which. I lie so still that Haider has to shake me from time to time to make sure I'm not dead.

On the fourteenth day Afrah calls from her home in Sydney. I am still catatonic on my bed. Haider answers the phone because I have ceased to do so, but I can hear her voice even from across the room.

'They have arrived! They are here!' she cries and I try to comprehend. Then Haider holds the phone out to me and I reach for it.

'They're alive?' I manage to get out as I begin to thaw.

'They are. The captain got lost so it took them seven days, then when they landed the Australians kept the news from the media so no one knew.'

Haider puts his arm around my shoulder and I weep like a child.

THE TIDE TURNS

So far everyone I have put on a boat has arrived in Australia safely. I now know the business, I have Haider and Jamal as trusted employees, and more importantly I have a respected name. There is no reason why I can't do one big final run, send Basim, and make enough to survive until I can work out a way to get myself there.

But it is becoming a race against time with Interpol and the Australian Federal Police in Jakarta after me. Somehow the AFP have found out Haider is my employee.

'They've asked me to spy on you,' he laughs.

'Great. Spy on me. Give them the right details, just the wrong days.'

So Haider goes to their office every two weeks and tells them what they want to know, but never accurately enough for them to catch me, and then we have lunch with the money they pay him. It is a dangerous game in many ways, but on the other hand Haider finds out from their questions what they know about me, and from that we can stay ahead of them. After all, it is better to stay close to your enemy.

There are so many asylum seekers waiting for boats we decide to go for broke and take two hundred. Jamal has good contacts in Iran and is soon sending me groups of twenty or thirty Iraqis at a time. Before long I have about eighty who have paid the full amount.

I don't ask them to help each other any more, I just use some of the money from those who can pay for the ones who can't, particularly lone women and children. The money is an amorphous thing that flows back and forth, so I don't have to say no to anyone. If they went with any other smuggler they would have to pay the same amount or more, and it would not go towards any worthy causes. The ones I help say they will pay me back but they seldom do, because I am a 'wealthy people smuggler'.

Buying the boat is hanging over me. The only person I have ever negotiated directly with to buy one is Mushbah. I don't want to work with him again, but despite our bad history, and issues of size and age aside, he has always delivered. They have been strong seaworthy boats with good engines, which have always reached their destination without problems. So I decide it is better the devil I know, and against my better judgement, I call him.

Sooner than expected Mushbah says he has found a boat for two hundred people. He needs a deposit of $US10000. I send it and tell him I will be coming to check the boat before we pay the balance. But this is Mushbah's checkmate. He keeps the money to pay himself and Francis for the last boat.

'I don't owe you nearly that much,' I yell down the phone. 'You know I'll pay you. I just need it to get the next boat up first.'

'I don't care if you need money or no money. I keep it,' he snarls. And then he disappears so I can't get my hands on him.

So there is nothing I can do about it. But then I get a call from a guy called Bambang I met when I was last in Kupang. He is older and more mature than Mushbah and must have heard what happened, because he wants to know if I need any help. Desperate, I accept his offer and within a week he finds a good boat in Surabaya, big enough for more than two hundred people, for $US26000. I buy it and put it in his name. He gives me the papers and I will pay him when the boat reaches its destination.

The next headache is finding a good captain. Bambang could do it, but since the fiasco with Mushbah I am determined I will employ each person to look after one area.

So I take a chance and call a fisherman Haider had met in Surabaya. He agrees to come to Jakarta to meet us. He is from Roti Island, just near Kupang, so any captains from there would know Ashmore Reef very well, as they go there regularly to fish.

'My God, I can't do business with this guy,' I whisper to Haider when I see him. 'Look at his feet, he came on the plane in rubber thongs.'

But as he talks I begin to forget his slovenly appearance. He is in his forties with a rugged face and quiet, thoughtful demeanour. Haider and I agree he seems straight and honest, but I take no chances.

'I just want you to get me a captain. You guarantee him, then I pay you when he arrives on Ashmore Reef.'

I realise I have finally become good at this business, and now on my last boat I can see how you should do it. 'I need some work done on the boat to carry people,' I tell the fisherman, and he agrees to find tradesmen to do it.

The boat is Bambang's responsibility, so he brings it to a small cove near Surabaya and helps them to fix it up. They take pride in their work and sleep on the boat at night to protect it.

Below deck we put a timber floor for the people to sit on and cover it with cheap carpet and piles of old pillows. We install lights, and block the engine so the people don't have to breathe the smoke. On the deck we construct a fence so the children won't fall overboard. We build a rough kitchen and put in a large drum of water for washing, gas cylinders, and a makeshift toilet.

I am beginning to trust Bambang enough that when he says he knows someone with experience in organising a location for departure and in handling the police, I agree to meet him. He seems like an honest guy, so when he suggests a suitable beach near Surabaya, not far from where the boat is moored, and says he has good contacts with the police, I employ him.

Back in Jakarta Jamal arrives, accompanying the last group from Malaysia. Our final count is two hundred and thirty adults plus children. The boat is large enough, but getting them to Surabaya will be a massive manoeuvre. Aware that I am now a target, we have to be extremely careful. One person panicking could expose us all.

It is the middle of August 2001. The weather is good, the moon is full, the boat is waiting at an isolated beach. Haider has told the Australian Federal Police there is a boat departing, but not, he thinks, until the end of the month.

Haider and Jamal start sending groups and I go ahead to meet them. Within a week all the people, including Basim, have arrived and are in different hotels around Surabaya.

Bambang loads the boat with food and huge quantities of bottled water. When it is dark we collect the people from their hotels in buses and drive south, down the coast. That is when someone realises we have left twenty-two people behind.

I am angry. I am running like a dog with too many sheep. They call me on my phone and I swing my rented four-wheel drive around and head back to Surabaya at 140 kilometres an hour. I burst into their hotel room and hustle them out into taxis. But the taxis won't go further than the edge of the city, so I have to stop and rent a minibus. I drive it myself so I won't lose them again. I wonder if maybe people get so scared at the final hour that they can't move. But what I really don't understand is why the others didn't think of them. These people are Mandaeans who came all the way from Iran together. They are like family, and then they leave some of them behind in the next room.

The beach looks similar to most of the other places of departure, except the main vessel hovering near the horizon is bigger than we have ever had before.

The local police are already here. I realise they don't only turn a blind eye, it is in their interest to make sure there is no trouble. If a different patrol, like the navy or the coastguard, come by, the police will have to share the cake with them. The ones at the top, the big fish, are very rich, but the small fish don't get much by the time it trickles down, so they are always on the lookout for more, and thus it all goes around.

While people smuggling is not a crime in Indonesia, the authorities are still meant to stop people departing without passports, and boats are supposed to have clearance. But these local police are the authority in this area, so there is no one to question the fact that they are letting a boatload of refugees with no passports go. If anything goes wrong it is easy enough to deny it. 'No, not from here, where is the evidence?'

Thus while the Australian Federal Police and the Indonesian National Police are supposedly working together to bust the smugglers, corrupt local police, immigration officials, and the lower ranks in the forces, are working with the smugglers to keep the business going. So what chance Australia would ever have of stopping any of it in a country this poor is questionable.

I hurry the latecomers to where Haider and Jamal have the last of the people in orderly queues, and are helping them climb aboard the small motorboats that lie purring and ready. Behind us the Indonesian police hover, which makes the people happy because they think it means they are safe, oblivious to the fact that that is where a large portion of their money went.

I leap into the last motorboat as it pulls away. When we reach the mother ship I climb on board and up onto the mast. I look down at their faces full of excitement and fear as they tussle for a few feet of deck to live on for the long days and nights ahead. I watch parents holding children, who are already seasick, and I think of the tragedy that this is the only alternative left to them.

'You are brave,' I call into the wind as the big ship rocks on the rise and fall of the swell. 'You didn't lie down and let Saddam destroy you. It takes courage to make this journey. But do as I say. This is meant to be a fishing boat, so don't climb on the roof so the navy can see it is not. It is a good boat with everything you need. And the captain is a good captain. He will take you to Australia, but do what he tells you, and don't argue with each other. If you fight and make trouble I can't help you. From now on you take responsibility for yourselves. This is your chance to start again and leave all the horrors behind you. So good luck and goodbye.'

I climb down to Basim. 'Do well in Australia, my brother,' I say, hugging him. Then I get off the boat, and watch it head out into the dark infinity of the ocean. This is the final one, with the last of my family on it, and I am determined not to get back on the treadmill again.

I am tired. I am only thirty years of age and I feel that at last I can move on with my life.

I want to go home to Eni to share her pregnancy but I stick to my rule of waiting until we know the boat is safe. So Haider, Jamal and I go back to Jakarta to sit it out. There has been no sign of the Australian Federal Police but they will soon find out I have dispatched a boatload of two hundred and thirty people on their watch, and they won't be happy.

After a week the news finally comes through that the boat has made it. I am elated. I have completed my mission, and not only have Basim and everyone arrived, but for the first time I have made a profit, with no debts to be paid off.

I return to Bandung and that night, as I listen to Eni breathing gently in her sleep, I rest my hand on her growing belly. Now that my family is safe, I can focus on my daughter. She will soon be coming into this world and I am anxious about her future.

So next day I give extra to Haider and Jamal, and then I buy a little house in Bogor for $US17000. I put it in Eni's name so now I know if anything happens to me, she and Nagis will always have somewhere to live. With what is left I buy a decent car, with the idea that I can make money as a driver, collecting businessmen and tourists from the airport. I have to lie low for now.

We move into our new house and life is good. We are not outside Bogor, where the rented villas are, but near the park that surrounds the old palace. We take long walks around the lake and sit under the shade of large fig trees to watch the deer grazing. They are so tame they nibble grass from our hands through the fence, watching us cautiously with their big doe eyes.

I have heard from Umi that Afrah is having a son about the same time that Nagis is due and now I can think of nothing else but children.

That night I am staring out at our small neat garden, trying to visualise a little girl created from my broad Arab features and Eni's delicate Indonesian ones, when my phone rings. I am inclined to ignore it, but it might be someone with word from my family, so I answer.

It is my father in Iraq.

I had heard from my grandmother he had finally been released when I was sending my last boat from Kupang, but he had not wanted to talk to anyone. He went back to our empty family home and now lives there alone. A decade of horror seems to have consolidated his fragile mental condition and finally broken his wild, fearless spirit. He now has trouble leaving the house, let alone coming to Australia, so despite a burning desire to see him again I have not attempted to bring him.

We seldom speak because he has no phone, and anyway it is dangerous for him to be caught talking to me, but he has urgent news.

'In two months your brother Asad completes his sentence and will get out of jail.'

It is hard to believe it is seven years since that terrible night Asad and Basim were picked up trying to cross the border into Kurdistan, having missed their rendezvous with Unis and me in Mosul. I have often punished myself for not waiting longer for them, so now I am elated. Asad will be freed. But then my father goes on.

'They will only release him if we pay money. They ask for $US10 000, and warn that when they let him go maybe the secret police will grab him again, so he has to get out of Iraq.'

My heart sinks. Suddenly the life I have been dreaming of is becoming distant again, as the weight of my family settles onto my shoulders once more.

Driven by the unimaginable thought of him ending up back in one of Saddam's jails, I allow myself to consider the unbearable. One more run to get Asad out of prison and Iraq.

Next morning I drive to Jakarta and tell Haider and Jamal. 'I want to send another boat,' I mumble sheepishly.

'Okay, but we'd better do it soon,' Jamal responds. 'Things are getting nasty since the *Tampa*. Have you been watching the news?'

I shrug. The truth is I seldom have time or the inclination. The asylum seekers keep up with the news about where they are going, but for the smugglers it is irrelevant.

'A boat sank with over four hundred and thirty refugees,' Haider says. 'At the request of the Australians a huge Norwegian container ship called the *Tampa* went off course and rescued them. But when they took them to Christmas Island the Australians wouldn't let them land because they don't want any more asylum seekers. I even heard they were threatening the master of the ship with prosecution as a people smuggler if he dares enter Australian waters with the survivors.'

'At least we are in good company,' I quip.

'If you want to do it I have seventy or eighty people in Malaysia waiting to go,' Jamal replies seriously. 'They are scared about what is happening in Australia and want to leave quickly, but Abu Quassey is the only person with a boat ready and they are unsure about him. If you did another boat they would go with you immediately.'

It seems too easy, and this is so often when I stumble, but I am experienced now, with a good team.

That evening I tell Eni I have to go back to work in Jakarta for a few weeks and while she is disappointed, she is happy money will be coming in. Whenever I am dealing with my job or family I speak in Arabic so she knows little about what I do. I have told her I am in import/export, which is not entirely untrue. I have also avoided telling her much about my past because unearthing the memories is such a painful business. But so long as it doesn't affect our relationship she seems happy not to interfere in my affairs.

I sit watching her chop vegetables for our dinner, her swollen stomach pressing out against her oversized T-shirt. I am imagining our baby curled inside her like a kitten, and dreading the idea of doing another boat, when my Uncle Kasem calls from the US.

'Did you hear the news?'

'What news?' I mumble, lost in my thoughts.

'The US has been bombed.'

'Now they'll know what it is like,' I say dismissively.

'Fuck America,' he explodes with pent-up frustration fuelled by memories of a bullet in his back and a terrifying escape during the Shiite uprising, which was encouraged then abandoned by the Yanks.

'They destroy us. Let them eat what we eat, let them feel what we felt for ten years.'

As he rants I turn on the TV, expecting nothing much. But I see images I will never forget. Jets plunging into skyscrapers, black smoke, fire and tiny human figures flailing through the air as they plummet thousands of feet to their death. Then, as I stand holding my breath, a massive glass tower folds into itself and collapses in a pile of rubble. A firestorm of choking white dust follows, engulfing New York City and its people. Then another tower crumples. I am horrified. There is no doubt my Muslim brothers who presumably unleashed this catastrophe will wound the pride of America so greatly that the retribution could change the world forever.

I had always avoided politics in Iraq until they killed Ahmad, and the same in Indonesia until now, but one way or another I keep ending up being forced to pay attention. I don't watch much Australian news because my English is so bad but now I begin to tune in. It seems that the Australian Prime Minister, Mr John Howard, who was in America at the time of this disaster, is using it to further demonise asylum seekers.

He appears to be trying to persuade his public that terrorists are disguising themselves as refugees and being brought in on boats by people smugglers, and that this attack on New York somehow verifies his fears.

It's hard to imagine why terrorists would embark on such an ordeal by boat, only to end up in a detention centre for years, when they can afford to fly in comfortably with false passports and visas. If you go to Australia by air, as ninety-eight percent of asylum seekers do, you are detained briefly, then released into the community. So if I was a terrorist, that would be the way I'd go.

It is unclear why Australians are so strangely unconcerned about asylum seekers arriving by airplane; maybe because there're no pictures in the paper or on TV. But they are so afraid of the two percent who come by boat that they lock them up like criminals. As with the Jews in World War II, the refugees' pitiful plight inspires irrational fear. If Australian people only knew the strength it takes to get on one of these boats, to keep holding onto life after the horrors these people have been through, they would be filled with awe and admiration.

Nervous about how this American tragedy will affect us, I go to Jakarta and join Haider and Jamal.

Such is the demand, we now have at least a hundred and fifty people waiting, so I meet with them in groups. The general hysteria that is being whipped up in Australia around 'boat people' is making them desperate to go before the door closes completely. I warn them I have heard that the Australian Navy might turn the boat back or send them to a place called Nauru.

'I have a baby and no money,' one woman says with desperation in her voice. 'My husband is in Australia. They give him a temporary visa, so by boat is the only way we can get to him.'

'I am sorry,' I respond impotently.

'To go back home is certain death for me,' a young man says, and everyone falls quiet as they reflect on their own fate.

'Okay,' I say. 'We share the risk but you must stick to the deal. I take you and if you are turned back within seven days I will pay you back half what you gave me. But only within seven days. After that I can't help you, because after seven days I have to pay everyone in Indonesia, so then it will be your problem.'

They are all happy with this, and when I tell my team they agree. Even if the boat does get turned back, with money from visas and what's left I should still at least be able to pull together enough to get Asad out of jail. So I take a room in the Matraman and get to work acquiring passports and travel documents. Meanwhile the Australian Prime Minister's hostility increases, with claims that Iraqi asylum seekers on another boat have thrown their children overboard in a ploy to be rescued and taken to Australia.

Anyone acquainted with our culture knows family is everything to us, and protecting our children ranks higher than our own lives. What we hear from relatives is that the people on board held their children up when the boat was sinking, to let the navy know they had precious cargo, and the children ended up in the water with their parents because the navy let the boat go down. But unfortunately the horse has bolted. Iraqi 'boat people' are now seen by most Australians as inhuman.

As we prepare for departure, some of the people from Abu Quassey's boat start coming to me.

'Look,' I say. 'He is only in it to make money. I am too but in a different way, for different reasons. You have to decide but I wouldn't advise you to go with him.'

Some of them have already paid him or are staying in his accommodation, which makes it difficult.

'I know it is a hard decision,' I tell them, 'but I warn you that he doesn't tell the truth.'

They ask many questions, and go back and forth while the numbers for our boat are growing. I want to tell them Abu Quassey was involved with the organisation that betrayed me when I first came here, but it is hard to warn people. It usually reflects worse on you than the other person.

'If you want to come as a group,' I say in a last attempt, 'I will only charge you $US700 each. But you need to decide because we will soon be full.'

Some of them come, some don't, but there is nothing more I can do.

Bambang has bought a good-sized boat that will take over two hundred people. The fisherman has fixed it up with his crew and got a new captain. I decide to depart from Surabaya again.

Our boat leaves on 15 October 2001, before Abu Quassey's. Perhaps because it all went so smoothly at our end I put aside concerns about the Australian Navy. And as Eni's pregnancy progresses she is finding my long absences increasingly difficult, so I break my rule and go back to Bogor.

Seven, eight, nine days go by and there is still no news. The Indonesians are wanting their money but I keep them waiting. Then at last on the tenth day we hear the boat has made it to Australia. I pay Bambang, the fisherman and everyone on our team. Then I send the money for Asad to Iraq, and there is money left over to bring him here when he gets out of jail. I am feeling very satisfied with our success and begin to think again about my own future.

Then four days later I get a call. I see the number is Indonesian. I know the guy is from the boat. I have to force myself to answer.

'Why are you here? What happened?'

'The Australian Navy, they push us back to Indonesia. Another boat with nearly four hundred people sank and most of them drowned. Australia is using it as an excuse not to accept any more asylum seekers. We were sent back to Lombok. Everyone is scared and we have nothing.'

'Look,' I say, 'we had a deal. I already waited three days more than we agreed.'

'Please help us,' he begs.

Once again I see my prospects evaporating.

To be a smuggler you need to have both compassion and a hard head. Haider is too caring. Jamal is the only one I know apart from me who is humanitarian but also has the capacity to be tough. It is possible to keep both things alive, but at this moment my two sides are at war. I can't turn off my mind to their misery, but we made a deal which, albeit not their fault, these people didn't keep and fifty or sixty of them had in the end gone for free or just paid half with promises for the rest. I send them $US4000, but I am afraid of opening the floodgates. There are over two hundred people. I can't possibly help them all.

Then, to make things worse, we hear that the boat that sank, which the Australians are calling the SIEVX, was Abu Quassey's boat, and it is making international headlines because so many people died. I hear they were mostly women and children, because Mr Howard's introduction of a Temporary Protection Visa means men who have already arrived are not allowed to apply for their families to join them. So the only hope of being reunited is for the women and children to be smuggled in by boat.

I turn on Al Jazeera and discover 353 people, mostly fellow Iraqis, drowned: 146 children, 142 women and 65 men. Only 45, mostly men, survived. I had been speaking to some of them only days before. It torments me that I wasn't more forceful in convincing them not to go with Abu Quassey.

If I had checked the size of the boat, and realised he was taking so many people, I would have known they would be unlikely to make it through Sunda Strait. Even with a large boat and a small load, it is perilous, then there is the vast Indian Ocean with its huge seas. There was a reason why we traipsed all over the archipelago searching for proximity to the calm waters of Ashmore Reef.

For the next two weeks I stay hidden in Bogor. I struggle not to be weighed down by the return of my own boat, and to keep the SIEVX tragedy out of my thoughts, but the faces of so many I met who are probably now dead hover in my dreams.

There is a rumour that Australia didn't respond to reports that the SIEVX was in distress because they didn't want to receive any more asylum seekers. I wonder if the woman who was taking her son to meet his father survived, or if he weeps alone in the land of opportunity.

Soon the lives lost are overborne by politics. I turn off the TV news and try to leave it that way. I hear from Afrah that Khalid has been released from detention in Woomera, which brightens me up. They knew he was a smuggler's brother, but when the asylum seekers confirmed he never took money from them, they didn't tar him with my brush. They found him to be a genuine refugee and gave him a visa.

But my mother and other siblings are all still there, and Afrah tells me Hashim is not coping well. He is surrounded by razor wire and guards, like the inside of a jail, and has been exposed to self-harm, hunger strikes and suicides. It is hard to accept that I have sent my little brother to somewhere that sounds worse than what he escaped from.

It makes me angry. But in January 2002 I have a distraction that is out of my control. Eni's waters break and we have to get to the hospital.

My adrenaline is pumping. It is like a drug. I am inebriated with the thrill of expectation. Our baby is about to be born and it becomes all I can think about. This time I am so swept up I am no longer afraid of women's hospitals. I am there, standing by Eni's side. Sleeping in the waiting room, by her side again. Until I am suddenly woken by the nurse.

'Quickly, she is coming.'

I rush to the delivery room just as Nagis appears, sliding into the world. Eni clings to my hand, yelling, but her cries turn to pleasure when she sees our baby girl. The nurse gives her to me while they clean Eni up and I gaze in wonder at this tiny little creature we have produced. There are no words to describe the happiness I feel, or the outpouring of love and need to protect her that I experience.

I spend two nights sleeping with them in the hospital. Listening with exhilaration to our baby's minute breaths. Then once we are home I have a small interlude in my life that is pure joy. I know it will not last for long so I relish every moment. I lie for hours beside this little child and run my fingers over her tiny body. She touches my face and pulls my hair as she begins to explore her world, which at this stage is Eni and me.

Every second day, I drive to Jakarta airport and chauffeur businessmen and wealthy travellers to hotels and shopping centres in my car. While it is not a lot of money it is enough for us to live, but I can never relax. Even though I am finished with smuggling, the Australian Federal Police are still after me. So each time I pull into the airport I have to circle a few times to make sure they are not lurking.

Late at night when the traffic thins I drive back home to Bogor, and next day I spend every minute I can with baby Nagis. I am besotted. I am love-struck. I am so drunk with her I am on another planet. She has tiny perfect hands like her mother's, the softest smooth brown skin, and an intoxicatingly sweet baby smell. Her very existence wipes away the misery of my life and I am reborn with the bliss of Nagis.

I am holding her in my arms, her little fingers grasping mine, when the phone rings.

It is my father again. 'I can't talk long but Asad has been released.

Can you get him to Australia?'

'Thank God,' is all I say. I don't want to tell him that in the current climate, even if I had money to get Asad to Indonesia, the only way out of here now is by plane. My contacts in Immigration all keep telling me it is very expensive and high risk now. 'We can't guarantee Asad won't be stopped by Australian officials,' they say, 'once he is in the air.'

Not that my father would understand any of this. Despite all his years of protest and punishment he never was a political man, he just knew about right and wrong.

'Tell Asad to keep his head down for the moment, while I work something out,' I say, knowing that I don't only have to get him to Australia, but first I have to get him out of Iraq, and it is a long time since I have used my resistance contacts.

Nagis, still lying nestled in my arms, murmurs and Eni takes her from me. Not wanting to be left with my concern about Asad, I relinquish her reluctantly, but I am soon overtaken with the pleasure of watching Eni release her perfect breast and feed her tenderly. How I long to immerse myself in fathering this child, but somehow I can never escape having to parent my father's children.

THE MOROCCAN PASSPORT

One morning at the airport a few weeks later, I pick up an Iraqi guy I met in Kuala Lumpur about five months ago. He was with a group who wanted to go to Australia. At that time in Jakarta, as often happens, an Australian government delegation had come to town to make a deal to stop the 'illegals', making it very difficult to get visas to Indonesia. So we had to wait and with time everything would return to normal.

So back then this guy, Rakin, knew me by reputation and took me aside. 'If you can get me a visa I have good connections and may be able to help you with something you need in the future.'

I had good contacts in Immigration so despite the drought I was able to get him a visa. I didn't see him again and I forgot about him.

So I am surprised when he climbs into my car. 'Rakin,' I say, shaking his hand. 'You didn't go to Australia?'

'No, I have relatives in Indonesia so I ended up staying here to do some business. But I haven't forgotten how you helped me. If you want anything from the Iraq embassy, if you have any problems I can help you with, my offer still stands.'

My first thought is Asad, but now he is out of jail, the problem is at the Australian end. The only thing I have ever wanted to know since the day I left Iraq is what happened to my brother Ahmad. Deserters were never spared, so I know he is dead. But, like my uncle the colonel, because I never saw his body, deep in my heart a flicker of hope has always resided. I have not let myself visit this possibility before as the finality of his death seemed easier to endure.

As I drive I silently consider whether to reopen this wound, but then I realise it is too late. With the very act of thinking about it the door is already ajar.

'There is one thing,' I begin hesitantly. 'My brother, Ahmad. For ten years we believe he is dead. But I want to be sure, and to know where he is buried.'

'I can try and do that for you.'

I go on and give him the details, but then I am too shaken to continue with social chatter.

'I will call you,' he says when we get to his hotel.

It is nearly three weeks before Rakin calls. It is night and I am driving back to Bogor.

'He is still alive,' he says nervously.

A dizziness comes over me and I swerve the car to a halt beside the freeway.

'I know a guy in the embassy who could help if you pay him enough money. I don't know his role exactly but I think he is secret police.'

'Can I meet him?'

'I will arrange it and call you.'

He hangs up and I sit staring into the headlights as they swoop by. I am back in Abu Ghraib with Ahmad, and I howl.

What will they have done to you by now, my brother? After a decade will any part of you still be alive?

I must have sat there for an hour in this state, then I begin to hear the cars rushing by, tooting their horns, flashing their lights in my mirror. And it suddenly hits me like a thunderbolt. Ahmad is alive! We can be together again. I will do whatever it takes.

It is hard for Eni to understand the enormity of what has happened and she is irritated by my distracted state and pacing. I wonder if I would have left Iraq if I had known Ahmad was alive.

It feels like a week but is only a day before Rakin calls with a time to meet his contact in the embassy. Muhtadi is a tall serious guy with an intensity that is frightening. The meeting is brief and I can tell it is important to do exactly what he wants. We discuss money and he agrees to arrange the release of my brother for $US25000.

Afterwards Rakin warns me that nobody can know about this deal. If anyone finds out, Muhtadi will be in big trouble. 'The people he is involved with, they are like a kidnapping business. So it is very dangerous for him. I will let you know when to bring the money. It might be a while, so you have time to get it.'

It seems almost impossible that after so many years of grief this could be happening. I call Afrah and she is also overwhelmed. Almost everyone in Iraq is lamenting over a relative, nobody expects them to come back from the dead.

'Afrah,' I say urgently, 'I have no way of making that sort of money any more.'

'We still have our house in Iraq.'

'That's hardly worth anything, and it would leave Baba with nowhere to live. Asad may have to take his chances and stay there too for a while. I'm still trying to work out how to get him to you.'

'I will get Umi to talk to our uncles. Now they are out of Iraq they may have some savings between them.'

'Make sure she understands absolutely no one but family is to know. It has to be kept secret.'

I try to collect some of the money promised by people I put on the boats for half-price or free, but most of them are still in detention or have more desperate needs. Now they have arrived it is easy to forget how they got there. There is one terrible choice, which I can hardly bear to consider. To sell the house I bought for my daughter. It wouldn't be enough, but the uncles may be able to make up the difference. But then if something happens to me, Indonesia is such a poor country, I am sickened by the thought of leaving my daughter with nothing.

A few days later, with an extraordinary sense of timing, a guy I know in Thailand calls to say he has a restaurant business which is expanding, and he is looking for a partner. I say I will come immediately to look into it.

Nagis is lying on her back on the floor, her feet in the air, discovering her toes. I am lying with her, trying to think of a way to break it to Eni that I have to go away again, when there is a knock at the door. I get Eni to open it in case I have to make a run for it, but it is Rakin. I know it must be serious if he is afraid to talk on the phone. I urge him to get straight to the point.

'Muhtadi has changed his mind.'

I stare at him, the blood running from my face.

'One of your family in Australia called Iraq and discussed it on the phone, and someone passed on information to the secret police,' he says apprehensively.

I sit down before I fall, and gesture for him to do the same but he stays standing. He clearly wants to leave as soon as respectably possible. I suspect he is now at risk because of this disastrous breach of trust by my own family.

'Who was it? Everyone knows our phones are bugged in Iraq,' I say bitterly, feeling I might be sick at any minute. 'We can't just leave him there, now we know he's alive.'

He winces at the look of desperation on my face.

'I can't talk about it, I am now in danger too.'

He says good night to Eni, apologising for the interruption, and disappears to his car for the long drive back to Jakarta.

I call Afrah.

'It would have been Uncle Karim,' she says, confirming my suspicion. 'He has always been a loose cannon since he got shrapnel in his head. We warned him not to speak to anyone but he can't help himself,' she sobs.

I hang up in despair.

My anguish is so overwhelming I will only keep Eni and the baby awake, so I jump the fence into the park and walk all night with the deer. I had sent Uncle Karim to Australia with Khalid and now I wish I'd left him with Saddam. But of course it is complicated. He has shrapnel in his head.

Next morning I drive into Jakarta to Rakin's hotel. He nervously lets me into his room.

'Please,' I beg. 'Could you try to persuade Muhtadi?'

'His life is now under threat,' he says with finality.

I stand there impotently. I can understand everyone's point of view but I just want my brother back. He never did anything wrong. If they were to keep anyone it should have been me.

'I'm terribly sorry for what has happened,' Rakin says with genuine caring. 'But the only thing you can do now is leave it alone until things quieten down, and then we'll see.'

He didn't close the door, which helps to salve the wound, but now I am in a new kind of purgatory.

I continue with my plan to go to Thailand, as the best possibility to make or raise money in case Muhtadi changes his mind. I meet Haider and Jamal at the 24-hour McDonald's where a lot of Iraqis and Iranians hang out, to see if they are interested in coming with me. Haider has to go back to Iran to see his sick mother, but Jamal is keen. Now the boats have stopped he is looking for work too.

'Indonesia is now full of desperate Iraqis stuck in limbo,' he says bitterly. 'They can't go forward, they can't go back. The Australians say they hate Saddam until we ask for help, then they abandon us or let us drown in the sea.'

From what Haider can ascertain from his meetings with the Australian Federal Police, they are still determined to catch me, even if the boats have stopped. I would have thought they would be too busy with Abu Quassey to worry about me, but evidently not.

'Be careful,' Haider says with concern. 'You've made fools of them and they don't like that.'

Nagis is nearly three months old when I leave for Thailand in April 2002. It will be hard to be away from her even for a few weeks. Every day there is something new in her development that I don't want to miss. Eni wants to come with me, but I know it is going to be hot trains and uncomfortable cheap hotels. It would not be good for a baby, so I manage to talk Eni out of it.

I find goodbyes so difficult I prefer to do it the night before then sidle out unnoticed in the morning. But now we have Nagis everything feels different. She knows I am her dad and looks me in the eyes, gurgling and exploring my face. I suck her miniature fingers and kiss her hands, her arms, her cheeks, until Eni has to take her away, and then I kiss Eni too. They are laughing, and I laugh with them but it is a terrible wrench to walk away, even for a few weeks. Our tiny girl has become the centre of my universe.

I leave the car with Eni and get a bus to Jakarta. I go to Rakin's hotel and make one last plea for a meeting with Muhtadi but he diplomatically rebuffs me.

'I will contact you if there is anything.' Then he adds reassuringly, 'I will try and speak to him while you are away.'

His tone of voice suggests a slight change in attitude. I sense with more money, Muhtadi may eventually come around. I leave with a lighter step and renewed hope.

I meet up with Jamal at the McDonald's to say goodbye to Haider before going to the airport. An Iraqi guy joins us with a passport he has for me. We quite like him, but amongst ourselves we call him the Weasel. He is balding, maybe ten years older than us, and had been hanging around for my last few boats. He occasionally brought me customers or bits of information, for which I paid him and offered him free passage to Australia, but he never took it. He was always short of money, and would take it from wherever he could get it, working for a number of people in the same capacity as me, but mainly with my old foe, Omeid. Then I heard he was trying to pilfer other smugglers' customers to take to Omeid, including mine. We had a blistering row and he denied it, so we still have somewhat of a relationship, in that we share CDs, he sets up meetings for me with people I don't want to meet, and hits me up for money.

I had run into him again soon after I decided to go to Thailand. He had a Nigerian friend who wanted to sell a Moroccan passport that had already been used to successfully enter Bangkok. Its Indonesian visa had run out, but the Weasel said he had a contact who could bring it up to date for me. I was short of time, and it was exactly what I needed so I bought it, replaced the photo and returned it to him so he could get it stamped. As he gives it back he says he will come to the airport for the ride.

I hug Haider. 'Goodbye, my friend. I hope your mother is okay. I will miss you,' I say, meaning it. 'If the business in Thailand works out you can join us there.'

Then Jamal and I head off with the Weasel, who just before we board says he is short of money. I give him another $US50 on top of the agreed $US400 I've already given him for the passport.

We transit in Singapore and I get off for a smoke, but as I walk around the cool, shiny terminal, festooned with delicate purple orchids, I feel like something is wrong. I stub out my cigarette and get back on the plane.

Once we are in the air again they serve us chicken for lunch and I tell Jamal about the joke we used to play on newcomers in Abu Ghraib. How we would take orders for our favourite food and the new guy would say, 'I'll just have a chicken kebab, thanks.' Then when the filthy prison food came we ate his share because he was waiting for his kebab.

We laugh. Then I look at Jamal seriously. 'When we arrive, if anything happens to me, you go on. Okay?'

Jamal looks at me, surprised. 'Okay. But why are you saying this?'

'I don't know. I just have a bad feeling, that's all. And if we are both caught we can't help each other.'

So we arrive in Bangkok, and as we approach Customs I go slow and let Jamal pass me, to get some distance between us. I watch as he reaches the checkpoint and presents his Yemen passport which doesn't need a visa. They stamp it and he goes through. I linger until he is well clear then I start moving with the queue again.

Soon it is my turn. I step forward and present the Moroccan passport. The guy checks it then looks up at me.

'You have no visa.'

'I am Moroccan. I don't need one.'

As I speak, four Thai guys appear in the booth. One of them leans over and takes the passport. He looks at it, then tells the first guy to step aside and repeats to me, 'You have no visa.'

'I don't need a visa to come here.'

'Yes, you need a visa.'

'No,' I say, trying not to get heated. 'I've come here before without a visa. You can check in my passport if you don't believe me.'

He looks at me as if I haven't spoken. 'You have no visa so we can't let you in.'

At this point three Western men appear and stand behind the four Thais. It seems I am outnumbered, so I concede. 'So what do you want?' I say, worried that I don't have enough American dollars in my little bag to get out of this one.

'You have to come with us to Immigration.'

Now I begin to panic.

'No, I'm not coming with you to Immigration. I have a return ticket. The plane is still here. I'll go back to Indonesia where I came from, it is not your business to stop me.'

The heavies start moving towards me, people scatter and gape.

'Let me go back to my plane,' I say with determination.

There are eight of them but all I can think of is my baby daughter growing up without her father, and I want to tear them apart. I foolishly abandon reason and let fly with a punch at the guy who won't listen. Jamal must have been waiting and watching, because as soon as I start fighting he is by my side.

'I thought I told you not to come back,' I hiss at him, but Jamal is already swinging.

Together we are a formidable opponent, even against eight, but there is no way we are going to win or get out of here, all we are likely to do is increase our punishment. In the end there are about twenty of them, so it is not hard to subdue and handcuff us.

The Thais take my Moroccan passport away and when they come back they poke it into my face. 'This is a false passport.'

They take me to a room and bring in a Moroccan girl who speaks Arabic. She has been watching the whole show and seems secretly pleased to meet me. I tell her in Arabic that she is pretty, which is true. She tries not to smile, then asks me simple questions about Morocco. 'What is the capital city, blah blah.' Then she turns to the Thai guards and tells them I am Moroccan. She smiles sweetly at me as she leaves and I throw her an undetected glance of gratitude.

But then the three Western men come in and identify themselves as Australian Federal Police. 'He's the one we want. He's not Moroccan, he's Iraqi.'

So clearly the game is up and this is about more than a fake passport.

They send us to the Immigration holding jail where there are four or five hundred men and women, some of them prostitutes, from Burma, Cambodia or the Philippines. There are three levels of huge dormitories and the noise is deafening. Poor Jamal is beside himself. He could be in a comfortable hotel by now, eating a decent Thai curry.

'I told you not to come back, but thank you,' I offer, but he is too wound up to hear.

'So who told the police?' he storms. 'They were waiting for you. How did they know we were coming?'

I am trying to stay rational but the reality is I am back behind bars again.

'"Your passport is false." Who the fuck makes this rule?' I explode. 'We didn't steal, we haven't killed anyone. A passport is for a human being to go from one place to another, but they decide this is my place, not yours. The truth is, nothing belongs to anyone. In the end we all go into the ground!'

'What are you talking about?' Jamal says, staring at me.

'My daughter is only three months old and I might never see her again!' I slide down the wall to the concrete floor and hang my head in my hands. He flops down next to me.

After a long pause I nudge him. 'So what would you like to eat?'

'I'll just have a chicken kebab, thanks,' he replies, and we laugh, then both go back to our misery. Not only have I lost my wife and daughter, but any chance of saving Ahmad is gone, not to speak of Asad.

In the morning we are taken to court. We are advised to plead guilty to using false documents or they are likely to get angry and give us a really hard time. So we say we are guilty and they give me two months and Jamal one month, which looks like a pretty hard time anyway, once we get inside their jail.

We are looking Hell in the face. We joke that if we die and go there, there will be no surprises. Men fuck men, the food is foul, the drinking water putrid. During the day we are locked out in the yard where the toilets are an overflowing fetid soup of faeces with five people in front of you watching, like in Abu Ghraib, and before long I get TB.

But more terrible than Abu Ghraib are the mites that come up from under the wooden floorboards at night and bite you. The space for each person to sleep is about one foot, so spooned together it is a hot steamy environment for the bugs to thrive. All night we scratch until our skin almost comes off, but the more we scratch, the worse it gets. We are like a seething pack of human maggots on the floor, tearing at ourselves, unable to sleep. In the morning when we wash for some relief the itching starts again with the water. So I go for weeks without a shower, until the stench of my own body is so repulsive I can stand it no longer and douse myself.

After one month Jamal is released, but when I finish my two months they tell me there is another charge.

'For what?' I ask but they ignore me, then they send me to Thailand's High Court and I am charged with people smuggling.

Of course I was expecting it, but this is not fair game. I was caught with a false passport. Not smuggling people. I have never smuggled anyone in or out of Thailand. It seems like anything goes when it comes to keeping asylum seekers out of Australia.

So they send me back to jail with my new charge of people smuggling.

Jamal stays in Bangkok and Uncle Karim pools together money to get me a lawyer. It could have gone to helping find Ahmad but instead we go back to the High Court.

I have no support from the Iraqi embassy, I am given no preparation on what to say in court, and I have no means to gather evidence with which to defend myself. I don't have a chance, and Australia makes sure I don't. They have their Thai lawyer, AFP witnesses, and six others from the Australian embassy to make their case.

During the proceedings it begins to become clear. They couldn't arrest me in Indonesia because people smuggling is not illegal there, so the Australian Federal Police have been sitting me out, waiting for me to make a move to a country where they can get me. Australia has an extradition treaty with Thailand, so all they needed was someone to notify them of my departure and a reason to arrest me, which the Moroccan passport provided, and they had me.

While they work out the details I still have to survive the Thai correctional facilities. I have raging TB, skin resembling raw bleeding meat, and I am losing weight rapidly. After a while I discover that if you have money you can order edible meals from a canteen. Jamal also brings food, but in case he doesn't come, I order prison food every day, so sometimes I end up with two meals. There is an Algerian prisoner who speaks English, French, Thai and Arabic that I have become friends with. One day he doesn't get his order and has nothing to eat. He is in another section but we can see through the bars, unlike Abu Ghraib where they tried to stop you seeing anything.

I go to where the chief officer sits in a glassed-in office between the two blocks. 'I want to give this to my friend,' I say, showing him the canteen food.

'No,' he snaps unreasonably.

'It's just food, there's no bomb, no drugs. Check it, you'll see.'

'No,' he shoots off again and I begin to get riled. Without speaking I go to the bars where someone is coming from a visit.

'Hey you, could you give this to that Algerian guy for me, please?'

He takes the food, but security comes running and he pushes it back to me. So I turn and walk towards the chief of the block with his gold lapels and sneering face, and I throw the plate at him. It hits the glass squarely at eye level and gravy, chicken bits and rice slide down in front of his face as he screams for the guards to shackle me. Two of them wrestle me to the ground, put me in chains, and I am led away to solitary confinement.

Soon after, before I do myself any more damage, Jamal manages to smuggle in a mobile phone in a packet of soap through some convoluted method of switching security's locked bags, which is not easy.

But the phone changes my life. I am able to talk to Eni and Afrah and hear how my daughter and family are. It doesn't stop me pining but it gives me something to look forward to. There is a toilet in the cell, which, unlike the ones in the yard, has a very low door, so they can't see you when you are sitting and using the phone.

I try to call Rakin, to find out if Muhtadi has changed his mind, but he never answers and I have to live with the fact that my arrest probably means Ahmad is lost forever. I try to advise Afrah how to follow it up but without Rakin they don't know where to begin. A black cloud of despair settles over me.

I languish for another seven months in this state. Then I learn I am going to Australia. My lawyer tells me Australia has recently brought in new laws for people smuggling, and I am one of the first to be tried under them. They are hoping for a show trial to prove how strongly they feel about our activities. People smuggling has been labelled by their Immigration Minister as a 'heinous trade in human misery', and I could get jailed for over twenty years.

For another two months I lie each night on my tiny piece of floor scratching and coughing, and longing to be with Nagis and Eni, but escape is impossible and I am powerless to return to them. When the day arrives and they come to get me, the irony is it is the hardest thing I have ever had to do, to walk out of that jail and onto a Qantas flight to Australia.

On the plane I sit handcuffed between two federal policemen. One of them has a huge stomach. The hostess comes by smiling and gives us each a bottle of water. I sip at mine and try to distract myself by pondering how this guy can bend over. If you run from police they should be able to catch you, but this guy would be hopeless. It would be easy to bash him and his friend and to take the whole plane.

But things are already complicated without a hijack to add to my offences, so instead, when I close the bottle, I let it fall to the floor. As I go to pick it up he yanks my handcuffs.

'No,' he says, immediately on guard. 'I'll get it.'

'Okay,' I reply, peering down between the cramped economy seats as he tries to bend over his big stomach. His face begins to go red, but as much as he tries he can't reach it.

The third time, just as the tip of his finger touches the bottle, I edge it away with my foot. He strains harder, but I keep inching it to the side until glowing red and panting he abandons the mission.

'Forget it,' he says. 'I'll get you another one.'

I am reduced to such small victories to keep my spirits up, in the face of such bleak prospects.

PART THREE

AUSTRALIA

2003—2012

A DANGEROUS MAN

The first thing the Australian police do, when I arrive at Sydney airport in February 2003, is to say they have to strip me.

'Take all your clothes off,' they demand through an interpreter, while they stand around fully dressed.

'No,' I reply. 'There is no reason to make any man naked in front of another man.'

'That's the rule.'

'Fuck the rule,' I say. 'Who makes this rule? This is not Abu Ghraib under Saddam Hussein. This a Western country and supposed to be civilised. You go to hell with your rule.'

But they force me to undress, then they hold me down while one of them puts on a latex glove and forces his fingers into my arse.

In my culture, when you make a man naked the shame breaks his spirit more than any bashing can do. It reduces him to the status of an animal. Even in Abu Ghraib you were only stripped for torture.

They have taken all my property so I ask for one of my cigarettes but instead I am marched off to the airport lockup for the night. The next morning they fly me to Darwin, where the Australian Federal Police are waiting.

'Ali Al Jenabi, we charge you with people smuggling. We finally caught you,' one of them crows.

'You didn't catch me, you motherfucker. I wasn't smuggling. I was passing through an airport like everyone else.'

They leave looking pleased with themselves and I still haven't got a cigarette.

It is Friday night, so they put me in a cell at the police station for the weekend. I am alone and uncertain about what I am to face. I know there is unlikely to be torture in Australia, but after the enforced strip search I am not sure what to expect, and I am plagued by images of Eni and baby Nagis waiting for me in a land I will probably never see again. My head throbs with nicotine withdrawals and my body has shut down from jetlag, so I curl foetus-like on the bed and sink for two days into a deep dreamless sleep.

On Monday they take me to the Magistrate's Court, where a guy comes to meet me. 'I am your lawyer from Legal Aid.'

I have not heard of Legal Aid before so I don't know if he is on my side or with the police. 'I don't speak English very well,' I reply.

'Are you Ali Al Jenabi?'

'No,' I reply, believing I have everything to lose if I admit it. 'I am not.'

He points to a picture in a newspaper. 'Is this you?'

'No, this is not me.' The truth is, the picture is taken side on and I don't recognise myself.

'Just a minute,' he says, looking confused. 'I'll get an interpreter.'

He finds a Lebanese guy who is up a ladder painting the court entrance. He brings him over in his splattered overalls and I begin to wonder what sort of show this is.

Then I am taken into the court to face the magistrate. She tells me I am to remain in custody until my case is heard. So that afternoon I am sent to Berrimah Prison, on the outskirts of Darwin, where I am to be held in Remand. It is a sprawling collection of old and new buildings surrounded by razor wire.

Once I have endured the humiliation of another strip search they escort me to Block C, a large concrete courtyard surrounded by about twenty single cells. One is unlocked and I am hustled in.

So I am back in another jail, another hell.

I soon realise it is normal for them to strip search us every time we leave or return. They don't use the latex glove, but they do make us hold up our genitals and squat over a mirror. This degrading procedure is carried out as nonchalantly as animals being inspected for slaughter. If you argue they put you in solitary for two or three weeks.

Because I speak so little English it is hard for me to understand what is going on, but I have managed to pick up that the newspapers and rumours are saying Ali Al Jenabi will get twenty years.

I am the first smuggler to be extradited to Australia, and the government will prove how despicable I am by the money I have made out of human misery. They are evidently saying I charged $US10000 per person, which is laughable when I think of how many came for less than a thousand, or on promises that were never paid.

The question of why anyone with $US10000 would go to sea on one of my boats seems strangely never to be asked. I want to tell them for that amount you could fly business class, be processed in the community and still have enough to buy a car. I know I can't endure another twenty years in jail, so my only hope is to keep denying I am Ali Al Jenabi.

The worst thing about remand is the waiting without knowing what is going to happen next. Fortunately my TB has by now abated; as soon as I arrived they gave me medication. But I still suffer from the kidney problems I developed in Abu Ghraib. And you are not allowed to work, so I fill my day as best I can, playing ping pong, volleyball, and some of the prisoners help me learn English.

You are permitted to use the phone but you have to pay, and long-distance costs a lot of money. So I borrow from one of my cellmates, but when I finally get onto Eni she weeps through most of the call. I can hear Nagis gurgling to herself in the background, so I ask Eni to hold the phone next to her. I say her name but she is too young to understand this disembodied voice, or perhaps she doesn't recognise it any more. I walk bleary-eyed back to my cell.

When I call my mother I try not to tell her how serious my situation is. She and my sisters and brothers have now all been found to be legitimate refugees and are living in Sydney with permanent residency. If the UN had granted us this recognition when we applied in Iran, we would all be happily together and rebuilding our lives by now.

After a few weeks she and Khalid come to Darwin to see me. I wait in the visitors' room and when they enter Umi is crying before she even gets to me. It is exhilarating to see them, but the possibility of me facing twenty years, and my helplessness to continue the search for Ahmad, or rescue Asad from danger in Iraq, hangs over us. We are only allowed fifty minutes together, so I try to keep it as cheerful as I can, but we all know the prospects for our family reuniting are bad.

Three weeks later, I am lying in my cell watching the news when I see the presidential palace in Baghdad blown to pieces. The next day the US, Britain and Australia invade Iraq. George Bush claims the purpose is to destroy Saddam's weapons of mass destruction, crush his support for terrorism, and free the Iraqi people. But there is no evidence of these weapons or Al Qaeda in Iraq, and we have lived under Saddam's repression for over two decades without any show of concern from the West. That is, until America fell out with him over chemical weapons and Kuwait, and their access to our oil was in jeopardy.

Khalid left me money for the phone, but after a few months I stop calling Eni. If you can't do anything it just causes pain. I don't know what is going to happen to me or if I can ever return, so there is nothing to say. I am powerless. Nagis has taken her first steps and I wasn't there to see it.

I pace the four metres of concrete floor for the long stretches that we are locked in our tiny hot cells. I cannot convince myself that I have done anything wrong. If I broke Indonesian law then I should get tried there, not by Australian law. If I got arrested because I did something wrong then John Howard should get caught too. He sent his troops into my country without UN approval.

If I broke someone's law it was for something good. I provided a path to safety for people who had few other options. Maybe Mr Howard thought what he did was good too, but the majority of Australians and millions of people around the world didn't think so. And who is going to take the wave of refugees the war in Iraq will create? Not Australia, according to him. He claims he has stopped the boats. If they want to give me twenty years I will do it, but I will not plead guilty. Why am I more of a criminal than him? He has more blood on his hands than me. I see it every night on the TV.

The invasion is rapid and the Coalition forces soon reach Baghdad. The Baath Party is disbanded, Saddam deposed and his statue torn down in the square, while Iraqis dance in the streets. Then we hear they are opening up the jails to release Saddam's prisoners. There is a chance Ahmad could be amongst them. I shut my eyes and wait – I will be called to the phone and it will be my mother telling me Ahmad has been found.

But when I open my eyes there is nothing. Just the heavy clang of metal on metal as someone locks a gate.

The weeks drag by with no word. It is over a year since we heard Ahmad was alive so the chances of his survival are remote. Then, in May 2003, we begin to get reports on the TV of mass graves being discovered. As they start to be excavated, hordes of decimated families crisscross the country in search of the remains of their loved ones.

So the wounds open again and my mother, whose torment over Ahmad's fate has never abated, wants to go back to scour every prison register, and, if Ahmad is not found, to sit in the dust with the weeping relatives as hundreds of thousands of decaying bodies of murdered men, women and children are unearthed. Or to enter the pits and untwine the decomposing remains with her own hands.

To be unable to go myself is agonising, even if he is dead. To give

him a proper burial would bring our family some peace. It is something I could have done for Ahmad. But instead I am trapped on my
concrete bed staring at a twelve-inch television.

By the time I am finally called back to the Magistrate's Court, in
August 2003, after six months in Remand, Iraq has been so torn apart
that the Shiites and Sunnis turn on each other. So the killing goes on
and the country becomes such a shambles that people continue to flee
in the hundreds of thousands, with no place to go.

My mother has returned from Iraq, and as is the case with thousand of Iraqis, she could find no evidence from prison records or
exhumed graves that Ahmad ever existed.

It is hot and muggy as we drive to the court. I have found out by
now that Legal Aid are not the police but are actually here to help
me, so this time I am pleased to meet my lawyers, Suzan Cox and
her junior Greg Smith. The Lebanese painter is not here, instead his
sister Nirvana is to be my interpreter. She and I sit behind my lawyers,
otherwise the court is almost empty except for the prosecution team
led by Ms Kelly.

'This is a committal hearing,' Ms Cox explains to me, 'which is
essentially only a pre-trial to establish if there is enough evidence for
the case to go to trial by jury in the Supreme Court.'

Then the magistrate, Ms Blokland, asks me to stand while the
charges are read. Nirvana translates for me and I remain expressionless
as I try to work out what is happening. The other prisoners told me
that the new mandatory sentencing laws, which the government has
brought in as a deterrent to smugglers, require a minimum of five years
for each boat. Seven of my boats made it here, which means I am facing not twenty but another thirty-five years in jail.

I stand to attention while I am charged with twenty-two
counts against the Australian Migration Act. I don't know what
they are talking about until Ms Kelly puts it into language

Nirvana and I can understand.

'The allegations in summary are that the defendant was a people smuggler who was involved in bringing to Australia on four separate occasions in 2000 and 2001 people who had no right of entry into Australia.'

I unwind a little. While this is looking bad they haven't charged me with all seven boats. Perhaps they think four is enough to put me away for the better part of the rest of my life.

Calmer, I sit down only to be stunned by the judge's revelation that there is a list of one hundred and eight witnesses to be called by the prosecution. So many people have been prepared to come and condemn me. Five or six maybe, but surely not one hundred and eight of them? How much manpower and how many thousands of hours would it have taken to do the interviews?

Ms Kelly then requests that some of her witnesses be allowed to stand behind a screen, for fear of retribution from me. I stare at her in shock. These are people I helped, and in many cases paid for, to get to where they desperately wanted to go. Why would I be a danger to them?

'Many,' Ms Kelly explains, 'are currently still in detention with their visa status undetermined, so they are particularly vulnerable and don't need any further stress of facing this man they are frightened of.'

It begins to dawn on me what I am up against. Now that Saddam has been ousted, the witnesses are afraid they'll be sent back to Iraq if they can't get permanent visas. The Australian Federal Police probably didn't have to tell them 'it would be good for you to help us'. In most cases they would have willingly told the AFP whatever they wanted to know. They have grown up in a world where a knock on the door can mean certain death or the loss of a family member, so sucking up to the government was essential. They would just assume that now they are in Australia, if they want to get a visa they have to help the Australian government get what it wants, which in this case is me. And aside from being terrified of coming into court, many would also assume the prosecution, judge and defence were all working for the government, as would have been the case in Iraq.

'My client has not committed a criminal offence,' my lawyer Ms Cox responds. 'He's charged with immigration offences, and he has allegedly *assisted* these people, who were more likely to be brave risk-takers than vulnerable.'

It is comforting to hear her speak in support of me. She goes on to say she cannot see how, in a case that is attempting to prove my identity, a screen between us is going to help the witnesses to do this.

Our first small victory. The magistrate rules against the prosecution, and the witnesses will have to look me in the eye when they give their evidence against me.

Because I have said I am not Ali Al Jenabi, it is up to the Crown to prove I am, but as I am the only Arab in court apart from the witnesses, there is a pretty good chance they will point to me when asked if they see Ali Al Jenabi in the room. So my only hope is that through their appreciation for my bringing them to Australia, they will say they don't remember, or that they are not sure it is me. But most of them can't wait to do their bit for the Australian government, and gratitude goes out the window.

The first witness confesses he was afraid of being harassed or tortured when he asked me to help him escape, which I did, and cheaply too. So I presume he is on my side but when the prosecution asks him to describe me he looks across the court.

'Why I describe?' he says. 'He is here.'

I try to keep a pleasant expression on my face while Ms Kelly goes on to enhance my 'bad smuggler' image.

'When the small boats were being loaded, what was Jenabi doing or saying? Were there threats uttered?'

'When the passengers began to crowd to one side of the big boat he got angry and started swearing and abusing,' the man replies.

I remember it well. When people are afraid they can be stupid. When they climbed on board they all clutched together on one side of the upper deck and the boat began to list dangerously. The Indonesian captain shouted at them in Bahasa but they didn't understand so he called me out on a dinghy. When I got there I yelled at them to go down inside the boat before it capsized.

When the prosecution asks another witness if he is sure it was me in a photo he was shown, he answers, 'It doesn't matter how many times he changes his clothes, I can always identify him. If I look at his eyes, I know him. This is Ali Al Jenabi.'

Like most Arabs my eyes are very dark, almost black I suppose. I turn to Nirvana and look straight at her. She giggles. 'They are nice eyes.'

'Thank you, but I'm not sure if that is what he means.'

Next day Ms Kelly plays her strongest hand. 'How much money did you pay for your family to go on Mr Jenabi's boat to Australia?' she asks a witness.

'$US1500 each.'

Ms Kelly wilts a little. She was expecting something closer to the $US10000 each, which the police and press have been circulating.

'The same for the children?'

'No, they go half price.'

Ms Kelly pauses. 'You went from Jakarta by train to Surabaya, then by plane to Kupang. Did you pay for these fares?'

'No, Mr Jenabi paid.'

As the days go by the prosecution continues to pursue this question, but they keep getting the same results. No one ever gave me anything remotely like $US10000 each. One man reveals he paid $US700 per person for three adults and nothing for his eight-year-old daughter.

'How much money did Mr Jenabi want?' Ms Kelly tries again with another man who travelled with his wife and child.

'We paid whatever we had.'

'How much was that?'

'$US2000 to Ali for us all. My cousin had even less, so they offered his wife's jewellery but Ali just took what little money they had and would not take the jewellery.'

This evidence is not presenting how the Crown expected, it is beginning to backfire.

'He was very good to us,' a witness says unprompted. 'He rescued us – the people who didn't have money. He helped them and he put food on the boat and he was good. Then he took us to the beach and farewelled us.'

I remember the boat sliding off into the night with a kerosene lantern swaying on the deck and the pleasure I felt at seeing them on their way.

It reached Australia in May 2000, and now I discover that the AFP had already begun interviewing asylum seekers about me back then. They took statements and showed them a board with several photos on it for them to point to the one they thought was me. So by the arrival of my third boat my passengers were already giving me away.

The photo-board was in the court and I could see it included my picture from the UN application we made in Iran. So much for doing things the right way. They not only rejected us but now they use my request for asylum to condemn me.

The Australian Federal Police had used these identifications to secure my extradition from Thailand. The Howard government had set up a special unit called the People Smuggling Strike Team, and a special agent was assigned to catching me.

I sit silently watching as witnesses come and go. The questions are the same. When and where did they meet me? Who bought their tickets? Who put them on the boats, and how did they know it was me? Did they stand by the statements and photo identifications they had made with the AFP? 'That is Mr Jenabi,' they declare, pointing my way as I watch bewildered. And so it goes, day after day.

But there are high points. One morning, as a witness looks at me intently and I wait to be damned again, I hear, 'This is not the person.'

I feel a surge of gratitude towards this frightened, sensitive young man who only just escaped with his life from Iran, and yet has the guts not to give me away despite the fact that his temporary visa has just expired and he doesn't know what will happen next. But of course this is not the main trial, just the committal hearing for the Crown to choose which witnesses they want if the magistrate deems the case should go to the Supreme Court, and no doubt this man will not be selected.

Meanwhile the press has been depicting me as intimidating, and physically threatening. But what can you do? Even if I get a chance to deny it, once said, the picture of me as a dangerous man is growing just like the government wanted.

Things go from bad to worse when, three weeks into the hearing, the Weasel is called as a witness. I had tried not to think about whether he had set me up when Jamal and I were caught in Thailand. So I am not entirely shocked to see him, but I am angered to hear him calmly confess to providing information on people smugglers to the Australian embassy since August 2000.

He testifies he only did it to get revenge against my old foe Omeid, who had taken the Weasel's money then abandoned the boat that was meant to take him to Australia. Instead of confronting Omeid, he agreed to work for him. Having almost gone down the same path myself I understand this. But then, while accepting accommodation, food, a phone and money, he sold information on Omeid to the Australian embassy to help them catch him. It seems he was making as much as $US200 to $US300 a week.

I have no sympathy for Omeid, but the Weasel, despite becoming a smuggler himself, went on to give the embassy information about other smugglers as well, which in the end included me.

Yet he is happy to testify that I was the person he would go to for money if he didn't have any news to sell to the embassy, or when Omeid was out of town, leaving him without work.

'Did you ring Ali Al Jenabi for money?' Ms Cox asks him.

'Yes.'

'And you were given $US300.'

'Yes,' he replies shamelessly.

Then I watch in shock as he testifies that he told the embassy when my last boat was leaving for Australia. The Weasel had been working for me at the time. He had brought me a few passengers and accompanied Haider with the buses to Surabaya.

'And then that boat was turned back?' Ms Cox asks.

'Yes it was,' he says flatly.

'Because you told them,' she adds.

Leaving over two hundred people doomed to a hopeless situation, I want to yell to the court, but the Weasel goes on brazenly to tell how, after the boat was returned to Indonesia, he wanted me to pay him $US1000 on top of his expenses, which he saw as his share. And how when the asylum seekers began desperately calling, he changed his number so he didn't have to 'hear them complaining'.

I am already sickened by this man's behaviour and lack of remorse. Then, at the end of the second day of his evidence, he tells the court that when acting as middleman to acquire the Moroccan passport I used to go to Thailand, he showed it to the Australian embassy before I bought it. Later, when I was ready to leave, he called his contact at the embassy and told him when I would be flying to Thailand. Then he came with us to the airport to make sure I got on the plane so the AFP could catch me in Bangkok.

I try to keep my face unruffled so no one can see the level of my fury, but I know with every fibre of my body that if I could get my hands on him I would kill him for this betrayal.

That night I lie on my narrow bed staring at the ceiling. Evidently while the Weasel was informing on my last boat he was also working with Abu Quassey on the SIEVX, whose sinking killed three hundred and fifty-three innocent people. No one died on any of my boats, in fact my mother tells me as far as she knows everyone who came on them has been found to be a refugee. Meanwhile the Weasel has been flown to Australia as a guest of the Australian Federal Police, fed, accommodated, and given an undisclosed payment each week. No doubt he will be given a visa and whatever else he wants, to make sure they catch and punish me.

After twenty-one days all the witnesses have been heard and the magistrate decides there is enough justifiable evidence to commit me to trial by jury in the Supreme Court and I am sent back to jail to anticipate the real thing.

One night, three months later, I am lying on my bed trying to shepherd my thoughts away from Eni and my daughter, when suddenly Saddam appears before me on the TV. Found by the Americans in a hole under a hut near his hometown of Tikrit, he now stands compliantly while the Americans swab his mouth and medically check him.

At first I laugh and shout with happiness, but then I am overwhelmed by sadness that I am not there. We tried to tell the people he was spineless, and together we could catch him. But they didn't trust us, and now the Americans are crowing that they 'got him' and Iraqis can see he is just a scraggy-bearded, pathetic old man, who nods subserviently to his captors after scrambling like a rodent out of an underground burrow. But now we have to watch the US playing the hero.

I struggle to stop myself banging my head against the wall. I feel no triumph, just a longing for my homeland, my brother, Intisar, and the life I could have had, in a place where I belonged, if it hadn't been for this gutless wretch.

MAKING A CASE

In June 2004, ten months after the committal hearing, I am finally
called to the Northern Territory Supreme Court. I am driven in chains
around the side of a towering white building set among lush tropical
plants to an underground dock, where I wait to be escorted down
hidden corridors to the courtroom.

This time my lawyer is Jon Tippett, with Greg Smith as the junior
council again. Mr Smith was a fearless combatant in the committal
hearing, with a rollicking sense of humour, and Mr Tippett, I soon
discover, is more of the same. He is direct and good-humoured with
an infectious laugh and fire in his belly. Like Smith he is slim and
muscular, with a shaved head. I feel like I am part of a football team.

I call them Jon and Greg and they refer to me as Ali, but my
instructions are that that is not my name, so they set out to prove it for
me, with the ferocity of full-backs who will try by any means to get the
ball.

'Prior to going before the jury, we are entitled to take legal points,'
Jon explains. 'During the committal it was raised that no videos or
tapes were made of the AFP showing the witnesses the photo-boards,
so now we will submit to the judge that some witnesses were led to
select a photo of you.'

'Some of the witnesses,' Greg adds, 'admitted they just picked the
one closest to a resemblance.'

'So we will claim,' Jon goes on, 'that the evidence to be given by the Crown to prove you are Ali Al Jenabi is not admissible, because it was gathered in an unfair manner.'

Then there is the issue of whether the AFP used the witnesses' uncertain visa status as a lever. It would be impossible to know, the witnesses are hardly going to admit this in court, but some of their statements are sufficiently ambiguous for Jon Tippett to try to disqualify them.

'I don't want to forestall any submissions Mr Tippett may want to make,' the Judge, Justice Mildren, says, 'but it looks to me as though he has got a particularly difficult road.'

'Your Honour,' Jon replies, 'I do, but it is one I intend to approach with enthusiasm and as much persuasion as I can muster.'

I smile broadly. I am beginning to feel I am in safe hands, and I like his strategy of trying to knock out as many witnesses as possible before going to jury. Fortunately the judge finds Jon's argument has enough basis to challenge the admissibility of evidence. So another kind of pre-trial called a *voir dire* begins.

'There is a limit to what we can do in the *voir dire*,' Jon warns me. 'Except to cause the Crown as much trouble as we can. We'll require them to get all the witnesses in again, and put them to proof on every issue. We'll admit to nothing, and with sheer bloody-mindedness we'll wear them down and hopefully push them to consider a plea so we don't have to go to the jury trial.'

So once again I have to watch sixty or so of the same witnesses turn against me, and I am back on a rollercoaster of acceptance and rage. I'm not expecting them to lie; all they need to say is that they can't remember. You can assist the authorities but you don't necessarily have to recognise the man. Even Jon would say, 'Why are they doing this when you genuinely helped them?'

I am shocked when the suave Iranian who took me to the nightclub in Jakarta, where we danced the night away and hung out like friends, is now falling over himself to identify me. 'That definitely is him.' It seems he blames me for being detained for years when he arrived because Immigration did not believe his story.

Then there is Mrs Talal, who stayed with my family in Malaysia and then in Indonesia, despite the inconvenience and expense, while waiting for the boat to be ready. And now she comes to court and not only denounces me, but insists on doing it from behind a screen. She claims she is vulnerable to my mother placing a curse on her for testifying and somehow thinks she will be protected if I can't see her.

At the end of the day I go back to jail alone with my anger. My English is improving but there is no one I want to talk to. When the other prisoners ask me what happened in court I just say, 'The same bullshit.' How can I describe the complexity of what I feel about the disloyalty of my own people? If the guards would let me I would scrub the floors and wash the walls of the entire jail but all I am allowed to do is lie on my bed, smoke cigarettes and stew.

The *voir dire* drags on for a month. After four weeks of objecting to every point, refusing to concede anything, and basically engaging in trench warfare with the Crown, we manage to get rid of five or six witnesses. But ultimately the prosecution puts forward thirty or forty they want, whose evidence Justice Mildren says will be admissible to the jury.

It is a small gain but that night, as I sit mindlessly watching TV in my tiny cell, I realise how hard Jon and Greg have fought for me. They are clearly in for the long haul, and are not going to crack or give up on me. I brush tears from my eyes. I don't remember this feeling of being looked after since before my father disappeared when I was ten.

Two weeks later we return to the Supreme Court, and over thirty witnesses plus interpreters are flown to Darwin for the third time. We are in a larger courtroom with a jury and public gallery, and are now facing another three or four months of trial before I get a verdict.

We have the same judge, Justice Mildren, who seems to be a fair man with high moral standards and a sense of humour, which, considering his position, surprises me.

'He is a conservative,' Jon tells me, 'but with deep concerns about liberty, justice, and the need for compassion and reason in the system. While he believes the authorities should get their man, it must be done correctly, with proper proof put fairly before the court, and only then does the government get the person.'

I am put in the dock with Nirvana my interpreter, and a guard, where I face a jury of twelve ordinary white Australians who will decide my fate. Considering the success of the government's demonising of asylum seekers and people smugglers, I hold little hope.

'The prosecution don't only have to prove to the jury that you are Ali Al Jenabi,' Jon explains, trying to put a brighter side, 'but that you are the person who organised the witnesses' trips. That you talked with them, took their money, accommodated them, and put them on the boats. Our job is simply to convince the jury the Crown can't prove it.'

So the witnesses are called to tell their stories for the third time. How I met them at the airport, put them in hotels, transported them all over Indonesia to various departure points and put them on boats. Jon and Greg cross-examine them ruthlessly. Whether they met me in a group, in a light or dark room, for how long, and in what proximity. What height I was, the colour of my eyes, the length of my hair, if I had a moustache or a beard are all dissected in detail.

Meanwhile I just continue to refuse to admit I am Ali Al Jenabi. It drives the prosecution insane because they don't have absolute proof. It becomes a toe-to-toe battle which Jon and Greg are not prepared to concede. They think if we can drag it out long enough, eventually the prosecution will make a deal to limit the charges to a couple of boats. As the days become weeks I often hear Jon say to the prosecutor, 'Well, are you going to be sensible and cut a deal, or are we going to continue with this?'

But the Crown is determined to make an example of me, despite the massive expense. I am to be a deterrent. So witnesses and interpreters continue to be flown from across the country, accommodated in hotels and fed. Some witnesses need more than one interpreter, to translate from one language into another, then into English and back again. It is a logistical nightmare for the Commonwealth but no one seems concerned about the cost so long as they get me. So on it goes.

After thirty-seven days Jon comes to me and says, 'Look Ali, I think we can get you a deal. The government want to lay blame for the boat people on smugglers like you, but you're not working out as a good scapegoat. You might be a bit of an outlaw, but it is becoming clear you are also a decent, kind and compassionate human being, and it's difficult to whack someone like that. So I think we can get the prosecution to the table.'

On one level I knew the gig was up once I saw how many people were prepared to turn against me. But deep down inside I still feel that if I stay dug in and refuse to admit I am Ali, by some miracle I might go free.

'You've seen the evidence,' Jon interrupts my thoughts. 'These pricks are going to keep coming into court and saying you are Ali Al Jenabi over and over again, and in the end the jury is going to convict you for four boats, and you could go down for as many as twenty years. If we can save you five, are you prepared to give us instructions?'

Terror slinks through my veins as I imagine doing even another fifteen years. I will be forty-eight and Nagis seventeen. Eni will have moved on, and my sisters and brothers will be middle-aged with teen-age kids. Little Hashim will be thirty, most likely my mother will be gone, and I will have missed all their milestones, celebrations and deaths. My hair will be grey, my skin slack, my body drooping with defeat. My dreams of a family business will have slipped away, I will no longer have the spirit.

'If you can get a deal, we'd better do it then,' I say in utter defeat.

The next day Jon is more optimistic. He has decided to make an offer of a guilty plea on a reduced charge of two boats. 'We'll fess up to the fact that you made a quid or two,' he tells me, 'but we'll want it taken into account that you did it for family and other humanitarian reasons.'

The prosecution flies to Canberra to discuss our offer with the Commonwealth Department of Public Prosecutions, the Department of Foreign Affairs and Trade, and Liberal Party politicians. It must be a disappointing result after spending millions on catching, extraditing and trying me, only to throw in the towel with so little.

When the Crown prosecutors return to court they accept the plea for two boats, that they were not unseaworthy or overcrowded, and that my purpose was mostly humanitarian, but they contend the people on my boats were jumping the queue.

'Your Honour, we're not going to cop this,' Jon objects. 'It's a lie perpetrated by politicians.'

'Okay,' Justice Mildren responds. 'Mr Prosecution, nothing supports your position. So I will give you a week to come up with evidence to support the conclusion that these people are jumping some sort of queue. I'll hear any evidence you wish to produce.'

This is the first time I have heard of queue-jumping. I try to imagine this queue. What do they think? That when the secret police are shooting at you, you run down the street yelling, 'Where's the queue? Where's the queue?'

Even if there was a queue to join, there is no UN office in Iraq. The nearest is in Pakistan, two countries away.

Anyway the belief that there are orderly queues where asylum seekers line up and wait their turn is extraordinary. Millions of people drift into shambolic UN camps all over the world, and only about two percent are ever settled. For some it takes a few years, for others decades, with many eventually giving up on the UN and finding a smuggler to take them on a boat.

The prosecution head back to Canberra and a week later return with no evidence, despite the extensive resources available to them.

'I gave Counsel for the Crown an opportunity to put before this court facts to support these allegations,' Judge Mildren says. 'The

Crown is unable to present any such material. I therefore do not find that the prisoner's activities displaced others by jumping the so-called queue.'

My plea is put with only two counts and the jury returns a verdict of guilty. So suddenly this gargantuan trial is over and now I must await the terms of my punishment.

A week later, on 21 September 2004, Justice Mildren hands down his sentence.

Nirvana interprets line by line and I wonder if we will ever get to the length of my imprisonment. The judge carefully lays out the background to the trial and then summarises my operations in Indonesia.

'I note that there is no evidence that he lived opulently,' he says. 'On the other hand, he did not live in the poor end of town, he was well dressed and presented and had four-wheel-drive vehicles at his disposal.'

He goes on to acknowledge that I had not acted like a secretive Mr Big, that I was well known in the Middle East and Malaysia, I did not have bank accounts with large sums of money in them, and that I had even been on the beaches getting my hands dirty, which was unusual from what he knew of people smugglers.

'Be that as it may,' Judge Mildren says, 'I find that he was heavily involved in the offending. He was at the very least the officer in command in the field and he had the power to negotiate the price. He exercised a great deal of control over each operation.

'On the other hand,' he goes on to say, 'in each case the vessels arrived at Ashmore Reef where they were expected to be promptly arrested, as indeed they were. There was no attempt to arrive clandestinely on the mainland.'

I recall what Jon said when we first met. 'Smuggling is the wrong description for you. You weren't trying to get people into a country without the authorities knowing. The Australians knew from their own intelligence the vessel had left Indonesia, because their Orion air-craft were out there looking for it. Then they picked the people up and took them to Australian territory for processing as refugees. That's not smuggling. Smuggling is about hiding people in containers and under vehicles like they do in Europe. You were not doing that. Nor were you human trafficking, which is the kidnapping and trading of slaves for sex or labour.'

Nirvana nudges me. The judge is noting that I have no prior con-victions and that in changing my plea to guilty the trial has finished as much as two months early. 'The savings in costs in this case are very, very considerable,' he says. 'So I will reduce the head sentence that I would otherwise have imposed by about ten percent.'

This is good, but ten percent of what? I wonder as I steel myself for the sentencing. But instead the judge proceeds to tell my whole life story, starting from the day I was born.

I soon realise that his summary is fair and quite sympathetic – at last I might be being judged in the context of my story. He talks of my father's mistreatment and our imprisonment in Abu Ghraib, of fleeing to Iran to join my family in a cellar, and of my family's failed applica-tion to the UN for refugee status in Australia.

Justice Mildren goes on to say he accepts 'that the prisoner was concerned to assist his family and that he did what he could on occa-sions to assist others who were unable to pay fully. I accept also that he did show special consideration for families with children. I also accept that humanitarian acts are not necessarily inconsistent with some financial award.

'As Mr Tippett QC submitted, Oskar Schindler saved many lives by employing Jews as slave labourers and he made a great deal of money out of their labour, although of course he did later repay many of those that he was able to save. But the point is a valid one; there can be mixed motives and I accept that the prisoner was not solely motivated by money, but was largely motivated by the need to get his family to Australia come what may.

'I think I can take into account that the prisoner has spent some seven or eight months in a Thai prison,' he says as I ready myself for what's coming. 'As to the prisoner's prospects of rehabilitation, I doubt if he will offend again when he is released. I accept that he has a remarkably stoic and positive outlook on life and will probably pursue his trade as a tailor.

'In conclusion,' the judge says as I hold my breath, 'there will be a sentence of imprisonment for six years, three months in relation to count 7, and eight years in relation to count 14, both sentences to be served concurrently.'

I guess that means eight years. I look uncertainly across the court but Justice Mildren is still speaking. 'I fix a non-parole period of four years. The head sentence and non-parole period are backdated to commence from 17 June 2002.'

Nirvana is smiling. 'Take off Thailand and the time you've served here,' she whispers, 'and you only have a year and nine months to go before you get out on parole.'

I want to run up to the bench where Justice Mildren sits under the Australian crest and throw my arms around him. But instead I look at Jon and Greg and beam gratefully. They grin and I call thank you and put my hand on my heart as I am taken away. Nagis, I might see you before your fifth birthday.

ASYLUM

I am moved out of Remand and into one of three large cage-like cells with ten other prisoners. They are built around a concrete musteryard with a glassed-in security room on the fourth side, manned by prison officers. The walls are made of steel mesh so that air can circulate, and it allows us to see out to a grassy square, which expands my world a little.

I am struck by how many of the other prisoners are Aboriginal. All my jury were white but in jail at least eighty percent of inmates are black, yet I understand they make up only two and a half percent of Australia's population.

Now that I know how long I must serve I become more relaxed. I draw a calendar on a piece of paper and cross off each day. But after two weeks I realise it is better to stop worrying about the number of days and just live in each one as it comes.

For the first time I discover marijuana, allowing me to transcend my miserable circumstances a little. The prisoners bring it in through their girlfriends. When they visit they kiss and swallow it in little bags, then vomit it up when they come back to the cell. So it becomes fun for a while and helps to relieve the boredom, but soon enough they break us up and I am moved to a single cell.

Without the drugs to preoccupy me I am going out of my mind. I talk to Mick the welfare guy, a real gentleman who will help in any way he can. Not everyone is allowed to work, but soon I am permitted to join another prisoner in painting the jail, after which we move to the welding workshop, a privilege given to prisoners who are not considered dangerous.

There are seven of us and it becomes a sanctuary with small new freedoms. We can make coffee or toast whenever we want, so whoever gets there first in the morning puts on a brew. But we seldom have any bread and are always watching at mealtimes for someone who doesn't want theirs. Then we are tantalised by anticipation of the next day when we can savour the smell and taste of hot buttered toast. But sometimes we get caught. 'Where are you taking that bread? Put it back,' a guard will snap.

There is a white guy in the shop called Simon. He teaches me English and how to build furniture. We are always laughing together. As none of us is a threat, our two guards are relaxed and friendly, so the place becomes somewhere we can work and forget our troubles, almost like normal men for a few hours a day.

But many of the guards want to make you feel you are nothing. In Iraq and Thailand it was physical, but here they play with your mind and there is no flexibility with their rules. One afternoon I fill a plastic bag with water and put it in a pillowcase to use as weights, to keep fit.

'It is not allowed,' the guards yell as they drag me off to solitary for seven days. I linger in a steamy concrete box warding off unbidden memories of Abu Ghraib, and of Intisar. I wonder how she is and if she married a good Iraqi man.

When I get out Simon moves into the cell next to mine and we discover we can talk via the sink. The pipe goes through the wall to the other cell before it joins the drain. So I rest my arms on the bowl and lean into the plughole, where we chat for hours when the long stretches of loneliness are getting to us. Other times we just yell from the door, 'What you say?' Then everyone in the jail gets involved, shouting their opinion until the guards shut us down.

On 16 June 2006, after I've been twenty-one months in jail, they come and say, 'You've made it. You are now out on parole.' I had done such a good job on my mind that I had actually forgotten my release date.

Two officers, a man and a woman, from the Immigration Department are waiting for me. The woman presents me with a pen.

'I need you to sign this paper saying you agree to being deported back to Iraq.'

I stare at her. I am flooded with images of those terrible years of trying to escape my homeland. Apparently, because I was brought into Australia on a Criminal Justice Visa, I have no status now that I have done my time.

'Just sign here,' she says again, tapping the pen in the right spot for my signature.

After my show trial falling flat, and the judge giving me the minimum sentence, it is not hard to deduce the government wants me out of the country as fast as possible, and that the woman has been directed to sneak me out the back door so as not to alert the press. I have no interpreter so she could easily have tricked me, but I speak enough English now to know what she is trying to do.

'No,' I say firmly. 'If they want to deport me, let them deport me. But I'm not going to sign any paper saying I agree.'

The guy indicates to her that she is getting me riled, and takes me outside for a smoke. After we light up he tells me I am not without rights.

'By law,' he says quietly, 'they are obligated to leave you alone once you ask for protection. If you are escaping persecution you have a legal right to request asylum.'

I thank him and when we go back inside I tell the woman that I am going to apply for a Protection Visa, and she backs off.

So I am released into the hands of two guards who are waiting to take me straight to a detention centre on the outskirts of Darwin, where there are about fifty Indonesian men who were caught fishing in Australian waters.

As soon as I see them every cell in my body begins to relax. I sit amongst them on the ground and they offer me one of their cigarettes. The pungent smell of cloves, which pervades all of Indonesia, fills my nostrils and I lean back remembering how much I grew to love that country and its people. Someone starts singing and others join in, then they begin to dance. It takes me back to my wedding day and I smile, teary-eyed as I long for my half-Indonesian baby and her mother.

Despite my loss being made more poignant by the company of the fishermen, I have three very happy days with them. Then this brief interlude ends and I have to say goodbye.

Immigration have sent their security company, Global Solutions Limited, to escort me back to Sydney. There is a man and a woman, but this time there are no handcuffs. It would be easy to escape if I wanted to, but why would I? My family is waiting for me in Sydney. I have done my punishment, all my relatives have been found to be legitimate refugees and have permanent residency so there is no reason I won't qualify. I want to take no risks, I want to go through the correct process to get a proper, legal visa and be free.

So I'm not thinking about running. I am thinking about food. I am finally liberated from four years of gastronomical misery and I want to eat everything. The GSL guard is a nice guy. 'Go ahead, have whatever you want,' he says. 'It's not from my pocket, it's expenses.'

This removes any inhibition, so I start eating at Darwin airport, then I have the in-flight meal on the airplane. In transit in Adelaide I eat some more, then again on the plane to Sydney. I love to eat but I particularly enjoy it because the GSL guy keeps up with me. 'Okay,' he continues to say, 'I'll have one too.'

When we reach Sydney it is the middle of winter and there is a thick white fog. As we descend I hope this void of nothingness is not an omen for my life. It feels eerie and cold after being in a perpetual summer for over six years.

I am put in a security van and driven through the outer suburbs to the Villawood Detention Centre. A Lebanese woman meets us at reception and records my details, but I am shocked by how much she swears. She speaks to me in Arabic but swears and talks to another woman about sex in English. I have never heard women talk like this before. I'm not sure if I should be scared – if the women are like this, what will the men be like?

But then she asks if I am hungry.

'Yes,' I say, forgetting her indiscretions. 'What do you have?'

'Chicken curry.'

'Could I eat one and take another with me?'

She grins and hands me two plates.

They put me in a room with a Chinese guy. We each have a bed and small cabinet and I am soon in a deep sleep. At three o'clock in the morning an officer turns on the lights to make sure we haven't escaped.

'What are you doing, you motherfucker?' I yell at him. 'I'm sleeping. Even in prison they just use a torch.'

He quickly switches the light off. But next morning I discover that whenever we swear at them, they fill out a report. I already feel like I am back in jail, where you accept the guards being nasty and having to stick to their rules, but people in detention are not criminals, and these officers are just security guards. They are here to ensure we don't run away, that's all. But they are recruited from the prisons so they treat us like prisoners.

The following day my family come for their first visit. They are living in a small fibro house nearby, in the suburb of Villawood. As I pace and wait I keep stopping to check myself in the mirror. I am only thirty-five but flecks of grey have crept into my hair and I am afraid I am looking old already.

Finally I am called and I go out into the grassy yard where picnic tables are scattered amongst eucalyptus trees. I see them coming in through the maze of gates and razor wire and hurrying towards me.

I throw my arms around each one in turn and we laugh and cry as we always do.

My first big shock is Hashim. He was just a boy of ten when I put him on the boat in Maumere five years ago, and that is how he has always sat quietly in my mind. I had told myself he will have grown up but I never imagined his face would be completely different. As I hug him I am gripped with sadness and a terrible guilt that I have not been there to help him through what must have been difficult years. But it is too late, he is almost a man and his youth is lost to me.

And then there are Afrah's children. She had her son while I was in Indonesia and now there are twin girls as well. I want to hug and kiss them but I have to hang back because they don't understand who I am. I try to talk to them but they can't speak Arabic. I am taken aback they don't know our language and are already little Australians.

My mother sets out a picnic with all my favourite food and we sit in a circle on a rug and eat together again. I speak to the children in English, and they gradually overcome their shyness and begin to compete for my attention. They, like Nagis, are the beginning of my family's next generation. I try not to let myself imagine them playing together.

We laugh and talk as we share my mother's food. The tastes, the familiarity of our little rituals, make me feel at peace for the few hours they are allowed to spend with me. We talk about setting up a small business, maybe a restaurant, a mixed business, or internet café. Ahlam, Inas and Hashim all attend school and are getting an education, so soon they will have their own skills to contribute.

By the time they leave I am in a warm glow of excitement about what lies ahead of us. We are finally going to have the life we had planned eight years ago in Iran.

Immigration require me to have an agent, so my family contact Dr Mohammad Al Jabiri. An Iraqi refugee himself, he is a lawyer who was once an Iraqi ambassador to Spain and chairman of a United Nations working group to find citizens who disappeared in Iraq. Four days after I arrive he comes to see me. I feel an immediate liking for him when we meet in the visitors' compound. He is not tall but his demeanour gives him stature. He is a softly spoken, dignified, urbane man, and we have in common surviving Saddam's prisons.

A few days later I get a letter to say I have an interview with an Immigration case officer on 29 August 2006, which is tomorrow.

I toss all night in bed. Everything hangs on this interview. I get up with the sun, dress in the new shirt my family have brought me and sit on my bed waiting. When Dr Al Jabiri arrives I am called over the loudspeaker. The guards usher us into a demountable building at the side of the visitors' compound.

A tall woman in her forties introduces herself as Kate Watson. She tells me I have a right to apply for protection under the Geneva Refugee Convention if I have a well-founded fear of persecution in my own country. If I meet the criteria I will qualify as a legitimate refugee and be entitled to a permanent visa. Then she says her job is to record my claims and to take a statement about my background.

It is difficult to simplify my past, especially in a second language. She asks me if I want an interpreter, but that can bring its own problems if they are from another culture, and I think my English is good enough.

I tell her my story the best I can, but she keeps asking for dates, which is like asking a refugee for their passport. You wouldn't be a refugee if you could get one legally. Each time I was in jail it felt like ten years, but of course it wasn't. You remember exactly what happened but seldom for how long. You don't ask the date when you are being tortured or running for your life. It is only with freedom that trauma settles and clarity comes.

We take a break and when we return Kate asks me to tell her why my life would be under threat if I returned to Iraq.

'If it was safe, with proper government and justice, I would be happy to go back,' I reply. 'But it is not. It is a lawless bloodbath. And not entirely of our own making,' I add with a certain amount of bitterness.

She nods for me to proceed. She is professional, like a lawyer. Not friendly or unfriendly, just doing her job. I like her. I feel she is listening to me, which makes it easier for me to dredge up my past.

'Many of Saddam's former intelligence officers are still there, hiding behind Islamic names, and involved in the bombings, kidnappings and killings that you see on the TV every night,' I continue. 'They want revenge for the information I gathered against them in the resistance. One of my neighbours returned from Canada last year and disappeared. Later his body was found.' I pause, remembering my mother's fear that I would be sent back and the same thing would happen to me.

'After I left the resistance I found out my group was not backed by the British but by the Syrian Baathists, and like Saddam's secret police, if you quit, you die. Some of these ex-resistance people are now in high positions and they don't forget.

'Plus,' I state the obvious, 'I am now known in Iraq as a smuggler who assisted nearly five hundred of my countrymen to flee, and the Baathists want revenge for that.'

This in itself should be enough, but I can see Dr Al Jabiri wants me to go on, so I force myself to open a door I thought I had closed forever.

'When they sentenced my friend Mohammad, they sentenced me to death as well. But I lived and he, the innocent one, died. His family were grief-stricken and assumed I escaped by informing on him, and they want retribution. Now his uncle, who was in the Communist Party, is in a position of power. It's not something you discuss in the coffee shop – in our culture it is shoot to kill.'

I look at my hands. The loss of Mohammad is still piercing.

'What about Indonesia?' Kate asks after a pause. 'You have a wife and child there.'

'I cannot return to Indonesia to live,' I explain. 'Women cannot give permanent residence to their husbands there.'

At the end of the interview Kate doesn't say anything to indicate I will be successful, but I have no reason to think otherwise. I am clearly running from persecution. I can tell she knows I am telling the truth, so I feel confident I will qualify.

Dr Al Jabiri tries to temper my expectations. 'Their decisions are not always rational. But by law they have to give you a decision within ninety days,' he says in a voice that has known disappointment and struggle. 'I would not expect anything sooner.'

So I set up a mindless routine that will get me through three months. I wake up, have breakfast and exercise until noon, which makes me so hungry I eat the unappetising lunch they provide in the canteen. Then I go back to my drab room to shower and wait until my family come. When they arrive at three or four o'clock we eat together. The meals in here are not as bad as in jail but still we hanker after Iraqi food. My mother, who has limited resources but feels sorry for the other Iraqis in detention, soon starts cooking for them too.

I like to talk about food, so I get to know one of the chefs in the kitchen. In Villawood the eggs for breakfast are boiled because you can serve a hundred at once. I tell the chef I haven't had a fried egg for four years.

'If someone sees you then everyone will want one,' he says. 'But if you come back in half an hour I'll make it for you.'

So I salivate for thirty long minutes of anticipation and when I return he cooks me two of the finest fried eggs I have ever tasted. When I thank him he replies, 'No worries, any time.' So my life improves by two fried eggs every few days.

Apart from the food one of the forms of persecution in Villawood is the loudspeakers. They are in every room throughout the detention centre, constantly giving directives and calling people's names for interviews, visitors or telephone calls. It is unrelenting and drives people to the brink. Not only is all silence threatened with an intrusion, but you think every announcement might be for you, and the cycle of anticipation and disappointment is ruthlessly debilitating.

On the ninetieth day, when I wake up and realise I have made it, I try to comply with my routine, but it is impossible. Every time the loudspeaker begins to blast a name it goes through my body like a bullet. With my excitement level pitching and plummeting like the Dunia Fantasi rollercoaster in Jakarta, I am a mess by the time my family arrive. They have been looking forward to a celebration. They stay with me until sunset, but by then we know nothing is going to happen.

The disappointment in the eyes of Afrah's children is the hardest. They have never understood why they can't take me home, and why they have to line up for hours in the sun to come through iron gates and a wire fence to see me.

'Why does Ali have to stay in a cage?' they keep asking their mother, but how can she explain?

Two more months slip by and still nothing happens. It will soon be Christmas. Dr Al Jabiri continues to write letters to the Immigration Department asking what is happening and when a decision is going to be made, but to no avail. I ask him for Kate Watson's number and I begin to call her myself, but she doesn't answer the phone. I get numbers for different case officers from other detainees, but when I try to explain who I am, they tell me to speak to Kate.

'She won't answer,' I plead.

'You'll just have to keep trying,' they say, refusing to explain. So I call and call and yell abuse down the phone while it rings out.

Then one day, just as I am about to slam down the receiver, some-one answers. 'She is on holidays and won't be back till the end of January,' a young man snaps and quickly hangs up the phone.

Okay, I say to myself. Now I know how long, I can get through that.

Each afternoon at least one of the family comes with my mother's food. Then once a week they all come together. But as time passes their visits become tainted by guilt and sadness. If it wasn't for me, none of them would be here, yet they are free and I am locked up like a criminal. They don't say anything, but I see the sorrow in their eyes.

When they are gone the loneliness returns, and the dormant wound of my daughter opens like a festering sore. With freedom having been in my sights, it is hard to keep her locked out of my mind as I had in jail. I lie awake at night asking myself, Where is the end to this?

Then a small miracle occurs. There are public phones in the Villawood main office but mobile phones are not allowed. One afternoon two friends, who travelled on one of my boats, come to visit me with a friend of theirs. We talk for a few hours, then as they leave they ask for my number so they can call me.

'I don't have a mobile phone. It's a rule.'

The guy who came with them, who I hardly know, pulls a phone out of his pocket. 'Take mine.'

'How did you get it in?' I ask, surprised. 'Visitors always complain about how ruthlessly they search them.'

'I was lucky,' he shrugs. 'Get your family to bring you a new sim card,' he says, taking his out and giving the phone to me. I protest but he insists. 'Take it, no worries.'

I am reminded of the kindness of strangers when I was hiding out in Iraq. Now I can make my phone calls at any time of the day or night, in the privacy of my own room. In my present circumstances he could not have given me a greater gift.

Christmas comes and goes and it is a happy day of sorts. All my family bring food and gather in the visitors' enclosure. Despite being Muslim they like to join in with Christian festivities. But it is bittersweet that they, too, have to spend the day behind wire to be able to share it with me. And when the children present me with their little gifts, I have nothing to give to them.

Soon after my mother brings me devastating news. My dear friend

Unis from my wrestling days, who helped me escape to the north, has been killed. He was beheaded, most likely by Al Qaeda, who made one of their headquarters in Mosul after the US invasion and targeted Shiites in their ensuing brutal rampage.

I begin to become part of the misery and depression around me. The days crawl by. I fool around with a football and others join in, but increasingly I play alone, kicking the ball aimlessly around the yard for hours by myself.

This is more terrible than jail. Criminals know exactly how long they are in for, they can count off the days, but these people committed no crime, and there is no limit to how long they will be locked up. They have come from backgrounds of persecution, torture and unimaginable traumas; they are separated from their families and are emasculated by not being able to help them. The only support on offer is antidepressants and sedatives, which I refuse.

With nothing to do during the day many of us spend the nights awake, staring into the dark, trying to hold at bay memories too frightful to relive. Or we play cards, hand after hand, smoking cigarettes until our heads ache and the sky turns red and another day begins. Then there is nothing to do and nowhere to go. And even if there was, we have lost the will.

The devastation on my mother's face at seeing me like this makes me so unhappy I tell her not to come. So now I become like all the others and lie silently on my bed as the interminable hours creep by.

When February 2007 comes around I begin to call Kate again but still no one is there. One day, after several rings, I am about to throw my phone at the wall when someone answers.

'She's not back yet,' the same guy says limply.

So now we begin a new routine, where they answer but tell me she is still away. I try to control myself but eventually I shout, 'Stop lying to me. Just tell me where she is. Someone has to answer for her if she's gone this long!'

'Okay,' he says and gets someone else who simply says, 'You're being processed,' and hangs up.

'How long?' I yell back but it is too late, she has gone.

A few weeks later, in the early hours of the morning, I hear screaming. My roommate rolls into a foetal position and covers his ears. From the window I can see a struggle going on in another yard. It looks like a woman is being held down by four guards while two others supervise. Then one kneels next to her. Suddenly the screaming fades, she stops struggling and they drag her away.

Next morning at breakfast everyone is unnerved. They are all too familiar with screaming in the night and live in fear they will be next. 'If they decide not to give you a visa they deport you after dark so visitors and the press don't get to see it,' the blank-faced man next to me says. 'The men are handcuffed and the women are forcibly injected with tranquillisers, sometimes the men too if they are too much trouble.'

I lose my appetite and go back to my room. How different this is to Iraq I am no longer sure.

The months go by. Kate Watson never comes back to her desk from holidays and appears to have completely disappeared. I am sinking into the same morass as all the other detainees. I have risen above so many incarcerations but I am drowning in this one. There is nothing to fight against and the boredom is insufferable; they kill you not by torture or execution, but by hopelessness and despair.

AN EGREGIOUS FAILURE

One day in the visitors' compound a woman approaches me. She is middle-aged with a kind, determined face. She introduces herself as Ngareta Rossell. I wonder what she wants but she is warm and friendly and we chat easily. She says she knows some people who want to talk to me, two journalists, Nick Farrow and Ross Coulthart, who are doing a story for the *Sunday* program on Channel Nine about Australian smuggling activities in Indonesia.

That night I ring Dr Al Jabiri. 'Do you know this woman Ngareta?'

'Yes, she is a friend. She's not going to spy on you, or do anything bad.'

So with Nick and Ngareta beside me I speak to Ross on my mobile phone and tell him what I know. He also wants me to talk about my background and how I am struggling to get a visa. Ngareta listens intently.

Next time she comes to Villawood she finds me and comes straight out with it. 'I've been speaking to Frances Milne from Balmain for Refugees and we think you should take the federal government to court for breaking the law.'

I gape at her. 'The Australian government?'

'They are obliged by law to give you a decision on your visa within ninety days, and you've been lingering here for nearly a year.'

'I have no money for a court case,' I say, somewhat in shock.

'We'll get Stephen Blanks. A human-rights lawyer who does pro bono.'

'Pro what?'

'They do it for nothing because they believe in your case. Anyone involved will have to be pro bono. No one can afford to do these things.'

'What things?'

'Fight the government. Stephen is also the secretary of the New South Wales Council for Civil Liberties. He'll be happy to do it.'

I feel light-headed. Is this how democracies work?

A few weeks later Frances brings Stephen Blanks to meet me. I learn that they and Ngareta are known as advocates. They work for nothing, helping refugees. I shake their hands with gratitude.

The months continue to drag by, but it is more endurable now I know people are working for me on the outside. Then one day in the middle of July I am called to the office and handed a letter from the Immigration Department. I stand frozen, reliving the day we received our rejection from the UN. Once again, with the stroke of a pen, my happiness or misery is in the hands of others.

I go back to my room and force myself to open it. It is hard for me to read English but there is no doubt it is a formal notification that they intend to refuse me a permanent visa.

I can't bring myself to tell my family so I call Stephen and inform him it is over.

'From a lawyer's point of view it has just begun,' he replies quite buoyantly after I read it to him word by word. 'They intend to refuse you, but they are offering you an opportunity to explain why they shouldn't.'

'What else can I tell them? They know everything about my situation.'

'That's right. It's just another delaying tactic, but a bad move on their part. Now that we have something formal from them, we've got the basis for a case. They should have given you a decision in ninety days.'

Five days later Stephen files my case in the Federal Court of Australia. Ngareta, who is becoming a good friend, begins to visit me once a week to keep me up to date.

'Stephen now has a top pro bono barrister, Shane Prince, on board,' she tells me victoriously next time she comes. 'He is young, ambitious, very talented, and committed to the rights of refugees. And Connie is going to keep writing up the proceedings in the press.'

Journalist Connie Levitt has already done a story on me, which attracted a lot of attention. Ngareta brought her into Villawood to do an interview, then organised a photographer to take a photo of me through the wire. Next morning there was a two-page spread in the *Sydney Morning Herald*, which created a flurry of interest.

Now people who came on my boats know where I am and come to visit me. When I ask them about their lives they are excited for their future. Whether they have good jobs or bad, they are content because they are living in a peaceful country and are free. Sometimes you plant a flowering tree but you never see it bloom. I lost four years in jail but when I see they have good lives it makes me happy. I haven't wasted my life for nothing.

Then I watch them leave and I think, I am not different to these men. They are just normal like me, no more handsome, no bigger or smarter. Why am I locked up and they are free?

I am pacing the small yard outside my room when my name is called to the phone. There is always a rush of adrenaline through your body when it is for you. You don't know whether it is going to be good news or bad, but at least someone remembers you exist. I go to the office and pick up the phone.

It is Eni. I hesitate. We haven't spoken since I have been here.

'Ali, Nagis needs to go to school but she is not allowed to unless I marry an Indonesian and make him her father.'

Indonesian women cannot pass their nationality to their children, so without me there, Nagis is effectively stateless. I stare out through the wire at the bleak compound where detainees drift aimlessly like ghosts around the grounds. It haunts me that Nagis has to pay for what I have done.

'I have waited for you for five and a half years, Ali,' Eni says after a long pause. 'I am arranging a divorce and planning to remarry.'

In detention with no visa I can do nothing to bring them here, or earn money to send to them. She says she still loves me and I believe her, but in Indonesia for a woman without a job it is very hard, without a husband it is harder. To survive she will marry him. Because of my impotence. The punishment of four years in jail is nothing compared to this.

I have always known why asylum seekers sew up their lips, hunger strike, and smash up the place, but now I can imagine doing it myself. I am lying on my bed when I hear glass smashing. At first I have no interest. But I only have to lift my head and I can look out the window, so I make the effort. I see the Chinese throwing rocks and breaking every window in their block.

I stand up and watch. I would like to throw a rock too. I would pick it up, lift my hand and heave it at a target of my choice, and for the split second in which I threw it, I would have taken back power and been in control of my life. I would not think about the consequences. I would not think. I would just erupt. And for an instant, I would have self-respect.

On 24 November 2007 Kevin Rudd is elected prime minister. I lie on my bed watching it on TV. I am astounded at how smoothly this transition takes place. Mr Rudd pays tribute to John Howard, who makes a gracious speech and offers congratulations. He doesn't fight or threaten anyone, he just steps aside. In Iraq by now someone would be dead.

There is a great deal of excitement as Kevin '07 assumes leadership. He promises to be prime minister for all Australians. Chris Evans becomes the new Immigration Minister. Everyone feels Mr Evans is a good man with decent humanitarian values. Ngareta shows me *The Age* newspaper where he is quoted as saying he is 'committed to helping people in vulnerable situations, in particular Iraqi refugees'. It looks like there could be hope after all.

A few weeks later preparations start for my case to be heard in the Federal Court. It is not like Darwin with witnesses; the evidence is all documents from the Immigration Department, and correspondence from Dr Al Jabiri, who kept up a constant stream of letters trying to ascertain what was going on.

One night Ngareta calls in a rage. 'The judge has required these materials to be handed over by the department, and amongst them we found Kate Watson's report.' She pauses and takes a deep breath. 'It says you met all the criteria for protection under the Refugee Convention. She recommended you receive a permanent visa over a year ago!'

I sit heavily on the bed. I feel like I have been bashed on the head.

'So why am I still in Villawood?'

'I can only assume the government has made such a hot issue of boat people and people smugglers that they can't be seen to be giving one a visa or they'll be savaged by the opposition, so they just want to bury you there.'

I hang up in stunned confusion. I am in Australia, not Iraq. I have done my punishment. Surely when they say you are a refugee, you are a refugee.

Next morning I call Stephen. He sounds frustrated but unsurprised. 'From the documents, it appears they worked extremely hard to avoid implementing Kate's decision. In fact the department seems to have spent a year trying to find a way not to give you a visa.'

'Was it the security check?' I ask.

'No, you were cleared by ASIO. From what I can tell they have been delaying things while they set up a new Character Assessment

Unit so they can move your case there. It's much stricter and can override the Geneva Convention.'

'But what about Kate's decision?'

'She has been taken off the case.'

'Can they just get rid of her if they don't agree with what she says?' I ask angrily.

'It would seem so. If they went with her findings they would have had to give you a visa. But with this new unit, if you have spent more than a year in jail you are deemed to be of bad character, and then only the minister himself can grant you a visa. So that's why we are taking the government to court, to force him to make a decision one way or the other, otherwise you will be incarcerated in Villawood forever.'

'What if he decides to ship me out?'

'Legally you're a refugee with nowhere else to go, so for the moment, while it is unsafe in Iraq, they can't return you. It is evident there are a number of significant people in the department who are sympathetic,' Stephen finishes, 'but it's much bigger than that. You've become a political football.'

When I think of the poverty in my broken country it is ludicrous. Mr Howard had already stopped the boats, and my family was safe so I was no longer smuggling when they caught me. The whole thing has cost the taxpayer millions, just to punish me for something I did in someone else's country, where it wasn't even a crime.

On the first day of the hearing I am allowed to attend. I am put in a van with two guards like a felon and escorted to the twenty-second floor of the Law Building in Macquarie Street.

The case goes round and round. There has clearly been endless infighting in the department over my situation. Shane Prince continues to argue that Kate Watson made a decision a year ago but that the department neglected to act upon it in defiance of the ninety-day requirement.

Then suddenly the Australian Federal Police show up with three barristers, who stride in wearing wigs and black robes. The judge comments that their attire is unnecessary, as this is not a criminal trial, but it succeeds in making us feel intimidated. Their evidence is only allowed to be seen by Shane and Stephen, who are sworn to secrecy, then it is to be shredded. As the failure to make a decision about my visa seems to hang on my 'bad character', the AFP must have come up with a serious allegation against me to justify such a dramatic presentation, but I will never know what it is, nor be given the right to deny it.

The case ends with Shane asking the judge, Justice Lindgren, to issue a writ of mandamus compelling the Immigration Minister to make a decision.

Now we have to wait for his response.

So I am returned to the van with my guards and I sit in a daze as we head back to the destitution of Villawood. I try to peek through a slit window at the streets of inner Sydney. I long to be out there walking amongst the people, looking in shop windows, drinking coffee on Macquarie Street, sitting in the park overlooking the harbour. If they would just drive around the block I might get a glimpse of the Opera House, but there is no possibility of negotiating a pleasure even that small.

Christmas comes and goes again, and in January 2008, after I have been in the detention centre for nineteen months, Justice Lindgren hands down his judgement. He finds that the former Immigration Minister, Kevin Andrews, committed 'an egregious failure' to obey Parliament's command by leaving my case unresolved for eighteen months. He says he will issue the order of mandamus to compel the current minister, Chris Evans, to make a decision.

Everyone is in high spirits and agrees Mr Evans will find it difficult to refuse me a visa now, especially under the new Labor government.

At last it seems there is an end in sight. I call Eni and talk to Nagis, who is now six, and when she asks, 'Daddy when are you coming?' for the first time I am able to say, 'Soon. I will be coming to see you soon.' I go to sleep dreaming of visiting her in our little house in Bogor, and wake with renewed energy to cope with another empty day.

A few weeks later Ngareta brings me a copy of the *Sydney Morning Herald*. Connie Levitt has written another article about me and I discover that Faris, whose son, mother, sister and brother I brought here, is still alive. He had very little money but he was a decent man. I told Faris I would take him and his wife and seven-year-old daughter as well for no extra, but he insisted he had to wait to settle a business matter. A few days later they went on Abu Quassey's SIEVX, and when it sank he survived, but lost his wife and child.

In the article, Faris says he will never forget me. 'I think he is a very, very gentleman. He is the best smuggler. He had a good heart. He was not hard, not a greedy person. I have a conscience about what I saw from Ali Al Jenabi.'

I am deeply touched. This poor man, from the depths of grief, is the first to speak out publicly in my defence, after so many others, even those who came for free, were unwilling lest it got them into trouble with the Australian authorities.

Next day my mother calls. She is just back from Iraq, visiting my father, whose years of brutal incarceration have left him with a heart condition.

'I heard that Intisar's family is living back in our area,' Umi tells me, 'so I went to visit them.'

It might have been remorse for obstructing my marriage in Iran that drove her, but more likely she desperately wants to see me happy. Either way I can feel my pulse begin to race.

'And Ali, Intisar was there ... and she is unmarried. She has been waiting for you all these years.'

My head spins. This is a second chance I never thought possible.

'You just have to get your visa and you can apply to bring her here.'

She gives me the number and I hang up. I sit down in a daze. It is like a lost gift being found. Part of me being returned. I call her immediately.

'Intisar,' I breathe. 'I will bring you here when I get my visa and we will marry after all. It's not too late for us to have our children.'

I hear deep, wrenching sobs of held-back sadness cascade over my pledge. Then, after a silence of remembering, she whispers, 'Yes.'

On 7 February 2008 minister Evans is finally due to announce his decision. After twenty months of detention my fate is to be determined. It is late morning when my name is called to come to reception and my blood is pumping. An officer from Immigration is waiting for me.

'I have good news. You are being released today.'

'Thank you,' I beam, and laugh involuntarily. 'Freedom.'

'You just have to sign here and you will have it.'

I take the pen. 'What sort of visa do I have?'

He looks at me sheepishly. 'The Minister refused your application for a permanent visa and gave you a Removal Pending Bridging Visa.'

'A what?' I say, shocked.

'You'll have to ask your lawyer.'

'Does bridging mean they'll give me the proper one in a few months?'

'Your lawyer will explain.'

I decide not to pursue it. All I can think about is being released, so I sign the document. I am determined not to ruin my first moments of liberty. I am getting out. I am going home to my family.

As I walk towards the gate I wave goodbye to friends still imprisoned. Many have asked me to visit but I said no. My father taught me never to look back, and now as I step out of this grave I don't want to step back in again. I take a deep breath and walk out into my new life.

Ngareta comes with Ahlam to drive me the few kilometres home. It is to be a surprise. No one has told my mother yet. It is pouring with rain and everything is drab, but the little rented fibro cottage looks like a palace to me. Everyone is there. As I get out of the car Umi sees me through the window and runs out, her black robes flying, and throws herself into my arms. Hashim and Inas are behind her. Afrah's children shriek with delight.

Ahlam stands by quietly. Tears streaming down her face. 'He is my brother but more like a father to me,' she says to Ngareta. It has been nearly ten years since I left them in Iran, and she has been waiting ever since for me to come home.

ROMEO AND JULIET

That night I keep waking, wanting to laugh out loud, and in the morning I hug them all too much before they go off on their various ways. Then my mother and I sit together over breakfast. We gaze out the window of our back room at the sun breaking through the last of the rain. I tell her how I am going to get a job, or set up a business, and maybe we can buy this house. And that I plan to bring Intisar here and marry her. Neither of us can stop smiling. With each word I feel my old spirit returning, and that everything is possible.

The next day we have a party in our backyard. We make a barbeque, and I am out there cooking kebabs, with Hashim assisting the way I used to help Baba. My mother and sisters are in the kitchen preparing kibbe batata and salads with khubaz. I quietly tell Afrah that I don't have a proper visa, but add that it is just until they see I am a good boy. We laugh. What else can we do? I am home and we are a family again.

After a few contented days I call Stephen Blanks to ask about my visa.

'I'm afraid it's bad, Ali,' he says. 'The minister has the power to grant it if he had wanted to. The only conclusion I can draw is he has it in for you personally, or he didn't appreciate being forced to make a decision. But effectively he has put you in the parking lot until Iraq is deemed to be safe and then he'll send you back.'

This is a devastating blow but I am used to disappointment. It will be some time before Iraq is safe, so I am determined to be grateful for what I have, and to hope that the minister will eventually see I am worthy and give me a proper visa. Then I try to put it out of my mind. At least for the moment I am free. Although certainly the edge has already been taken off my glee and once again I'm under threat of losing Intisar.

For now what I need to do is get a job. It has tormented me that I have been unable to contribute. Khalid has had to not only support the family, but has also been sending money to Eni and Nagis. So each day, with great enthusiasm, I get the newspaper, ring up and make appointments.

But every time I apply for a position they want to see my visa status, and it falls through. And even if I could find a job where it doesn't matter, I need them to allow me to work around my other commitments, which are complicated.

There are three different government departments I have to comply with. Every two weeks I need to report to Immigration in the city as a condition of this visa. It is an hour each way on the train. Meanwhile if I'm not out looking for a job Centrelink will cut off my benefits, and the parole office require me to report once a week to complete my sentence.

Each department has its own measure of humiliation. My parole officer keeps threatening to report me to her manager because I am not co-operating.

'Do you want me to write down how many times I go to the toilet or have a cigarette?' I level back at her.

'No, but you must have something to tell me.'

'Well, I have a tooth coming out which I can report, and today I went to the shop and bought some food, then I went back home.'

She glares at me but I don't understand what is in her head. I have no job. No life. I have nearly two years of parole to get through. I am doing time again. What is there to say?

So next she puts me into a drug and alcohol program.

'I'm Muslim!' I say to her, conveniently forgetting my youthful forays into my uncle's arak. She replies by giving me a request form for a piss test. So the following day I have to go to a clinic where a woman asks me to pee into a tiny cup while she stands next to me, watching.

I look at her bewildered. 'It is impossible for me to do this in front of you.'

She is very nice. 'Just forget about me,' she says politely, giving me water. But it is not about nice. I drink until I am ready to explode but I still can't pee.

When I finally do fill the cup I can't stop, and it goes on my hands and everywhere. We laugh, but the whole thing is utterly degrading.

I am told I have to go back there every two months, or whenever they decide they want me to. Even worse, parole officers come to my house unannounced to do breath tests. If I'm not there they call me and I have to come home. If I'm absent or don't pick up the phone more than three times, they can arrest me and put me back in jail.

It soon becomes clear a job is not possible until I have completed my parole, so I decide to set up something on my own. There are plenty of Iraqis in the community with skills in the building trade. I borrow money to register a company, get insurance and make a business card. I visit building sites and try to get a contract to supply labour, but whenever they ask to see my visa they go cool.

The rosy glow of liberty begins to dim and I realise I am back on the treadmill of endurance. The reality is the minister is going to leave me on this removal visa and any day I could get a knock on my door and be flown out. Until I get a permanent visa I am told I definitely can't apply to bring Intisar here as my wife, and if I leave the country to visit Indonesia I will not be allowed back in. I call Nagis and try to explain to her, but what does a six-year-old understand? She waits each day for me to appear. The responsibility

I feel for her pain is crippling.

I tell Intisar and she remains stoical, but the next day she sends a message through Afrah that her brother will no longer let her speak to me. He says it will only fan the flames and make her more resistant to marrying somebody else. Her refusals have already shamed her family. Her mother is jeered at when she walks down the street. They think I am just playing games and will not take me seriously again.

Ngareta, who is like a terrier with a bone, is determined to get the minister to see beyond the politics to the human factor. She is going to put a submission to the Commonwealth Ombudsman, and needs me to come and sign some documents.

I catch the train to Bondi where she lives, and stare into back-yards as they flash by. Small cosy houses with kids and families. I look around the carriage at the young women chatting about their boy-friends, clothes and TV. I wonder if any of them could even imagine Intisar's life. She is a teacher and had the tenth-highest score in her year in Iraq when she graduated. But her family takes her wages and because she is unmarried, she is a disgrace. She should not have waited for me, I never expected her to, but it is impossible not to blame myself. My eyes well as the train pulls into Bondi Junction.

I feel dizzy as I stand up. The doors open and I step out, then sud-denly I can't breathe. Someone asks if I am all right but I cannot speak. I nod and they hurry on, but as the station empties, a burning pain shoots across my chest. I wheeze empty-lunged, arms clutching and wrapping around myself as I slide into the pain and onto the concrete platform. A train glides past soundlessly, then everything is a blur. After all I have survived, is this how it will end – so silent, so clean, undramatic, and quick?

Black becomes light and I look up. Someone standing over me helps me to my feet. 'Would you like me to get you an ambulance?' he says and I shake my head. I don't want to cause a fuss if it is just reflux from a stomach that has suffered years of starvation and abuse.

I walk slowly to the other side of the platform and get a train home. I lie in bed for two days, then my mother insists I go to a doctor. After X-rays and blood tests he sends me straight to Liverpool Hospital telling me I have had a heart attack.

They rush me in, prepare me for an operation, and I am put in a ward with three other people to wait. A surgeon arrives to see someone in the bed next to me. He is Iraqi and as he consults his patient I think I know his voice, then when he turns to leave I recognise him. He is an asylum seeker I brought here on one of my boats. His face lights up when he sees me.

'If I die now it is okay,' I say, sitting up. 'To see you a surgeon in an Australian hospital makes everything worth it.'

'Thanks to you.' He laughs and hugs me. 'But you had better lie down or you may well die.'

'And your brother-in-law who came with you?' I enquire as I slump back.

'He teaches in a university.'

My smile widens.

An orderly hurries in and politely interrupts. He wheels me out and down a corridor to the operating theatre, where a tiny instrument is inserted into a vein in my leg and fed up to my heart while I watch it on the TV. When they find the blockage they release a liquid that sets my body on fire. Afterwards I collapse into a hospital bed for three days in exhaustion.

A few months later, when I am healthy again, I visit Ngareta.

'We are going to take a complaint to the Human Rights Commission,' she announces. 'We'll ask them to find that the time it took to resolve your visa was a breach of your human rights.'

I am sceptical but relieved to discover there is still another chance.

'Sister Aileen Crowe, a Franciscan nun, is going to assist us. She has helped dozens of refugees get their visas and knows how to work the system better than most lawyers.'

As soon as I meet her I can tell she is a fighter. Her two feet firmly planted on the ground, not much is going to get past Aileen without her noticing.

'Ultimately all they can do if they find your human rights have been breached is recommend the government pay you compensation and make an apology,' Aileen tells me.

It's not money that I am after, and an apology is hardly going to help me as it's not my pride that is at stake, but she goes on to explain that they initially get the parties together to try and work out a solution, which can become an opportunity to discuss face to face with the department another application for a permanent visa.

The first meetings are fruitless, until a senior officer from the department gets to know my case and begins to look more sympathetically at it. So, in an atmosphere of renewed hope, the work begins to draft a new submission to the minister.

But I balk when the department suggests it would help my case if I apologised for my crime. I always said I would take my punishment, and I have, but I'm not prepared to apologise for what I don't believe is wrong. How can I see helping my family to safety as a crime? Or giving a new life to nearly five hundred other Iraqis who were fleeing Saddam as an offence? When I see the happiness on the faces of my siblings, safe and free, marrying, having children, studying and getting jobs, setting up businesses, paying tax and joining the Australian way of life, no longer living on the run and in perpetual fear for themselves or the ones they love, how can I say I am sorry for this?

So I agree to apologise for breaking Australian law, because I didn't know that was what I was doing when I did it, and it seems to be an acceptable compromise. I have now completed my parole, and my entire family have permanent residency or citizenship. Ten children have been born to us with Australian nationality, and in the absence of my father I am head of this extended family.

Ngareta and Aileen pull together a multitude of letters of support from high-profile people in the community, and in early 2010 the most persuasive application we have ever done goes off to Minister Evans, requesting he use his power of ministerial intervention to finally grant me a permanent visa.

Meanwhile Dr Al Jabiri applies for a tourist visa for Intisar. If she could just visit she could see for herself why I can't bring her here to marry immediately, and why it is worth waiting.

And I could see her again. At last I allow myself to revisit those cherished days of first love. Her family's belief in me revives and they help with the documents we send Intisar to sign, and she is allowed to speak to Afrah on the phone again.

We discover that at the school her students heckle her for being unwed. And she is watched, escorted, or locked in her room when she is not at work. But now that she is able to say she is going to see her future husband in Australia, all that will change.

The months slip by while we wait for her visa to be approved, and for a response from Mr Evans to my submission, but nothing happens. Then one night I get a call from Ngareta.

'The Immigration Department have rejected Intisar, they won't even let her visit.'

I want to run from the room and howl like an injured dog. Instead I stand holding the phone in silence.

'Are you all right?'

'No. I feel like my world has broken,' I say and hang up. How can I tell Intisar I have let her down again? If I had wanted to torture her I couldn't have found a more effective tool.

Desperate, I go with Aileen to a talk Minister Evans is giving prior to the upcoming federal election. Prime Minister Kevin Rudd had been unexpectedly deposed by Julia Gillard in June 2010, and she has announced the country will go to the vote again to legitimise her standing as leader.

When the minister's presentation is over there is an opportunity to meet him, but the queue is long and we are at the end of it. It inches along and just before we reach him, Mr Evans announces he has run out of time and has to leave. Determined, I push forward. I am sure it will help my case if I can put a human face to it.

'Please, before you leave office, give me a proper visa,' I call to him as he gathers up his papers.

He doesn't recognise me, but then it dawns and he looks around, as if he is worried reporters might be listening. 'Smuggling is a serious crime and the Australian people won't forget it.'

'Australian people are my family. My mum, my brothers, my sisters, my neighbours, my nephew's teacher, are all Australian people.'

He looks unprepared for this response. Aileen quickly jumps in.

'If he could have brought his fiancée here it would have helped.'

He looks at her stony-faced. 'If he is to be deported what would be the point?'

I watch him go. I was told he is a man with empathy for the plight of others, but I see little evidence.

'Gutless,' Aileen mutters as we head off.

Shortly after, I get a formal letter from Mr Evans, refusing my application again.

When I call Intisar to tell her and break the news that she has been rejected as well, for the first time she becomes angry. 'My family won't stand it any longer,' she says bitingly.

'You must believe me, I am doing everything I can,' I plead. 'I will send you a mobile phone so we can talk.'

This makes her happier. But with the news of her rejection, Intisar's brother forbids her to speak to any of us and takes it from her. So my contact is completely cut off.

The election is set for 21 August. The issue of the few thousand asylum seekers who arrive here by boat continues to be one of the most important in the campaign. Billions of dollars are allocated to the problem, and people smugglers are seen as the cause of this evil. Kevin, who seems to be a nice enough guy, labelled us before he was overthrown as 'absolute scum of the earth … the vilest form of human life' who should 'rot in hell'.

Yet as reported across the media the Weasel, a confessed people smuggler himself, has received $250000, Australian citizenship, and indemnity from prosecution, as a reward for informing to the AFP.

Whichever party can stop the boats has come to be seen as good government, and the way to beat the other is by generating public fear, so Julia runs with it and wins the election by an inch. But people smugglers don't create the demand. They only exist because refugees are fleeing for their lives and there is no one else to help them. I never had to beg anyone to get on one of my boats or promise them a good life in Australia. Most of them were devastated to leave their own country and would not have if they had a choice.

In her new cabinet Julia Gillard replaces Chris Evans with Chris Bowen as Immigration Minister. Despite the relatively toxic environment, with Labor still in power and a new and possibly more liberal-minded Mr Bowen at the helm, our optimism is returning. Stephen, Ngareta and Aileen quickly submit another application for ministerial intervention for a permanent visa.

At the end of 2010 my father is hospitalised and my mother decides to go to Iraq to be with him. I know there is no killing my father. I have spent my life imagining him cut down by one means or another, only for him to re-emerge as fit as ever. I long to see him again, but without a proper visa I cannot go to him even if he is dying. So we decide Ahlam will accompany Umi, and she can also try to visit Intisar and explain to her family that my intentions are true.

Soon after arriving they go to Intisar's house bearing gifts so they will be let in. Her brother and his wife, plus his sister and husband, live there with their mother.

'Intisar is not allowed to speak to anyone alone,' Ahlam tells me over the phone from our old home in Diwaniyah. 'So we had to sit with her mother and sister, which meant she could say very little. It is like she is in a prison. Her mother told us that by staying unmarried Intisar degrades their entire family.

'"She is not a whole woman," she said in front of poor Intisar. "She is not my daughter. She is just an animal, like a donkey. We have brought home many suitors over the years for her to marry but even when my son beats her she refuses. She says she is engaged to Ali Al Jenabi who is in Australia. That one day he will come for her."

'Then her mother showed me the stick they use to hit her with. It is the length of a broom. It is called a punishment stick and is especially made for beating women.'

Ahlam's voice is raised and tremulous. She left Iraq when she was too young to experience how hard it is for women there, and now that she lives happily in Australia with a loving husband and a baby, she is having to confront the cruelty she escaped.

'I followed Intisar to the kitchen when she went to make tea,' Ahlam continues. 'So for a minute I was alone with her. I saw the palms of her hands as she put out the cups. They were blistered and purple. She noticed me looking and quickly lifted up her hijab and took off her veil to show me the rest. There were black bruises all over her white skin, on her back, behind her knees, on her arms and head. She begged me to take her with me. She is beautiful, Ali. But if she doesn't marry soon they will kill her.'

To know torture is being inflicted on someone you love, when you are helpless to do anything, is unbearable.

Ahlam is holding back tears as she finishes. 'When I left they told me I wasn't allowed to talk to Intisar again, and they have issued you an ultimatum. Either you take Intisar by March or she marries a man they have chosen. If she refuses, her brother will flog her, this time maybe to death. She is trouble to him, he wants her gone. He will go to jail for it, but he will only get six months.'

Aileen and Ngareta panic and decide to apply for a Woman at Risk Visa to bring Intisar here. They spell out the urgency of her situation, but while the people in the Immigration Department are sympathetic there is no category in which to fit her. Intisar will have to stay where she is.

Then Aileen calls and tells me Minister Bowen has rejected my application for his intervention with the same old language as Chris Evans. I hang up the phone and stare at my reflection in the living-room window and I see an image that is no longer a man. Chris Bowen, like Mr Evans, is killing me.

I want to go out and beat someone senseless, but there is no one person I can punch out. Chris Bowen would say, 'It's not me, I'm advised by the department,' and the department would say that thousands of people work here, so you can't go and punch every one of them, and even if you did, each person would say, 'Why hit me? I have nothing to do with your problem.'

But I would look at them and say, 'Do you know what it is to live in limbo? To be knocking your head on the wall? Every day seeing friends with their wives and wanting to say, "Why don't I have a wife?" Or seeing a couple with kids and thinking, Why does he have children and I don't? And if someone has a small business, wanting to yell, "Why can't I have proper job like you?"'

Then I look at myself and I realise I am different, I am not like these people. I live with them, but I do not belong. I have nothing to work for because any day I could be gone.

It is a week after my fortieth birthday and ten days before Christmas. I wake up late with a jolt, as if something is wrong. I go into the living room where I see my mother sitting horrified in front of the TV. She reaches out to me and as I slump down next to her she gestures to the screen. Together we stare in silence at a wooden fishing boat being smashed by wild stormy seas against the jagged cliffs of Christmas Island.

Men cling to the vessel as it breaks up and waves crash over them. A boy is swept from the deck and disappears amongst the debris and dead bodies. Children are torn from their parents' arms and flung against the cliffs or left floundering in the churning sea. Local residents are trying to help but the backwash keeps hurling the asylum seekers into the turbulence and battering them with pieces of wreckage before the islanders can reach them.

Over the next few days this tragedy becomes a competition between both sides of parliament to show how much they care about boat people. They announce with renewed intensity that this disaster was entirely the fault of people smugglers, who must be stopped in order to save lives like these. There is little talk of what the refugees are running from, or recognition that most of them would prefer to die in the ocean while attempting to escape than at the hands of torturers or executioners in their own country.

Surely the fact that they keep coming, even after terrible disasters, is proof of that. Does the government imagine asylum seekers hear about changes to Australia's border protection policies but not about the SIEVX?

During the debate that follows, Prime Minister Gillard and Minister Chris Bowen coin the phrase *the people smugglers' business model.* They declare they are going to smash this mysterious identity by any means. I laugh out loud when I hear it. Do they think there are men in suits sitting around boardroom tables somewhere devising strategies? Has no one told them people smuggling is an amorphous rag-tag network run by word of mouth and mobile phones? There are no records or bank accounts. No spreadsheets or business plans. They pop up wherever people are trying to escape and disappear when they are no longer needed. If you want to stop people smugglers you have to do something about what causes people to flee their own countries in the first place.

Meanwhile preparation has gone on with the Human Rights

Commission report, which at last, in May 2011, is sent to the Attorney-General with strenuous recommendation for compensation and an apology. Both requests are denied and on 16 August the rejection is tabled in parliament.

For a brief moment my story is in the newspapers again. ABC TV's Heather Ewart does a stirring segment on me and the government's response that night on *7.30*, and I am hailed as a hero by one of the people who came on my boats for free. And that's the end of it. All those amazing people who have fought for me can see nothing more to do.

It is a week later, just a few days before the end of Ramadan and some five months since the ultimatum from Intisar's family expired. There has been no word of her forced marriage. It seems that it could have been a bluff, so I am beginning to relax. Her brother would have enjoyed making sure I knew she had a husband, as revenge for keeping his sister unmarried for twenty years. So somehow she must have managed to resist him and be still waiting for me.

It is a perfect sunny late winter's day with warm rays shining through the windows. I sink onto a worn tattered couch in our family room at the back of the house and drift into a peaceful slumber. I am soon floating over the yard, where my mother hums to herself as she picks flowers from a camellia tree which I hadn't noticed was blooming.

I glide past Hashim who is up a ladder painting our fibro cottage. Between us we have raised a mortgage and it is now our family home. I gaze at the small neat granny flat we have built for my mother which looks onto a bed of flowers and a garden of herbs and vegetables. Jasmine grows along the new timber fence we have built in preparation for the wedding.

When Nagis arrives she will stay in Umi's little cabin because Intisar will want her own space with me. I can't take Nagis from her mother but Eni trusts me and she wants Nagis to have a better life, so we will share her. Sometimes she will be here with me, and sometimes

Intisar and I will visit her in Indonesia.

I tend to a young pomegranate tree which Intisar and I will plant together when she arrives, just like the one her balcony overlooked in our garden in Iraq. From the fruit we will make our own juice to sell at our restaurant. My kebabs and my mother's cooking attract half the Middle East community as well as our Australian friends.

My phone rings, jarring me from sleep, and as I put it to my ear I hear the sound of Afrah's voice. 'Ali,' she says urgently. 'She called.'

I see a flash of black hair swirl from under Intisar's scarf as she runs with her sister after the gasman's donkey cart, and I smile.

'Ali,' Afrah says again, but this time more tenderly. 'Intisar is married.'

I sit frozen as my dream dissipates and becomes another nightmare. I am wrenched by guilt and sadness for what Intisar has endured for me, and for what I cannot have. I had only wanted a simple life with a wife and family. I never sought what befell me, but like my father, I was drawn in by standing up for what I believe. All that is left now is my daughter, who I cannot ever see.

A cyclone of fury threatens to engulf me. 'Saddam, you bastard,' I shout into the drab interior of our house.

Then I fall back into the embrace of our decrepit couch and sigh. I see my mother's phone on the coffee table. I pick it up and go to the video she and Ahlam took of my father when they last visited him. He dances in traditional clothing to the throb of Arabic music in our old home in Diwaniyah. He twirls, arms poised, robes and turban swirling as he circles. He is happy. Like a nail, the more they hit him, the harder he got. Once again he has stood back up and now he has outlived Saddam.

Opposite me Ahmad's soft-eyed boyish face looks down from its frame on the wall. I am swamped with memories of the good times, not the bad. 'Eventually,' I whisper to him, 'there will be someone in power that has a kind heart and a family he would do anything to protect, who must understand how I got into this situation. So for you, my brother, I will keep on going. For you I will go on doing time.'

ACKNOWLEDGEMENTS

My sincerest gratitude to Ali Al Jenabi for sharing his life with me and the three years of hard work that it took to do that. And to his family who so graciously allowed me to explore their story. And especially to Ngareta Rossell whose idea this project was and who supported me throughout, with Stephen Blanks and Sister Aileen Crow as our backing team. My heartfelt thanks to my wonderful publisher Ben Ball and editor Meredith Rose for giving their all to this book, and to Anyez Lindop, designer Adam Laszczuk and everyone else at Penguin. Special thanks to Rosie Scott for her editing in the early days and her constancy of support. And for their endless reading and occasional editing, my dear and generous friends Kristin and David Williamson, Adam and Pen Shaw, Kate Milner and my precious sister Zoe de Crespigny. And for their unwavering love and support Sophia Turkiewicz, Virginia Duigan, Ann Brown, Sandy Kogan, Terri Condon, Helen Malinowski, Ros Washington, Ross McGregor and Angela Punch McGregor. My sincere gratitude to my lawyer Lloyd Hart Jon Tippet QC, Matthew Hubber, and Angela Bowne SC. for their generous legal assistance, Wayne R King from Merrill Corporation, and Suzan Cox and Sue Ready at the Northern Territory Legal Aid Commission for assistance with court transcripts, and to Cybele and Justin Malinowski at Blue Murder Photographic Studios. My thanks and appreciation to Hugh Sykes, Sabas Banggabean, Sue Hoffman, and Paul Greenway for their kind research and reading, also to Jamie Grant and John Collee. Finally my sincere thanks to Michael Armstrong and Prof. Arun Aggarwal, and to the source of my strength, my amazing agent, Margaret Connolly, and my beautiful husband Christopher Gordon, whose wisdom and love carries me through.

Ali holding Asad on his shoulders, with (left) Basim and (right) Ahmad

Hassan Pilot with (left) Ahmad smelling the flowers and (right) Ali

Ahmad, just prior to Abu Ghraib

Nagis

Cybele Malinowski

Robin de Crespigny is a filmmaker and lives in Sydney. She spent over three years writing Ali Al Jenabi's story.

Ali with Afrah's children, twins Malak and Narges, and Hassan, named after Hassan Pilot